IMAGES
of America

VISTA

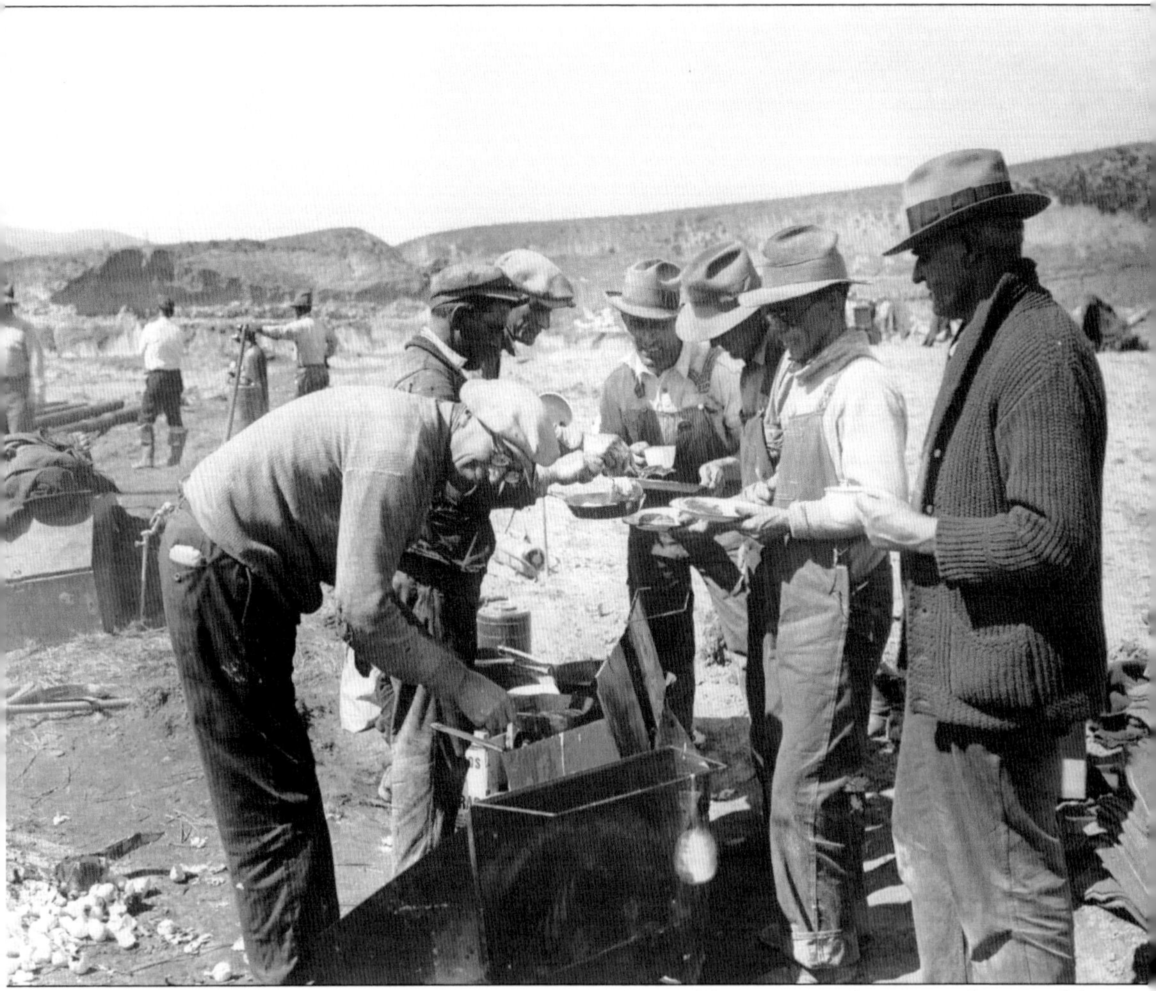

These men, pausing for a meal cooked on a small portable stove, are the unsung heroes of the plan to bring ample water to Vista. They labored in rugged terrain from the ground-breaking ceremony in May 1925 to the formal dedication in February 1926, building the flume and reservoir that would ensure delivery of water from Lake Henshaw, 40 miles away.

On the Cover: In the 1930s and 1940s, Vista was the avocado capital of the world. This first branch plant of the Calavo Growers of California was considered to be the most modern and efficient of its type. Many wives of servicemen worked here during World War II, and to them and other employees, it was known as "a family place." (Courtesy of Vista Historical Society and Museum.)

IMAGES
of America

VISTA

Lois Vaughan Cavalier

ARCADIA
PUBLISHING

ISBN 978-0-7385-5939-1

Published by Arcadia Publishing
Charleston, South Carolina

Printed in the United States of America

Library of Congress Catalog Card Number: 2008922698

For all general information contact Arcadia Publishing at:
Telephone 843-853-2070
Fax 843-853-0044
E-mail sales@arcadiapublishing.com
For customer service and orders:
Toll-Free 1-888-313-2665

Visit us on the Internet at www.arcadiapublishing.com

This book is dedicated to my children, Gary and Patti,
from a mom who loves the poesy of words and the smell of printer's ink,
but not nearly as much as she loves them.

Contents

ACKNOWLEDGMENTS

Unless otherwise designated, all photographs in this book are treasured memories that were donated to the Vista Historical Society and Museum by longtime residents and remain part of the museum archives. The support of the Vista Historical Society board of directors and staff, all of them multigenerational Vistans, was invaluable to the groundwork for this book. During the photograph selection process, the society's museum was unexpectedly displaced and demolished for a new fire station. Decades of memorabilia had to be packed and stored posthaste pending the search for a new permanent site. As we worked, board members and volunteers rescued framed photographs so they wouldn't disappear into cardboard cartons. They kept a special box for me in which they stowed pictures and documents and were generally kind and helpful as is their way. The unparalleled chroniclers of Vista's written history are my heroes, *Vista Press* publishers M. Z. and Everett Remsburg, who lived in and for the community every day of their lives from the first edition of the *Vista Press* on September 24, 1926. Invaluable references were also provided by Harrison and Ruth Doyle in their 407-page *A History of Vista*, published in 1983, and by Donna Harper's *A View of Vista*, written for Vista Unified School District elementary school students in 1991. Leaders of the Parks and Community Services Department of the City of Vista, and most particularly director Cathy Brendel, producing artistic director Kathy Brombacher, and community senior services program manager Mary Dreibelbis, enthusiastically provided information and photographs. Ashley Jaques, curator of collections at the Antique Gas and Steam Engine Museum, also was most generous with her time. Warmest thanks also go to the members of my writers group: Dave, Don, Lina, Paula, Selma, Susan, and Todd, devotees of the English language who supported me and, most of all, listened. And I am most grateful to have such a wonderful, supportive friend and fellow connoisseur of words as Betty Wieser.

INTRODUCTION

To study the history of Vista is to fall in love. Fact by fact, footprint by footprint, there emerges a people of extraordinary integrity, ingenuity, and generosity.

Vista was truly a "late bloomer." With the exception of the two original land grants by Gov. Pio Pico, Rancho Buena Vista and Rancho Guajome, and the arrival of such industrious individuals as Bernard and Jules Jacques Delpy from France in the late 19th century, Vista remained a small, sleepy village.

The first real sign of awakening was the arrival of the Vista Land Company in 1912. The quarter-million-dollar corporation, organized by the Hartley-Martin Real Estate Company of Redlands, bought a major portion of Rancho Buena Vista land, laid out some streets, and built the 26-room Vista Inn. The showplace hotel, later termed in a *Vista Press* advertisement as "the Ritz Carlton of San Diego County," became a center of social and business life for the entire northern San Diego County area. Old Highway 395 passed through Vista then, and the inn sat on a knoll at the corner of Santa Fe Avenue and what is now Main Street, where the highway made a turn. It took two days to travel from San Diego to the Riverside–San Bernardino area, so the inn was a popular place to spend the night.

It wasn't until the early 1920s that other astute land developers began to understand the potential of the gently rolling hills, fertile soil, and near-perfect climate. They also discovered that there was very little irrigation water and that most of the town's domestic needs were provided by the Vista Water Company, founded in 1911, from some wells near Buena Creek.

Until 1923, when the Vista Irrigation District was formed, most of the land was only good for the dry farming of such crops as oats and hay. By 1926, the Vista Irrigation District board of directors had found a way to slake the thirst of the rich soil by bringing water from Lake Henshaw, 40 miles away. After a grandiose celebration in February 1926, which brought thousands of visitors from all over the region, Vistans began to till and plant and nurture until Vista was the avocado capital of the world and extolled as well for its abundant citrus groves and field crops.

Many of these early settlers were experts in their field, in horticulture or land sales or building or publishing. They were mainly family people, so they secured their own land and built their own homes along the newly laid-out dirt roads. It was a glorious mix of races and nationalities, all working together for the common goal of creating a thriving community.

The *Vista Press*, the community's first newspaper, stalwartly supported every good undertaking in the burgeoning community starting on September 24, 1926, the day experienced newsman M. Z. Remsburg and his son, Everett, published their first edition. No story was too insignificant to make the news in those days. People didn't just die, with a few statistics recounted about their lives. In bold headlines, often on the front page, the sorrow and support of the entire community were extended to the grieving family. The April 3, 1930, *Vista Press* bragged, "Vista has produced enough rhubarb this season to make 835,600 pies." There was no information about how that accounting process was conducted.

Those who wanted a new business simply put an advertisement in the *Vista Press* and opened their doors; there was no need for an address, for everyone in town knew where to find everything.

If there was need for a building to house a new enterprise, they built it. If there was need for a church, citizens of like mind got together and met where they could until they raised funds for their own place. The ladies created the Vista Garden Club and the Women's Current Events Club, later renamed the Woman's Club of Vista. When there was need for a library, Nellie Acker willingly housed the 50-book collection in her own home.

An amazing number of these early families, and subsequently their families, generation after generation, have remained in Vista. Most of them say they simply can't find a place that is half as nice.

After World War II, the verdant groves began to give way to houses. Servicemen and women who had been stationed in the area went home to places like Minnesota and North Dakota and remembered soaking up the sun in January on the beach in Oceanside or Carlsbad. They decided that a community like Vista would be a great place to raise a young family.

Early Vistan Ervin Ries and his family, who first arrived in Vista in the 1930s, recall hearing the bells of Mission San Luis Rey and the Pacific Ocean surf from their home on the hillside above West Vista Way, in the center of town. Then Highway 78 was built from Oceanside to Escondido in the early 1960s, right through the center of Vista, and the sounds of traffic replaced the sounds of chimes and breaking waves.

Vista was governed by the San Diego County Board of Supervisors, who made decisions about local issues that residents felt it was time to control themselves. In 1962, Vista led all unincorporated cities of San Diego County with building permits totaling $5,596,600, and by the early 1960s, the decision was made to incorporate. On January 28, 1963, the community of Vista became the city of Vista. It later also became home to the San Diego County courthouse complex and the community of Shadowridge and developed the prospering business park in the southern part of the city.

The Vista of today is a family place at the hub of northern San Diego County. The city has six times the national average of parks and an exceptional recreation program for all ages that is run by the Parks and Community Services Department. When mobile home parks proliferated in Vista in the early 1970s, a whole new age group emerged that was in need of services. Vista met those needs with a program designed for senior citizens and, ultimately, a modern two-building complex.

Vista Unified School District continually upgrades its scholastic and sports programs, and when students graduate, they have a choice of nearby Palomar Community College, California State University at San Marcos, or National University in Vista.

Vista continues to grow and change, but as it does, there is always, always the echo of the footsteps of the brave people who came here when the land was barren and created the spirit of their chosen community. Longtime and new, Vistans share the roots put down by these early settlers and by the inhabitants of the romantic ranch homes of Rancho Buena Vista and Rancho Guajome, which have been painstakingly preserved for our education and enjoyment.

The Vista Historical Society offers a museum that is abundant with memorabilia and photographs that honor our past. Most of the docents and staff who man it are longtime Vistans themselves, many second or third generations, and they are the keepers of fascinating stories that bring the past to life.

Come and learn about Vista. You will fall in love.

One

The Home of the Ranchos

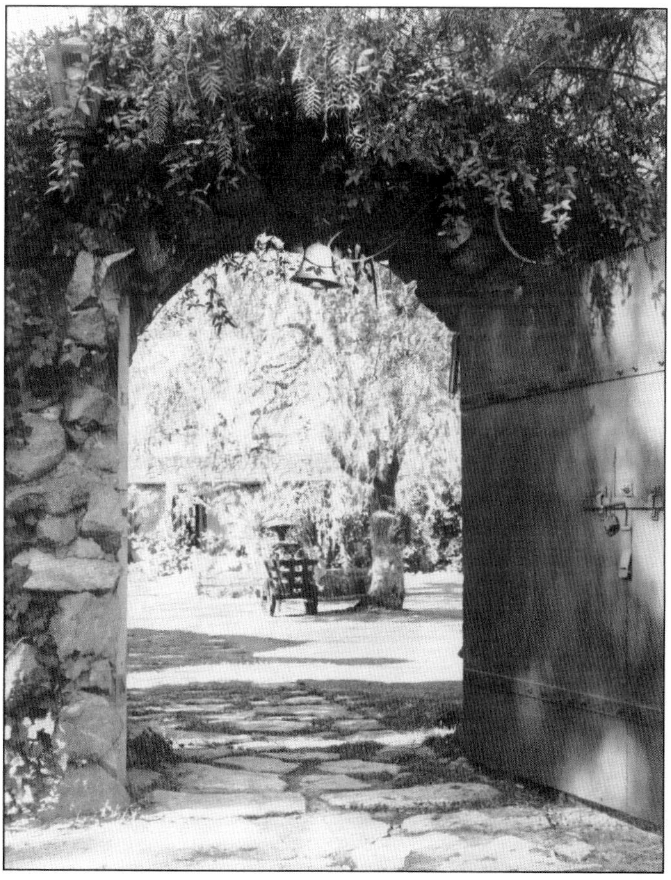

Thanks to the care taken in preserving historic Rancho Buena Vista and Rancho Guajome, anyone who wishes can step through a Spanish-style archway and into the past. Rancho Buena Vista, now owned by the city, had many caring owners; Rancho Guajome, run by the San Diego County Parks and Recreation Department, stayed mainly in the Couts family. Both haciendas are within the city of Vista's boundaries, fully restored as a living legacy.

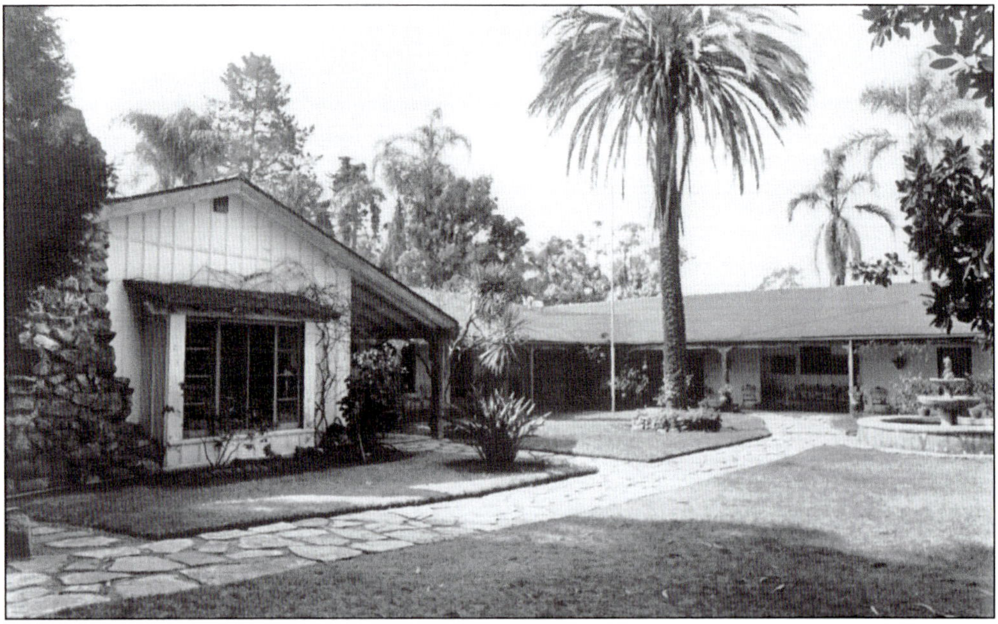

Anastasia Weil said it was love at first sight when she and her husband, Dr. Walter Weil, found Rancho Buena Vista in 1957. They purchased the house from geologist Frederick Reid and lived in it happily for the next 15 years. When they moved here full-time, they built Vista Medical Center and Pharmacy so Dr. Weil could continue his successful practice as an eye surgeon.

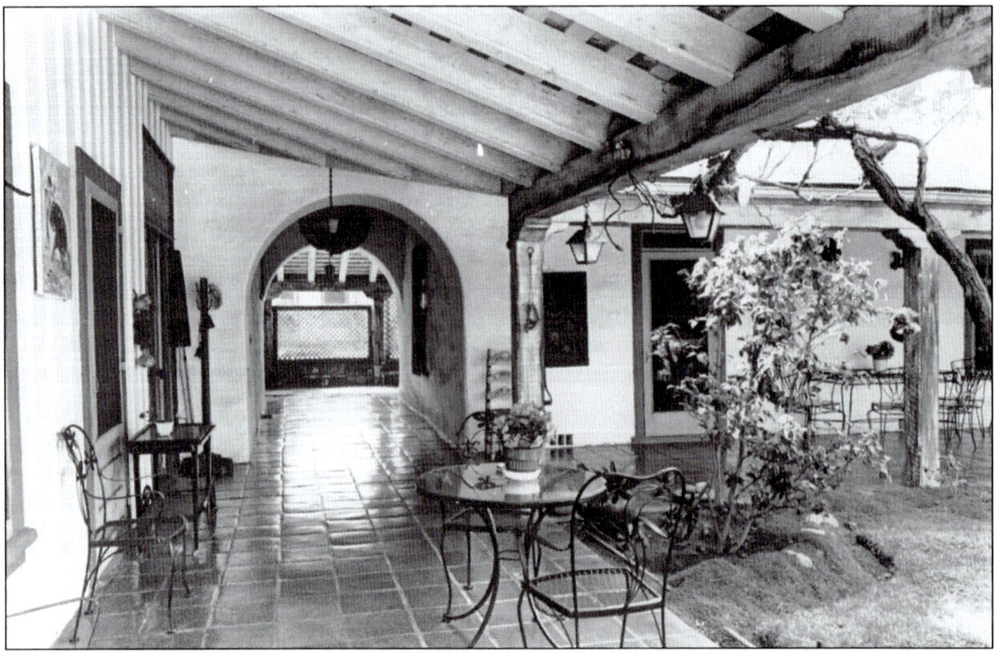

The rancho was originally a 1,184-acre land grant from Gov. Pio Pico to Felipe Subria and was later owned by Col. Cave Couts, who built Rancho Guajome. Restoration and improvements were made by each ensuing owner. This photograph provides a view along the patio, past the courtyard, and through the archways to the swimming pool beyond, which Dr. Walter and Anastasia Weil created from a small reservoir.

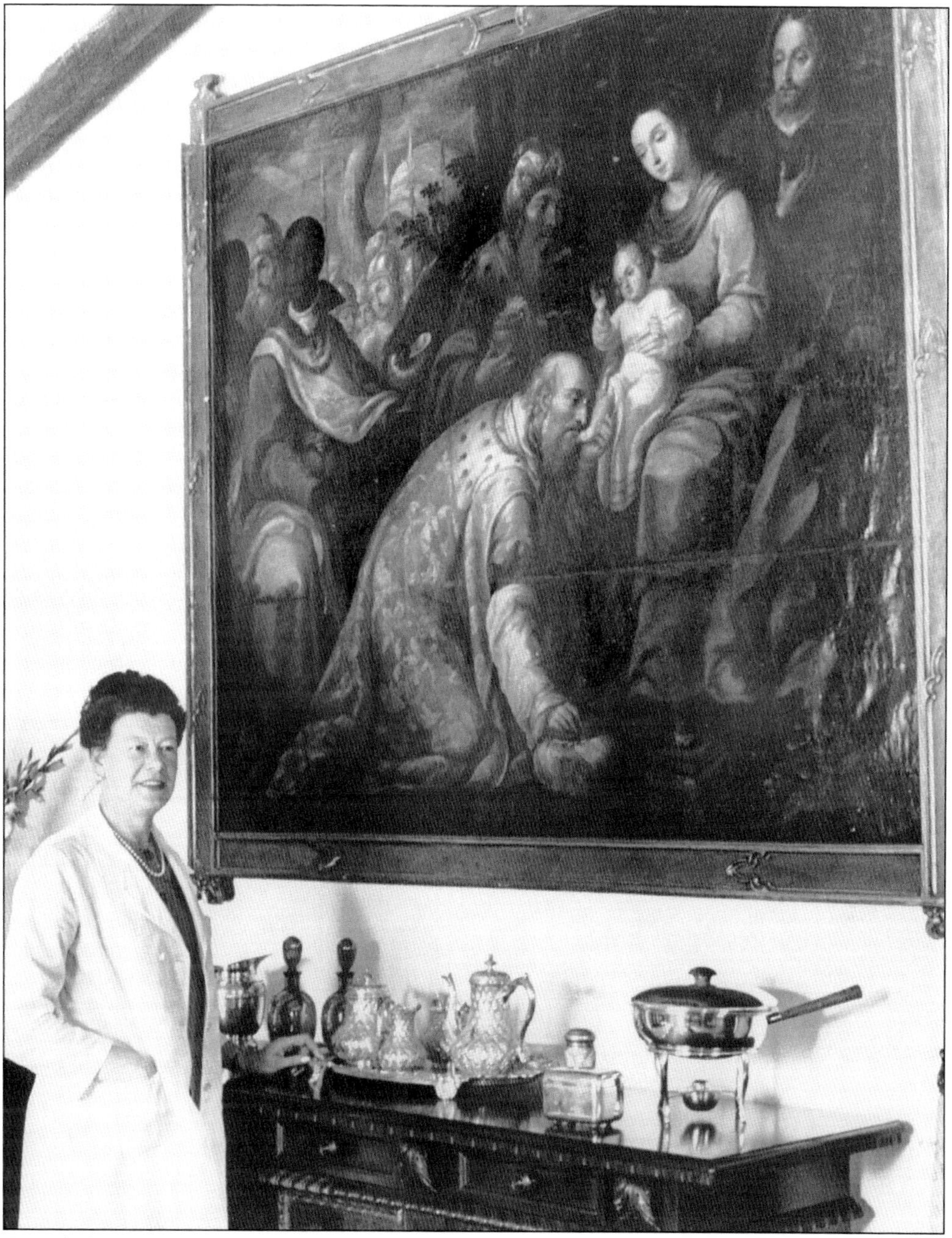

Famed photographer Joe Rosenthal took this picture of Anastasia Weil in the dining room of Rancho Buena Vista when he was a guest there in 1970. Rosenthal came from San Francisco on Flag Day and presented a copy of his famous picture of the raising of the flag on Iwo Jima to the Vista Ranchos Historical Society. Dr. Walter and Anastasia Weil had many notable guests during their 15 years of living in the historic adobe, including physician members of the Doctors' Symphony from Los Angeles on weekends; Ramon Navarro for dinner most Sundays; and Joan Crawford, who planted a magnolia tree on the rancho grounds.

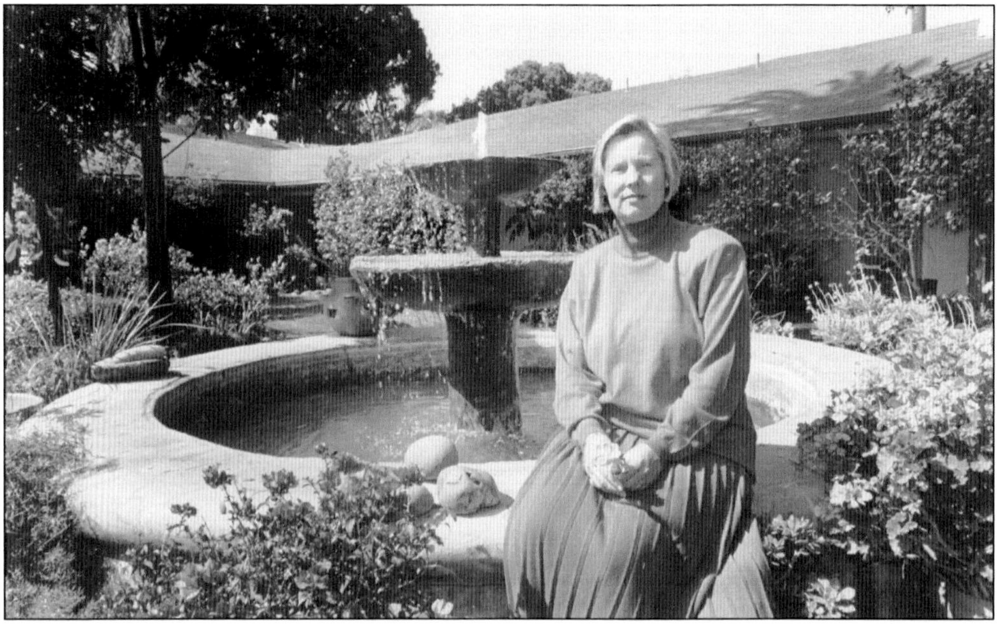

Rudd and Elizabeth "Sally" Schoeffel purchased Rancho Buena Vista from the Weils in 1972. Sally Schoeffel is pictured in April 1988, seated by the fountain in the ranch house courtyard. They added a guest house, and in 1981, they built a complex of professional buildings on Escondido Avenue, adjacent to Wildwood Park and Rancho Buena Vista. (Courtesy of *Escondido Times-Advocate.*)

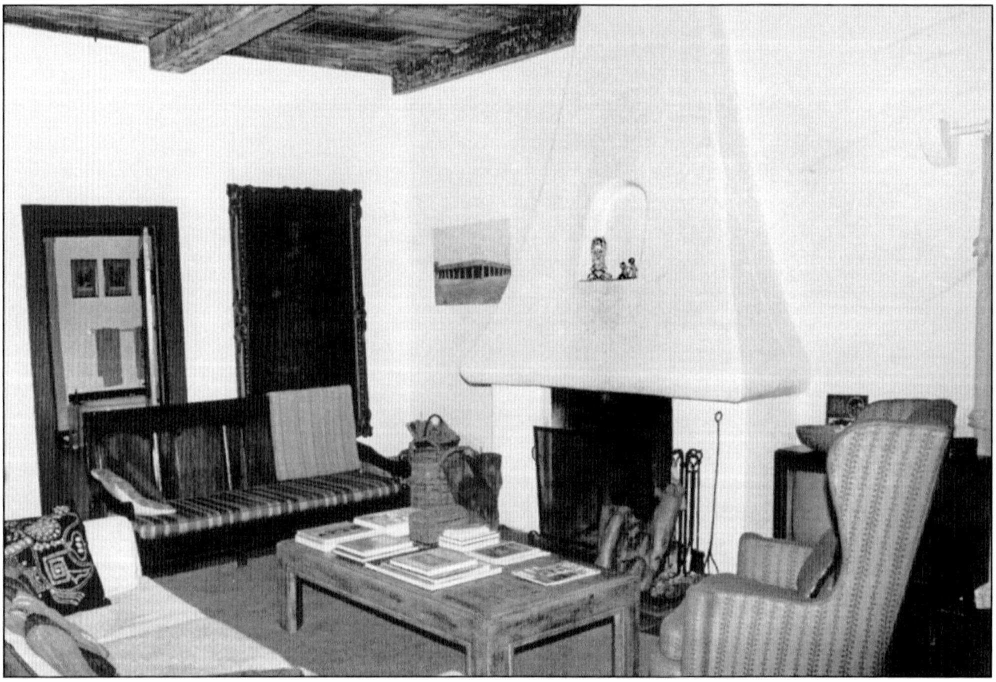

The historic Rancho Buena Vista adobe owned by Rudd and Sally Schoeffel was chosen in February 1985 as Home of the Week by the *Escondido Times-Advocate* and featured in their weekend section. Pictured is the comfortable living room of the ranch house in the mid-1980s, accented with pieces authentic to the time of the early ranchos. (Courtesy of *Escondido Times-Advocate.*)

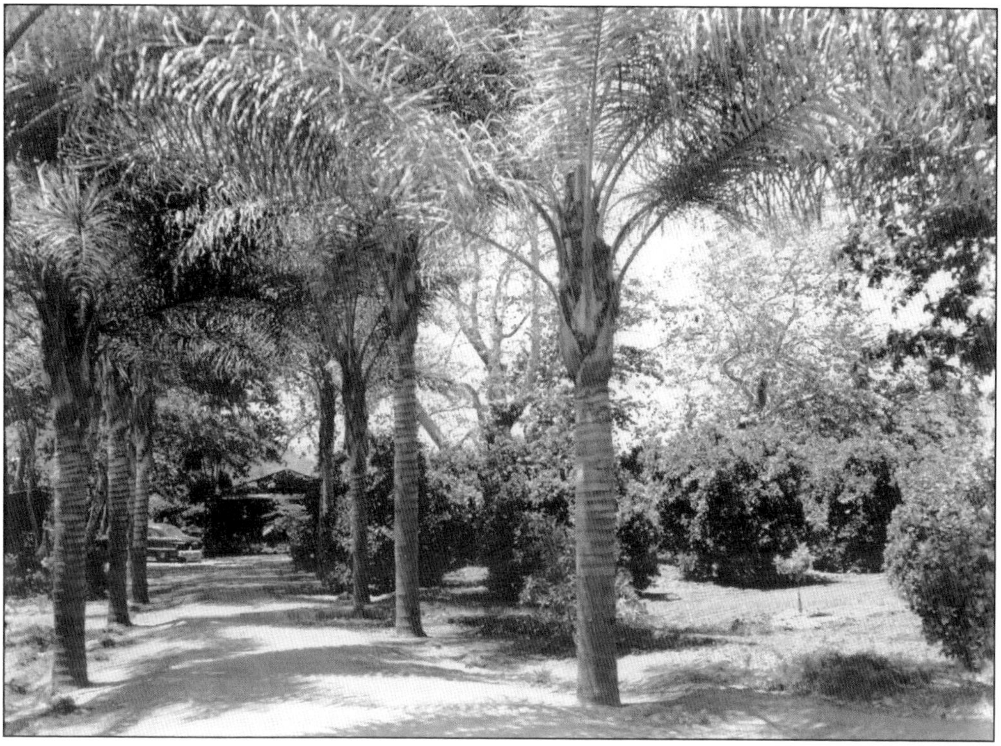

Until the 1970s, the palm-tree-lined entrance shown above led to Rancho Buena Vista from Escondido Avenue. The entrance below, relocated around the corner to Alta Vista Drive by the Schoeffels, was paved using 60,000 bricks from an old Alcohol and Beverage Control building in Salt Lake City. Two-thirds of the bricks were used in the driveway, with the remaining 20,000 sold to finance their installation.

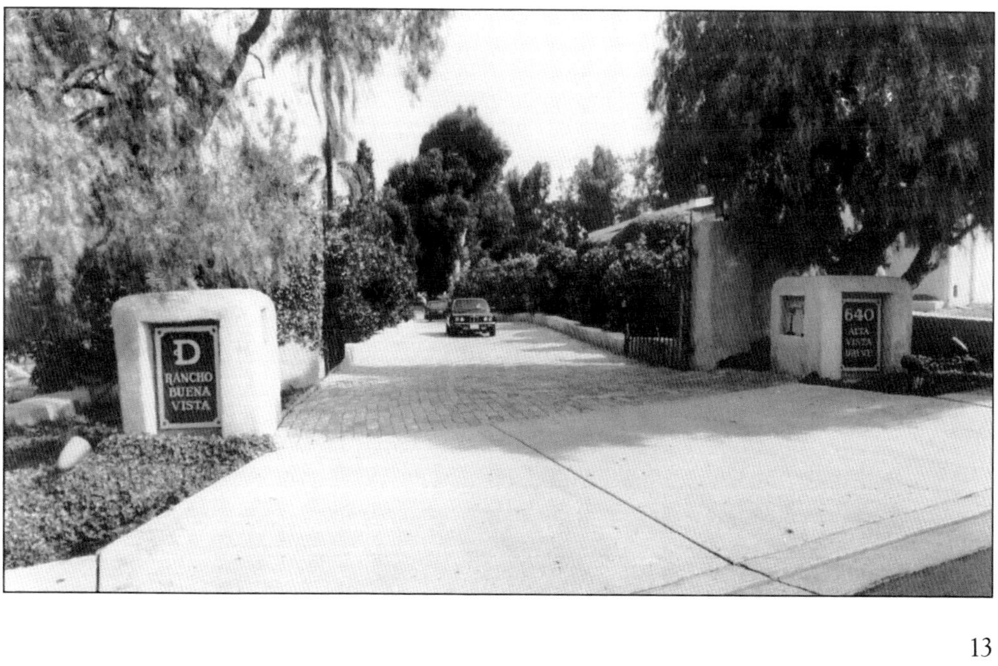

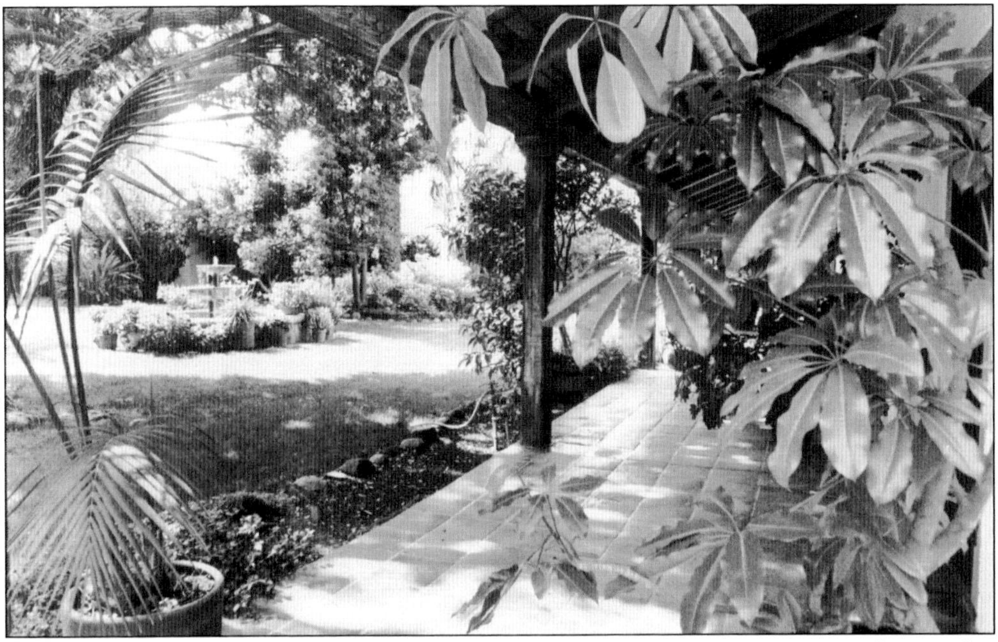

The City of Vista purchased the remaining 1.9 acres of Rancho Buena Vista in 1989, the year this photograph of the carefully tended courtyard gardens and fountain was taken by longtime *Escondido Times-Advocate* photographer Dan Rios. The garden was first enhanced, and the courtyard fountain installed, by silent-screen actress Margarita Fischer Pollard and her husband, Harry, during their ownership of the rancho from 1931 to 1951. (Courtesy of *Escondido Times-Advocate*.)

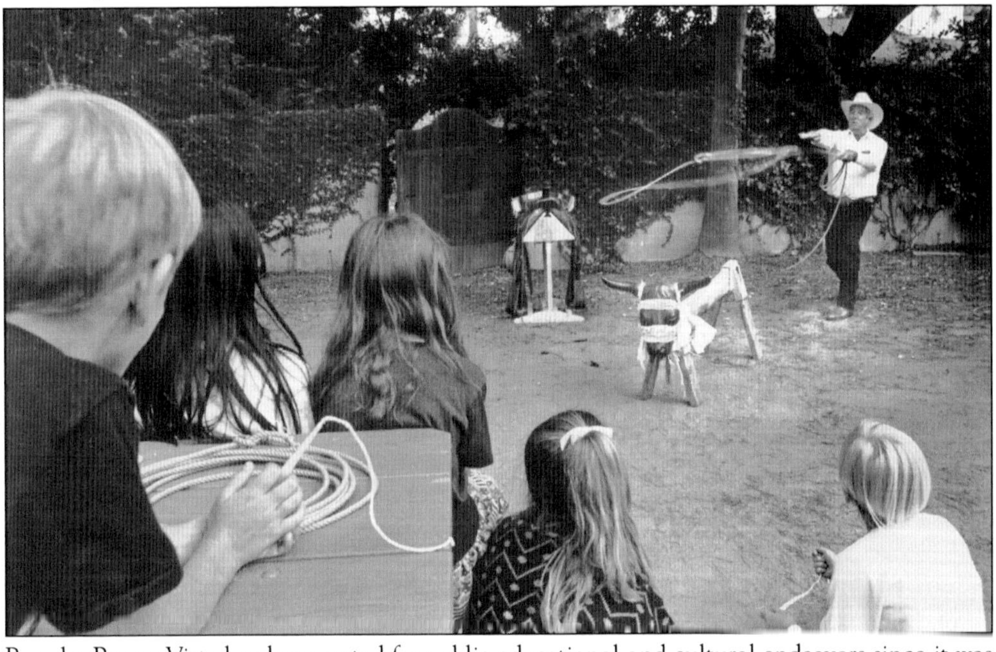

Rancho Buena Vista has been noted for public educational and cultural endeavors since it was purchased by the City of Vista in 1989. Pictured here in June 1991 are visiting schoolchildren as they get a steer-roping lesson and learn about saddles and other Western gear that were used in the late 1800s, when the rancho was in full swing. (Courtesy of *Escondido Times-Advocate*.)

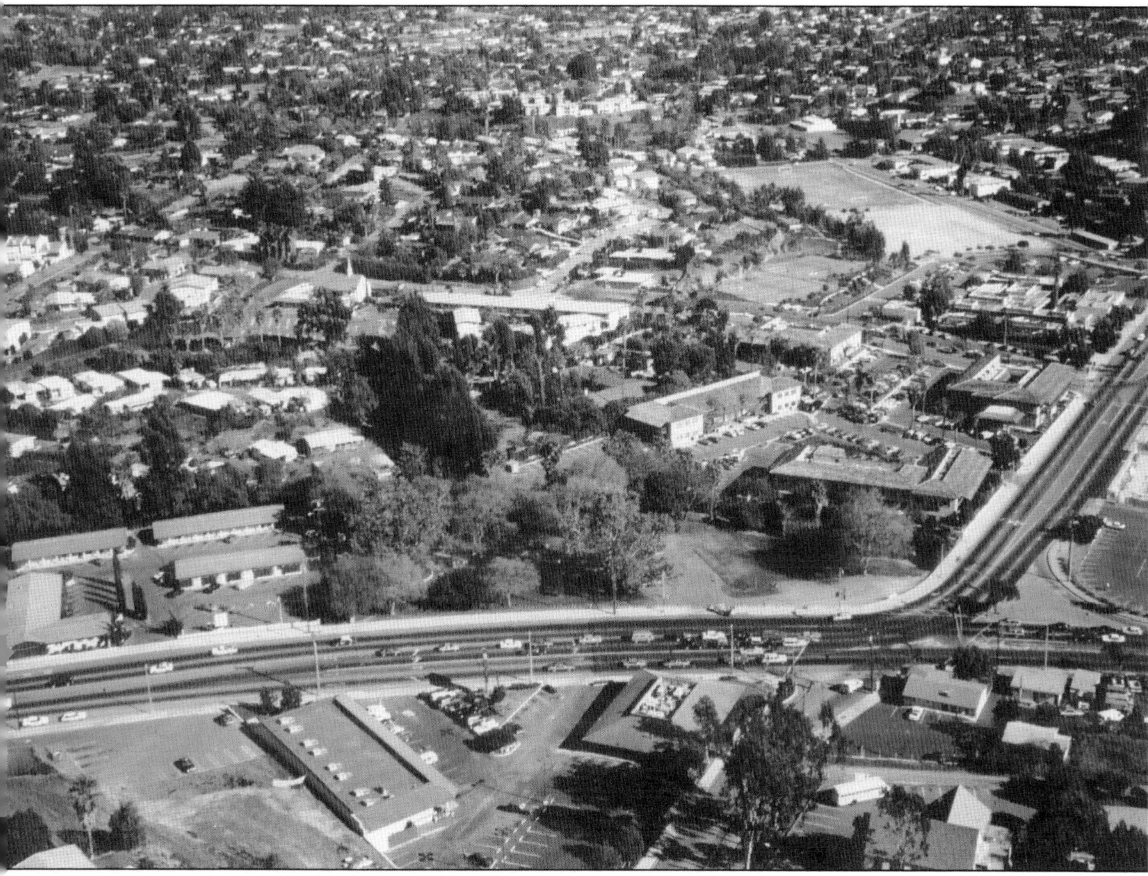

The configuration of new and historic Vista sites is shown clearly in this early 1980s aerial view of East Vista Way and Escondido Avenue. The group of trees on East Vista Way, at the lower center, is Wildwood Park. Two of the former professional buildings to the left of the park were razed and the remainder used for a community center and Vista Historical Society Museum until 2008, when a fire station took their place. The office buildings at the right of the park, on Escondido Avenue, were built by Rudd and Sally Schoeffel during the time they owned Rancho Buena Vista; the roof of the historic ranch house can be seen directly behind the rear office building. The empty field at the upper right is the location of the library and the new city hall complex.

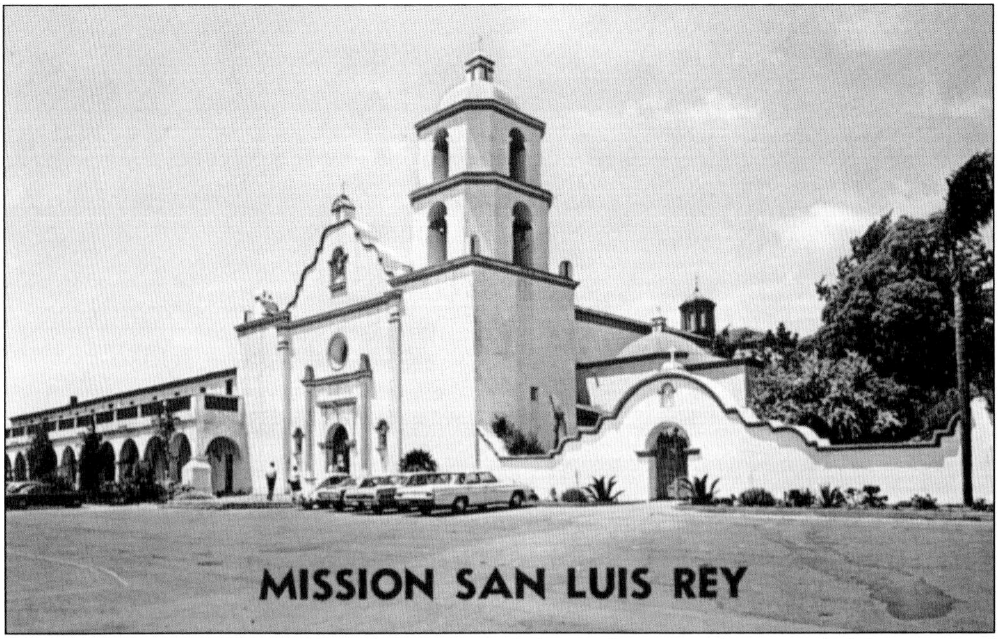

Mission San Luis Rey was established in 1798. Until the Civil War era, the original El Camino Real ran in a circuitous route from Mission San Diego de Alcala through Vista. It passed along North and South Santa Fe Avenue, past Rancho Buena Vista, and about 9 more miles to the mission site. Fully restored, Mission San Luis Rey is today a keystone in the chain of 21 California missions.

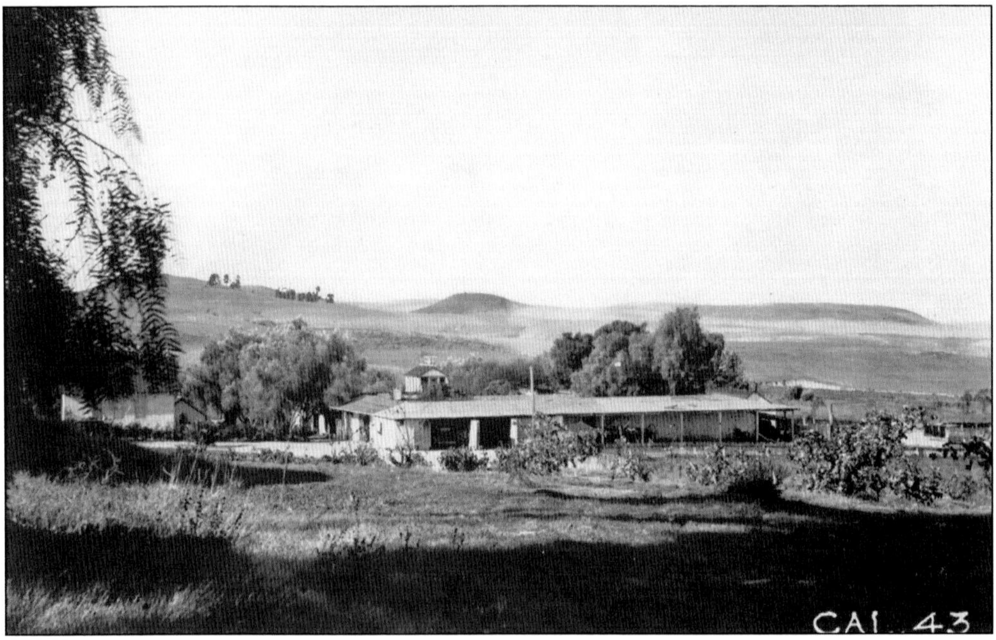

This view looks across Rancho Guajome land from the northeast. Ysidora Bandini received the property as a wedding gift from her brother-in-law, Abel Stearns, when she married Col. Cave Johnson Couts in April 1851. Stearns purchased the 2,219-acre ranch for $550 from two Luiseno Indians, Andres and Jose Manuel, who received it as a land grant from Mexican governor Pio Pico and named it Rancho Guajome, "home of the frogs."

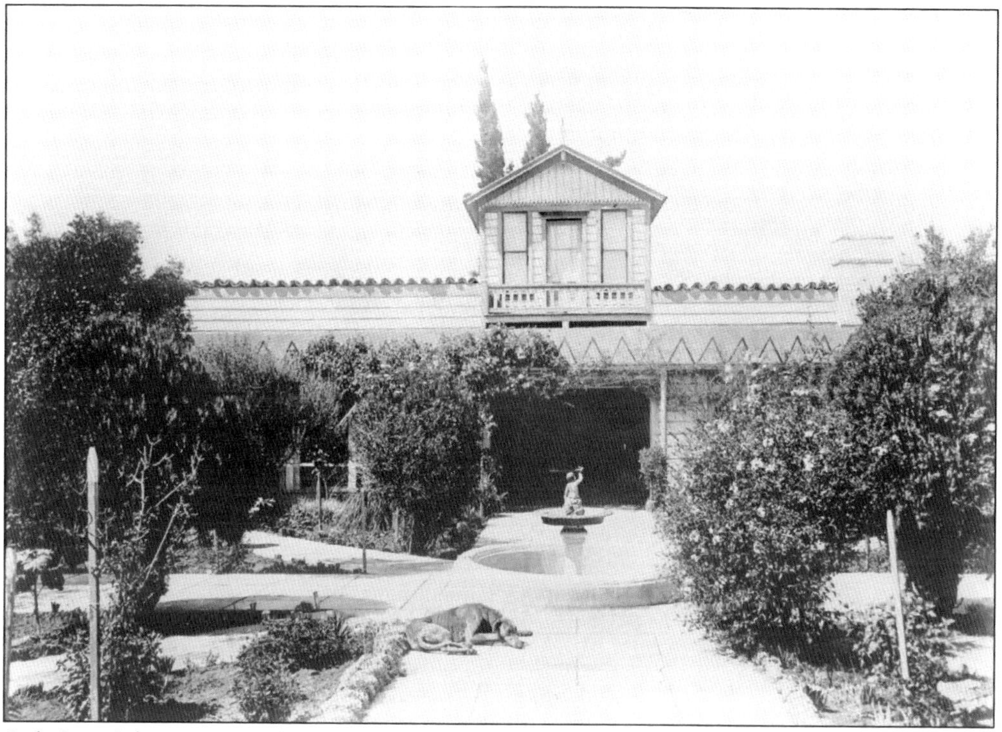

Col. Cave Johnson Couts built this 20-room home in 1852. An outstanding example of Anglo-Hispanic architecture, it is constructed of wood frame and adobe bricks, with 4-foot-thick walls in some places. Four long wings surround the landscaped patio and fountain. The second story was a sewing room. There were always guests, and Helen Hunt Jackson spent time here as she gathered material for her famous novel *Ramona*.

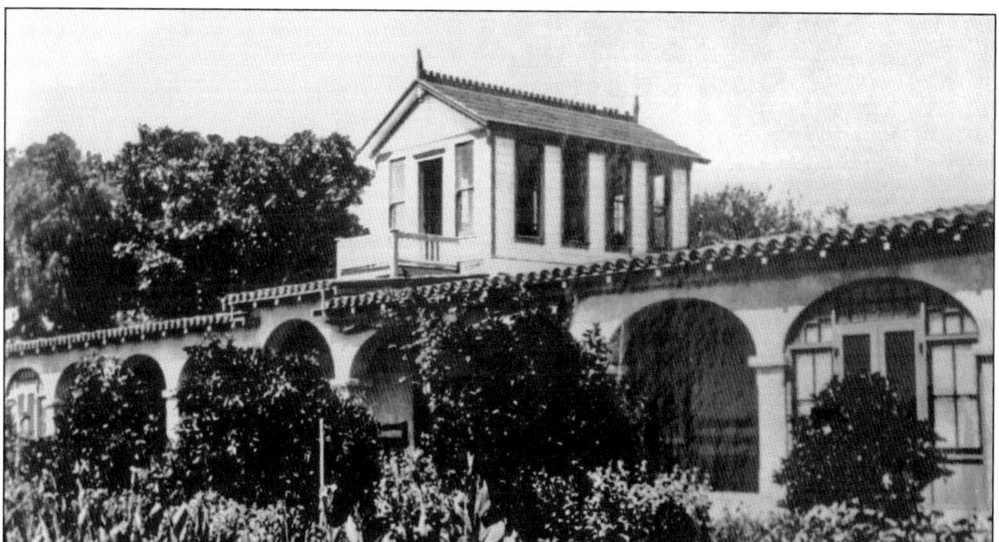

Spanish-style archways face the patio along the wings of the ranch house. The home and 600 remaining acres were purchased in 1973 by San Diego County, which runs it as a museum and sponsors special events. The annual Thanksgiving weekend "Rancho Christmas" features children's activities from the rancho era. Rancho Guajome is a National Historic Monument.

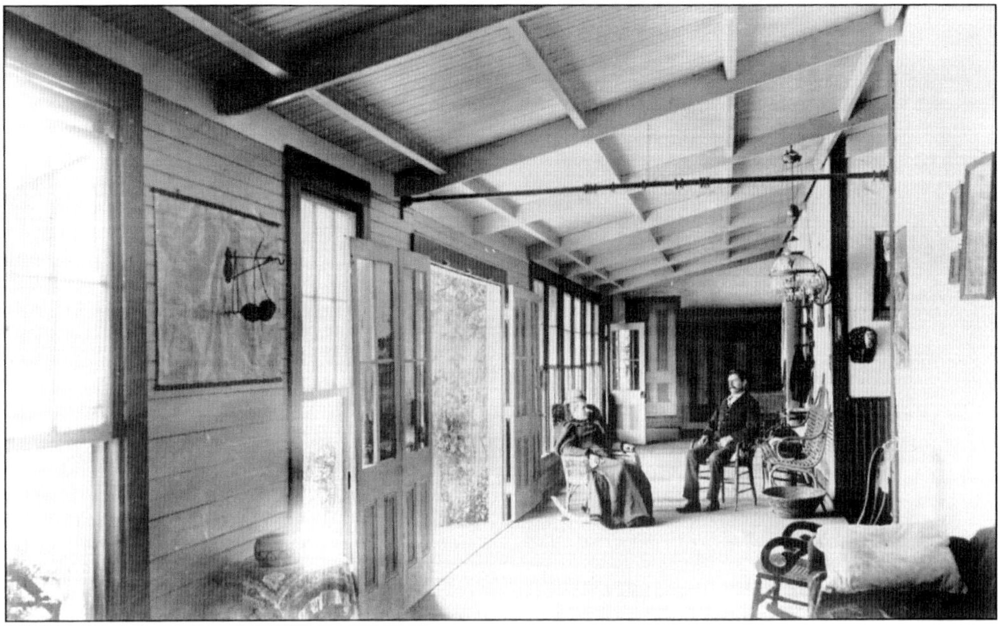

Cave Couts Jr. visits with an unidentified lady in one of the wings of the Rancho Guajome hacienda. He married Lilybelle Clemens, niece of Samuel Clemens, and had one son, Cave Couts III. Cave Couts Jr. spent his entire 87 years at Rancho Guajome and died in the bed he was born in. In the 1920s, he fully restored the house, using his father's original plans.

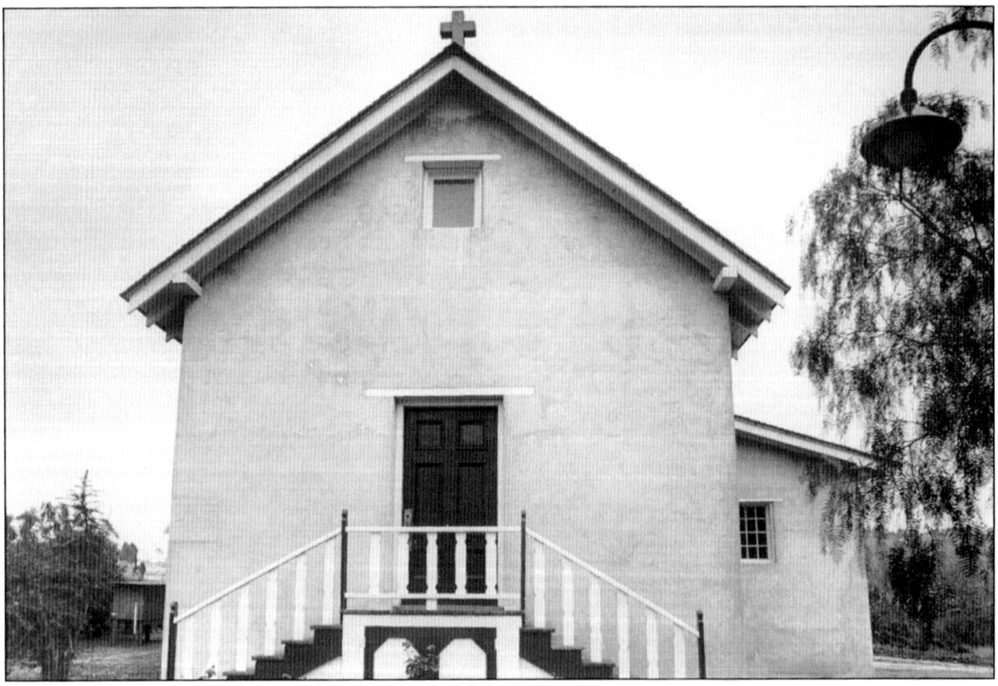

Although he was a Protestant, in 1868, Col. Cave Johnson Couts received permission from Pope Pius IX to build a chapel and bring in a resident priest so he could raise his 10 children as Catholics. The original adobe chapel collapsed, and this wooden building was reconstructed by Cave Couts Jr. in the 1920s. (Courtesy of *Escondido Times-Advocate.*)

Two

A Corner, an Inn, and 60 Miles of Concrete Pipe

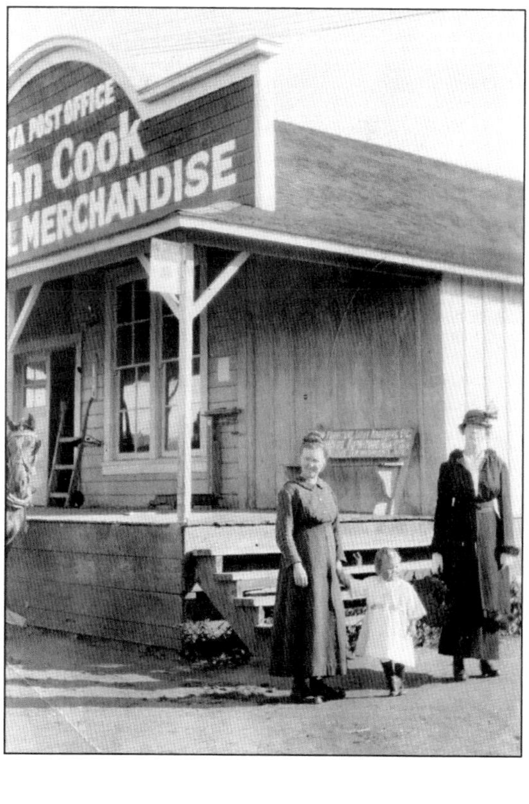

Gertrude M. Cook became Vista's first postmistress on May 5, 1917. She was appointed upon the death of her husband, John Cook, who had served as postmaster since January 30, 1915. The Cooks at that time owned the general merchandise store, which housed the post office. This photograph, taken in 1917 or 1918, shows Gertrude Cook (left) with her little daughter, Pauline. She served as acting postmistress until May 9, 1918, when Joseph A. Flower Jr. took over the job.

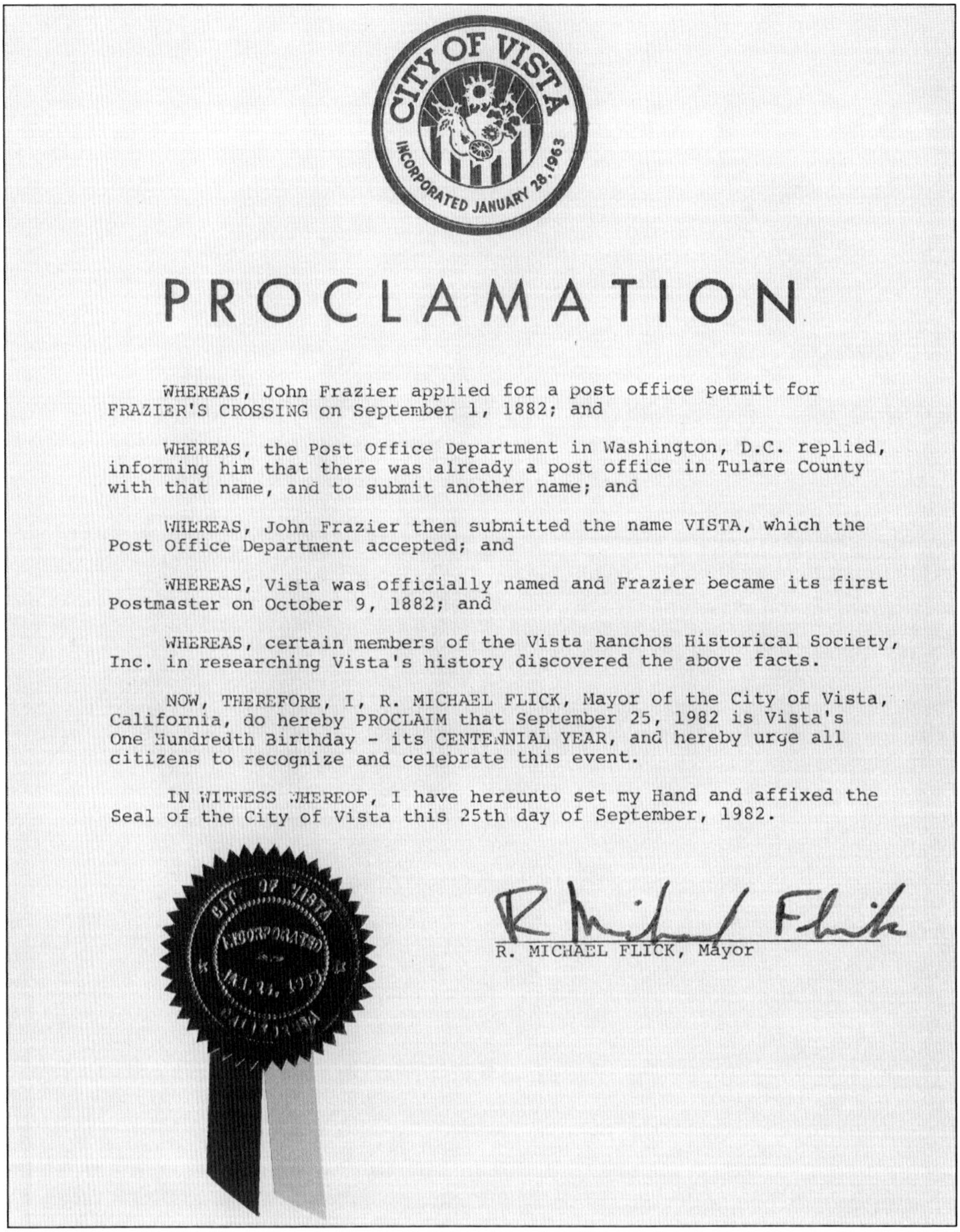

CITY OF VISTA
INCORPORATED JANUARY 28, 1963

PROCLAMATION

WHEREAS, John Frazier applied for a post office permit for FRAZIER'S CROSSING on September 1, 1882; and

WHEREAS, the Post Office Department in Washington, D.C. replied, informing him that there was already a post office in Tulare County with that name, and to submit another name; and

WHEREAS, John Frazier then submitted the name VISTA, which the Post Office Department accepted; and

WHEREAS, Vista was officially named and Frazier became its first Postmaster on October 9, 1882; and

WHEREAS, certain members of the Vista Ranchos Historical Society, Inc. in researching Vista's history discovered the above facts.

NOW, THEREFORE, I, R. MICHAEL FLICK, Mayor of the City of Vista, California, do hereby PROCLAIM that September 25, 1982 is Vista's One Hundredth Birthday - its CENTENNIAL YEAR, and hereby urge all citizens to recognize and celebrate this event.

IN WITNESS WHEREOF, I have hereunto set my Hand and affixed the Seal of the City of Vista this 25th day of September, 1982.

R. Michael Flick
R. MICHAEL FLICK, Mayor

John Frazier came to town in 1882, acquired a mineral well, and decided to immortalize himself by giving the fledgling community his name. He applied to the U.S. Post Office in Washington, D.C., for the name "Frazier's Crossing" but was notified that there already existed a Frazier Post Office in Tulare County, California. He tried Buena Vista, too, before submitting the name Vista. It was accepted, and on October 9, 1882, he was granted permission to open a post office and become the first postmaster. In 1886, John Frazier moved on to Carlsbad. This 1982 City of Vista Proclamation commemorates the 100-year anniversary of the town's naming. There are a few other tales about how Vista got its name, but this one is by far the most popular and authorized version.

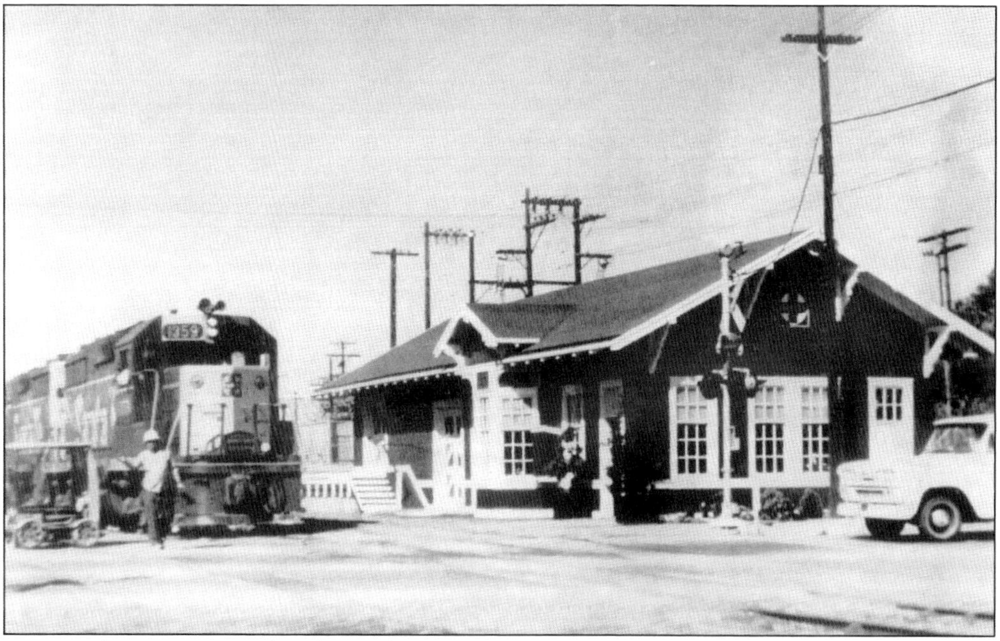

In 1887, the Santa Fe Railroad completed its freight line from Oceanside to Escondido, passing through Vista and San Marcos. Vista had only a freight platform, located near what is now North Santa Fe Avenue and Jefferson Street, until April 1913, when the railroad announced it would build the new siding and depot shown above at a cost of $8,007. After more than 80 years of continuous operation, the station was closed in December 1969 as a result of a major reduction in local freight. In early 2008, the $477-million Sprinter passenger line began daily runs along the same route. After sitting empty for a decade, the depot was moved to the corner of Indiana and Jefferson Streets, authentically restored as pictured below, and dedicated as new headquarters for the chamber of commerce on July 2, 1981.

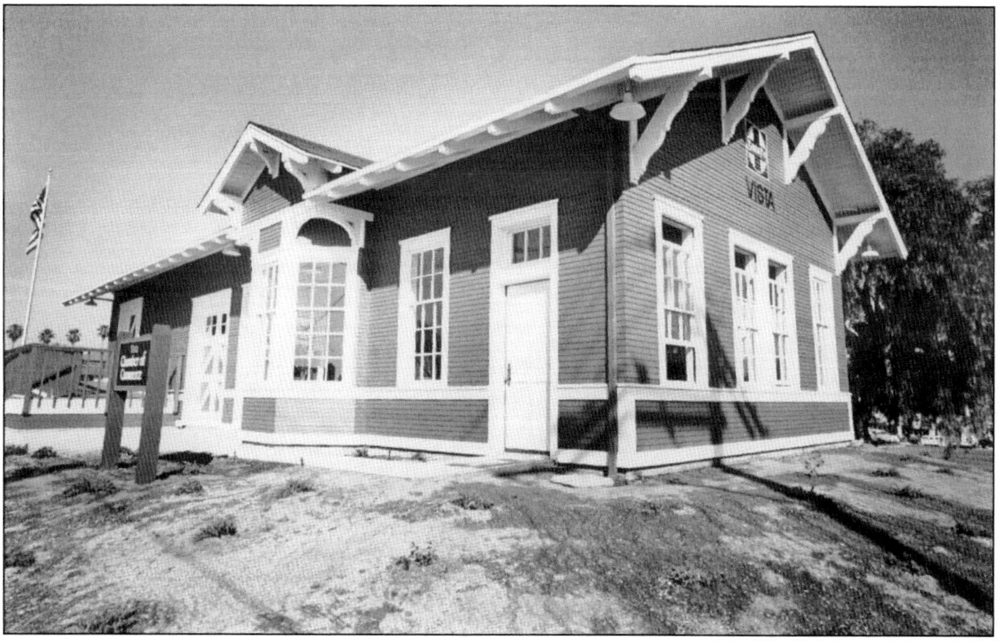

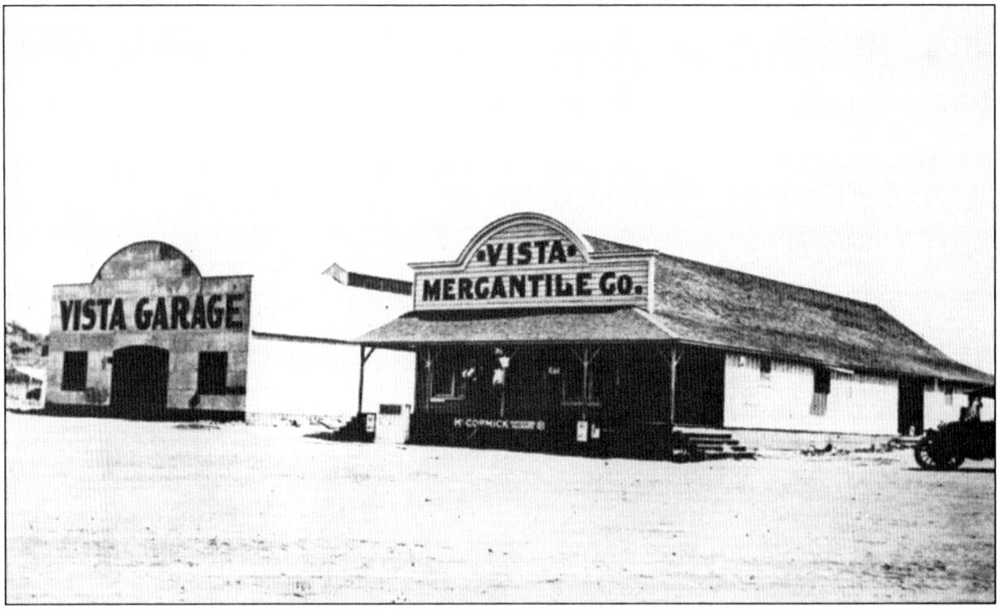

The Vista Garage and Vista Mercantile Company on North Santa Fe Avenue, pictured here in 1912, were among the first businesses in the community. They were located across from where the new Santa Fe Railroad depot and siding would be built the following year. Later called the Red Barn, the garage building housed an assortment of businesses over ensuing years.

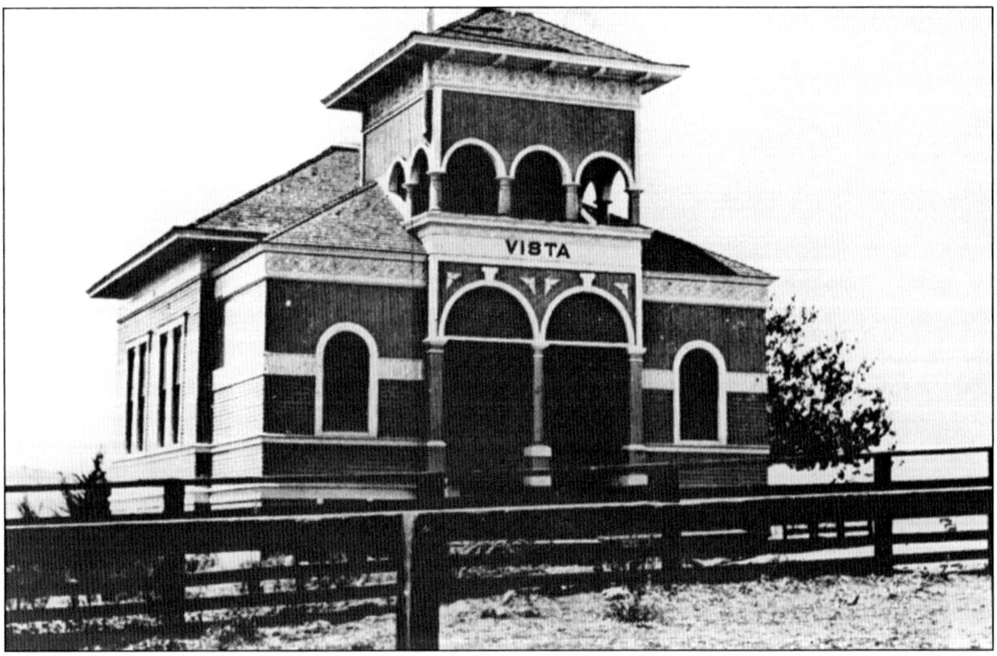

Lily Irwin was the first teacher for children living in the Buena area in 1887. It wasn't until 1914 that this permanent, Victorian-style schoolhouse was built on South Santa Fe Avenue, across from the railroad tracks at Buena Creek Road, by William A. Pechstein, who also formed the first school board.

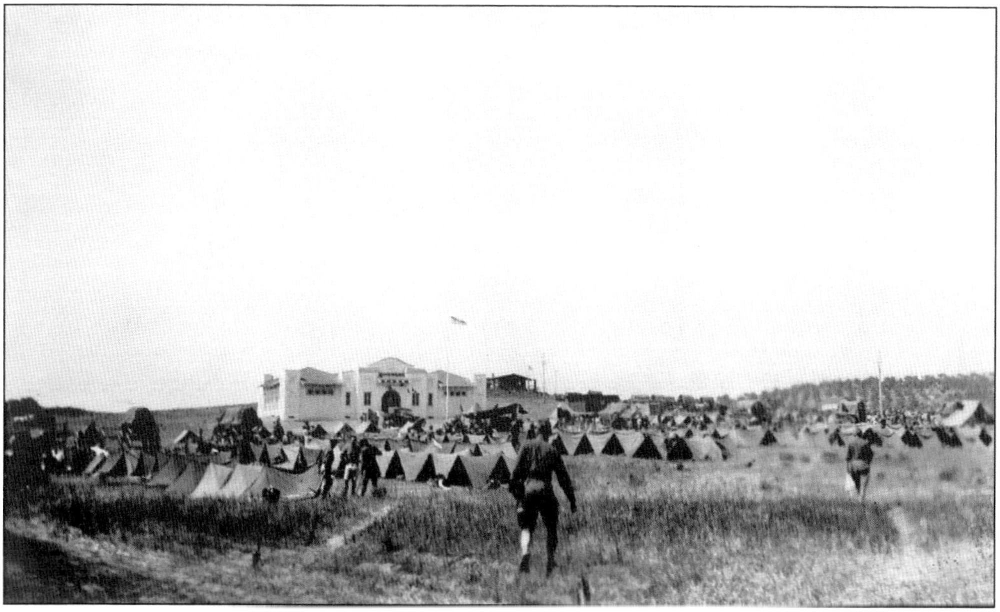

A World War I unit of the U.S. Army is shown as it encamped in Vista in this extraordinary photograph, taken about 1918. The tents are set up where downtown Vista is today. In the background is the new Vista Union School, opened in 1917 and renamed Jefferson Elementary School in 1930.

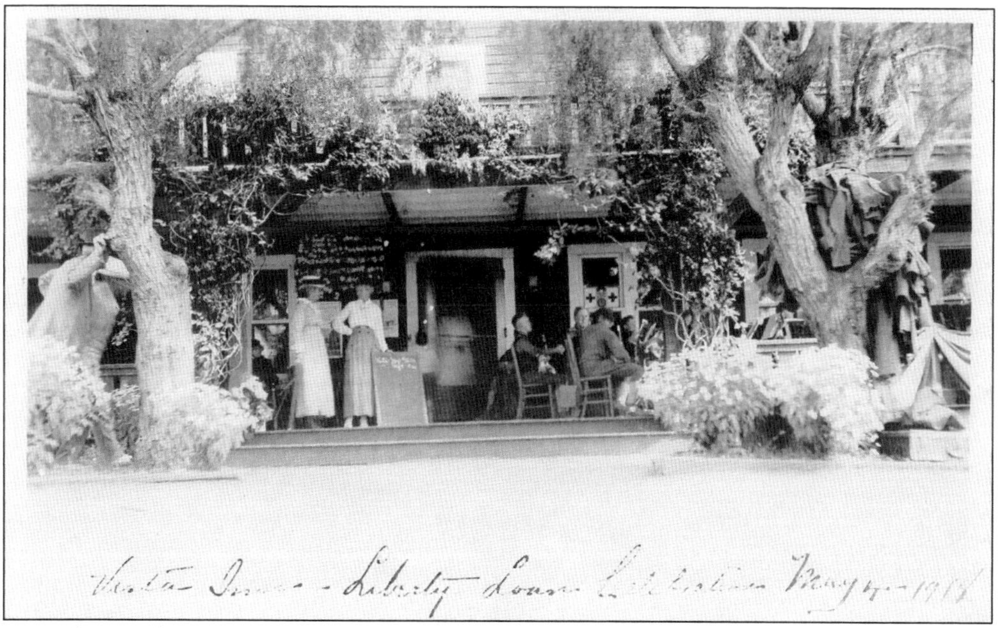

According to the *Oceanside Blade* of May 11, 1918, "Vista did herself proud in the celebration of the Third Liberty Loan Drive." Pictured here is the Liberty Loan Celebration held at the Vista Inn on May 4, 1918. The Woman's Club sold Liberty Bonds and sponsored fund-raisers, bringing in $4,000 instead of the $600 allotment hoped for by the Women's Division of the National War Savings Committee.

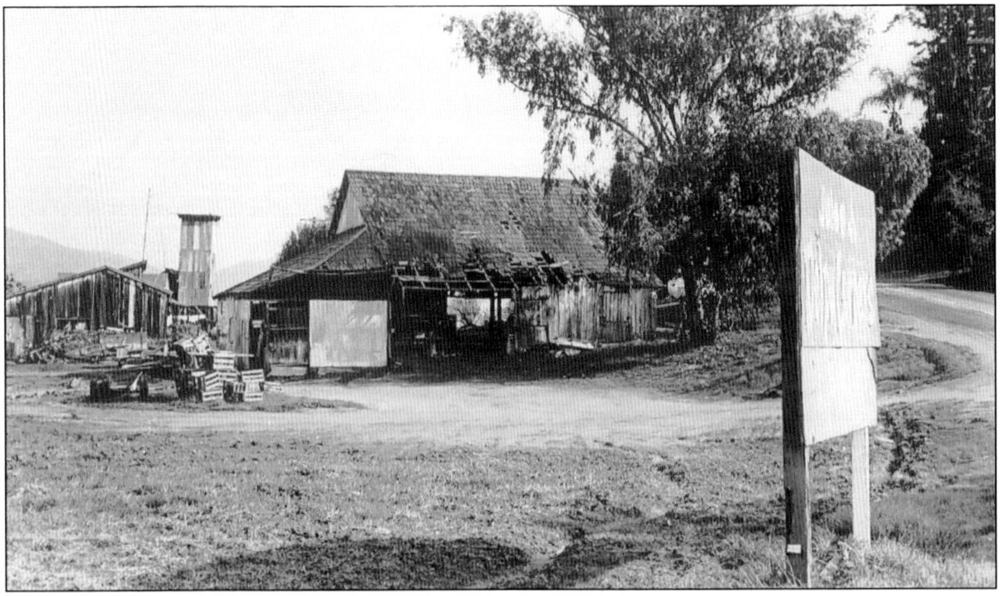

Bernard Delpy came to Vista from France in 1873 and homesteaded the land that is still called Delpy Corners. His nephew, Jules Jacques Delpy, joined him in 1879, and they dug wells and planted vineyards and groves. This photograph shows the winery before it was razed in the early 1970s. The sign reads, "Jules J. Delpy Corners, Since 1879."

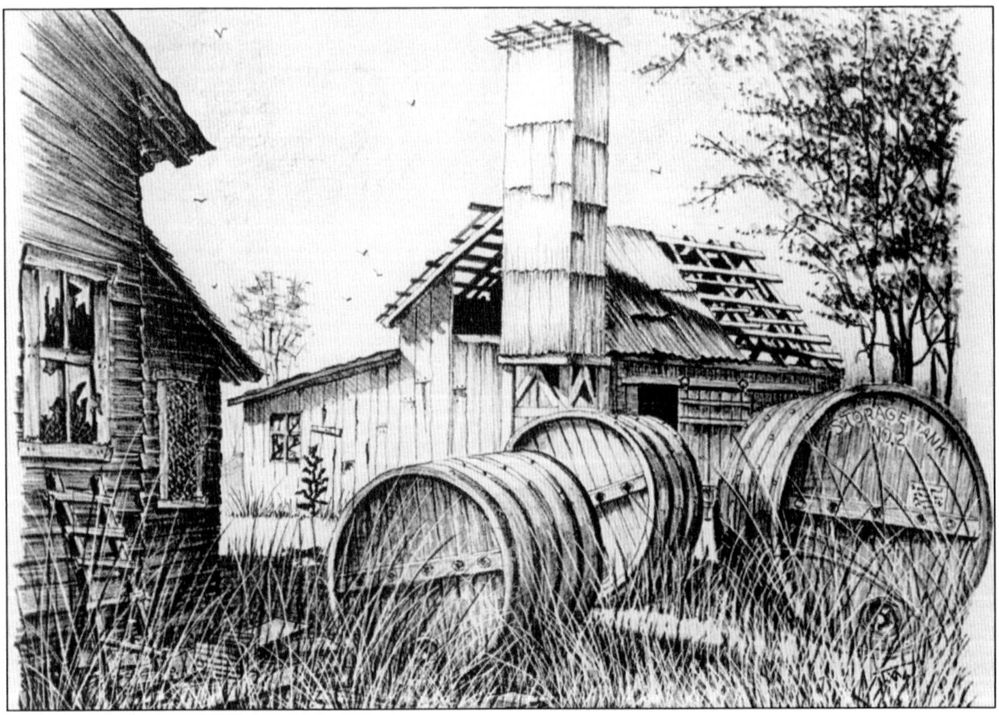

This lithograph of the old Delpy winery was created by famed local artist Ted Wade, who captured many historic scenes like this one. In 1884, Bernard Delpy and his nephew, Jules Jacques Delpy, opened Buena Vista Winery, the first successful winery in northern San Diego County. Noted for the quality of its sherry, the winery operated for several decades until Prohibition closed it.

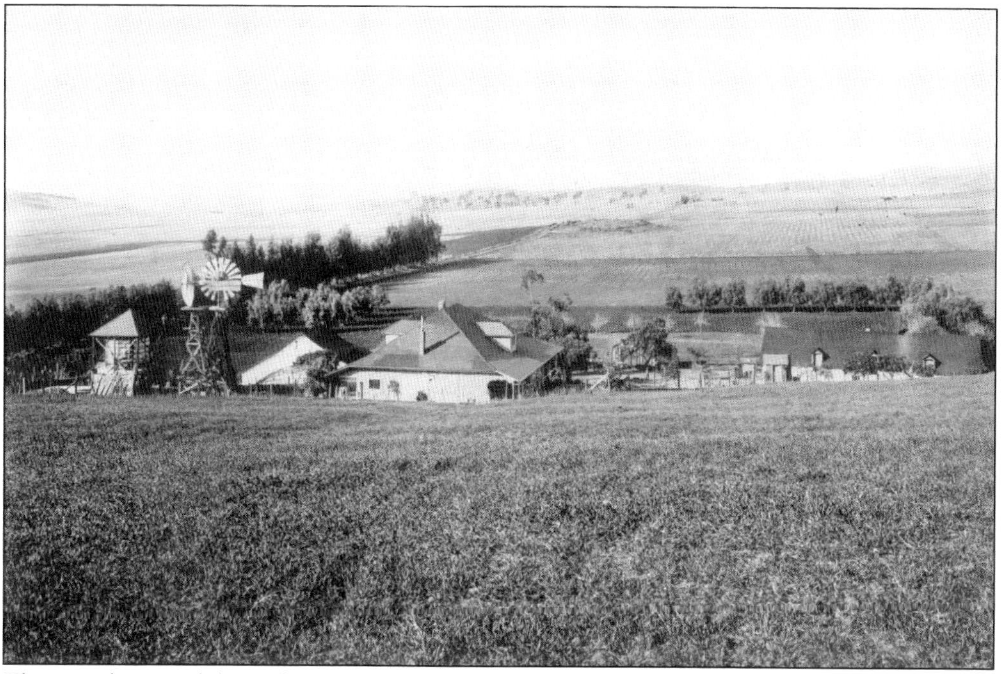

This aerial view of the Delpy property was photographed in 1927. The house, which was later remodeled and enlarged, sat on the south side of Foothill Drive near what is now East Vista Way. This photograph encompasses the Delpy land to the north, with the Rancho Santa Margarita hills in the background.

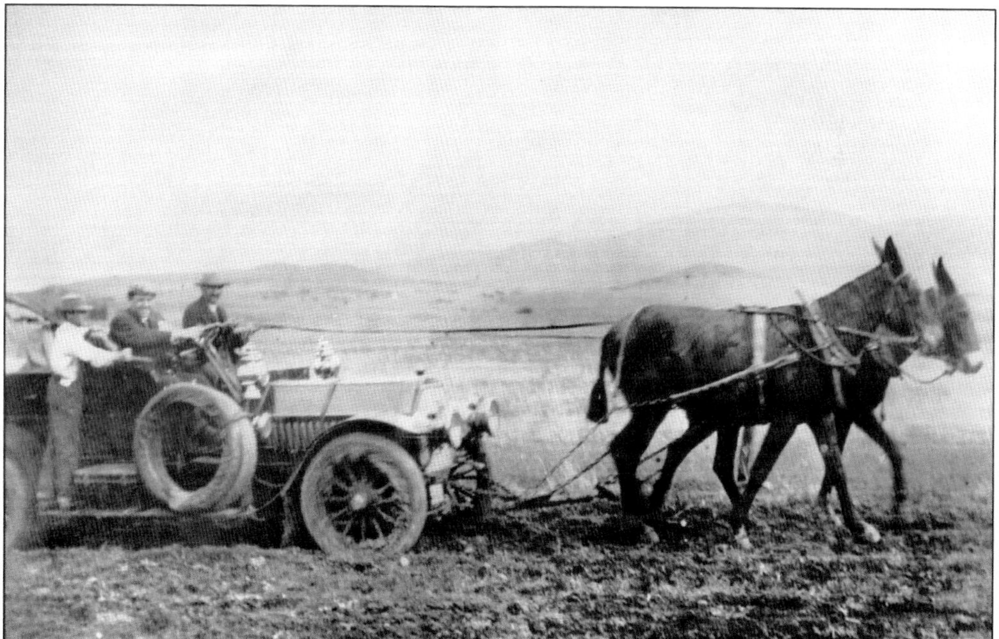

The first automobile in Vista, a Moon, was owned by Jules Jacques Delpy. Rains were heavy and streets unpaved in the early years of the 20th century, and vehicles and cattle often became mired. This is believed to be Ambrose DeBard's mule team pulling the Moon out of the mud.

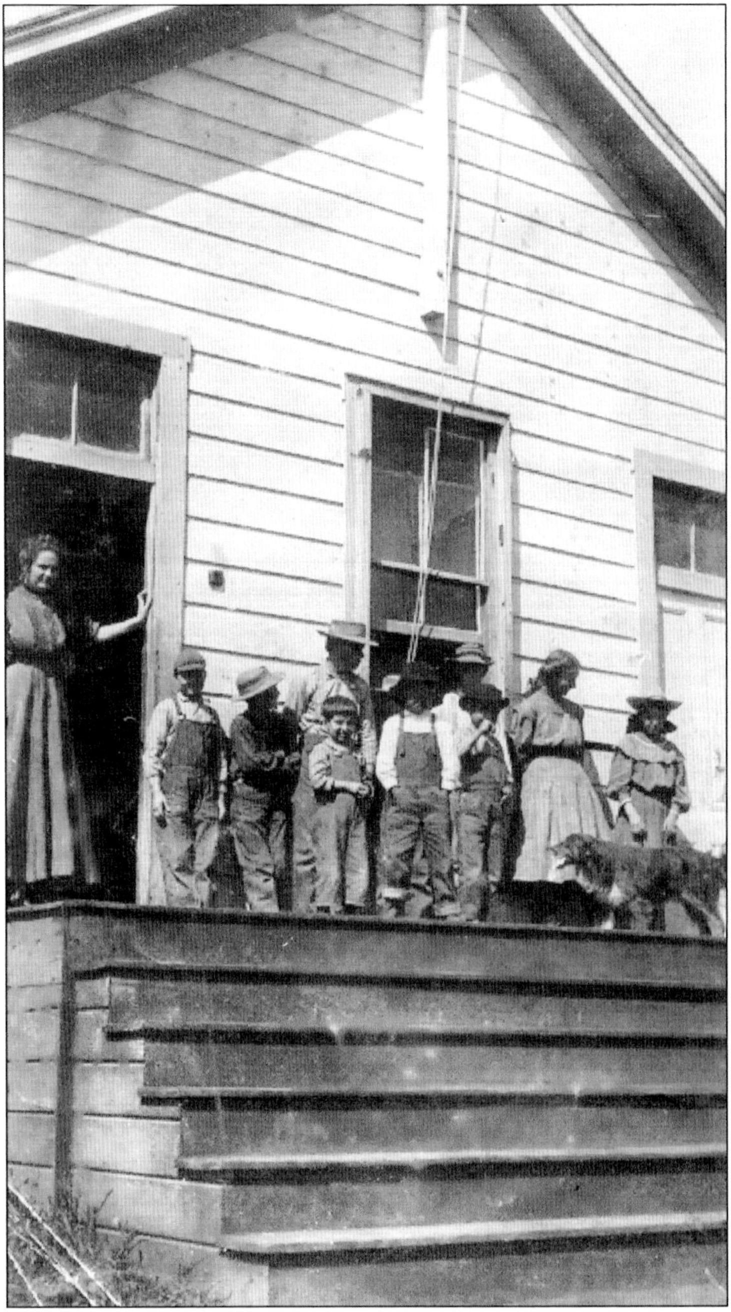

Teacher Lydia Winters stands in the doorway of Delpy School in 1907. The school, located on what is now the 1500 block of East Vista Way near Palomar Place, was founded in 1894 on the property of Bernard and Jules Jacques Delpy to provide an education for their own and neighboring children. Seventeen-year-old Maria Delpy, newly married to Jules Jacques Delpy, qualified as a student so there would be eight children and they could legally hire a teacher. Dances and parties were held to raise funds so the teacher could be paid. The first teacher lived with the Delpys and received a salary of $8 per month. Among students pictured here are Frank, Louis, Jack, Henry, and Clara Delpy and Emily Itzaina.

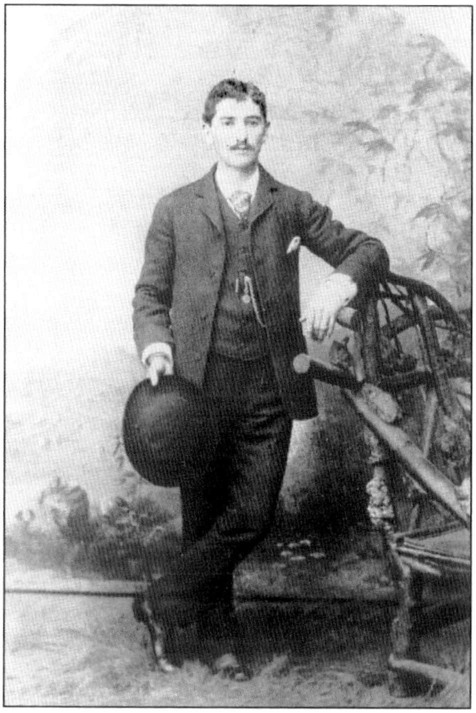

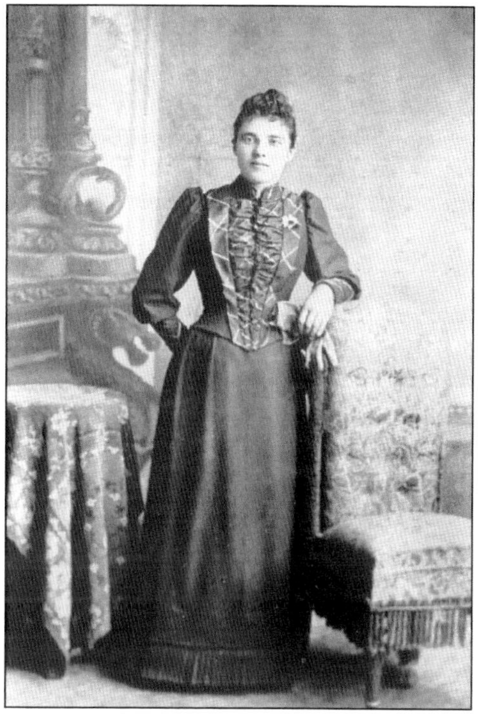

Jules Jacques and Maria Delpy, married in Los Angeles in 1894, posed for the portraits above as a young couple and again on May 5, 1944, their 50th wedding anniversary. Maria is gowned in the dress and veil she wore when she married in Los Angeles at age 17. Over the years, the industrious family prospered in Vista and remained active in civic, business, and social affairs. Jules Delpy lived to be 94 and Maria 105.

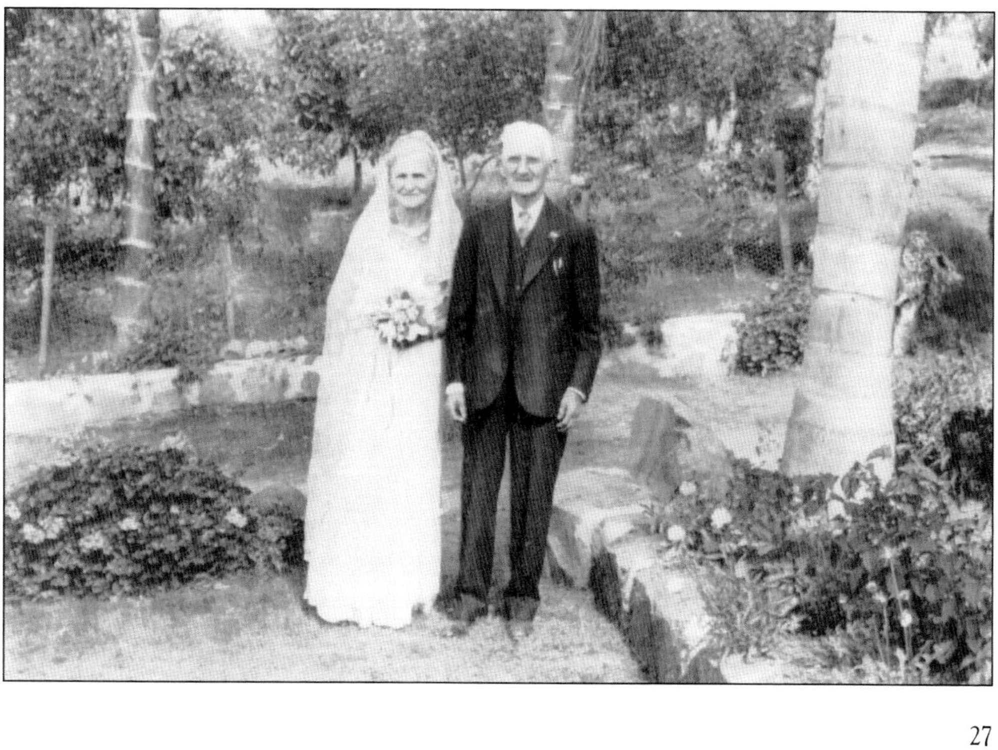

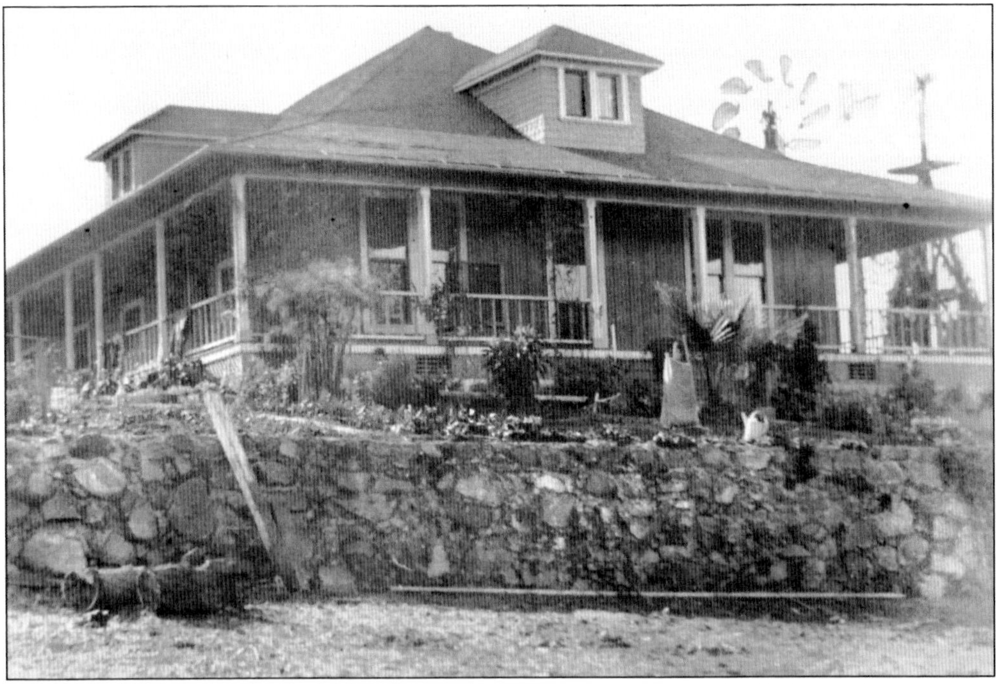

This is the first Delpy home, a wood-frame dwelling built in the early 1900s on the southeast corner of what is now Foothill Drive and East Vista Way.

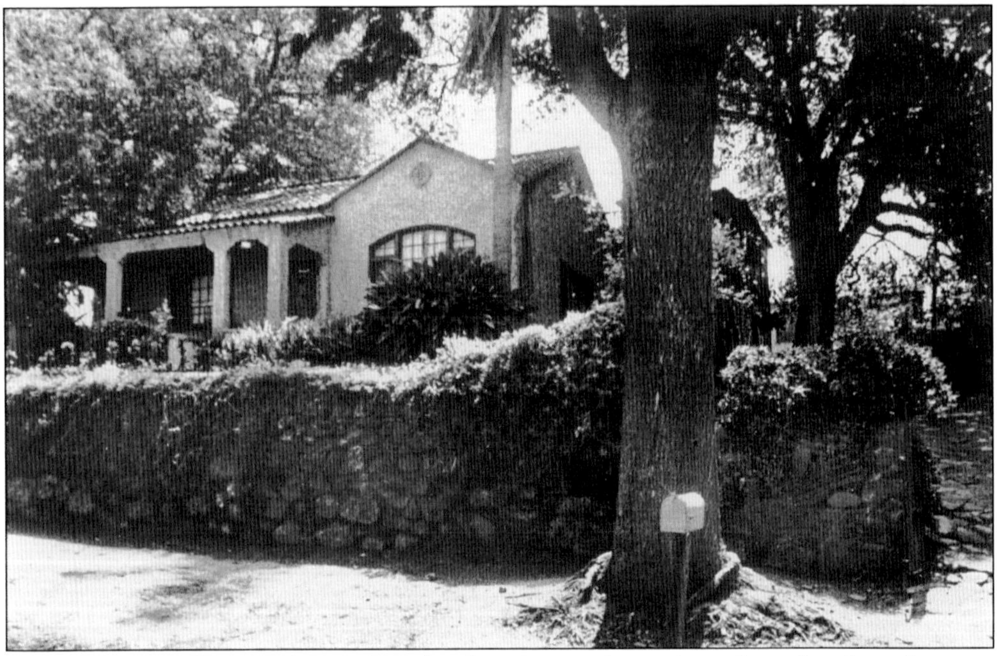

The home shown above was later enlarged and its exterior changed to a Spanish style, with stucco exterior and tile roof. It stood as a Vista landmark for many years. The winery and other buildings across the street on Foothill Drive were razed in the early 1970s for commercial construction, but the house remained until it was removed because of its deteriorating condition. This photograph was taken in March 1983. (Courtesy *Escondido Times-Advocate*.)

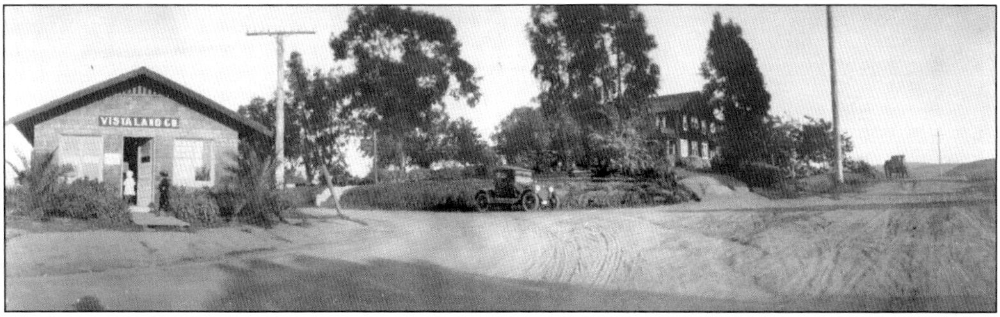

The 26-room Vista Inn was built in 1912 by the Vista Land Company. It stood on what is now the corner of Santa Fe Avenue and Main Street, which at that time was Highway 395. This photograph of the Vista Land Company and the Vista Inn shows clearly the elevation on which the hotel sat, proclaimed a "commanding knoll" by the *Oceanside Blade* on August 24, 1912.

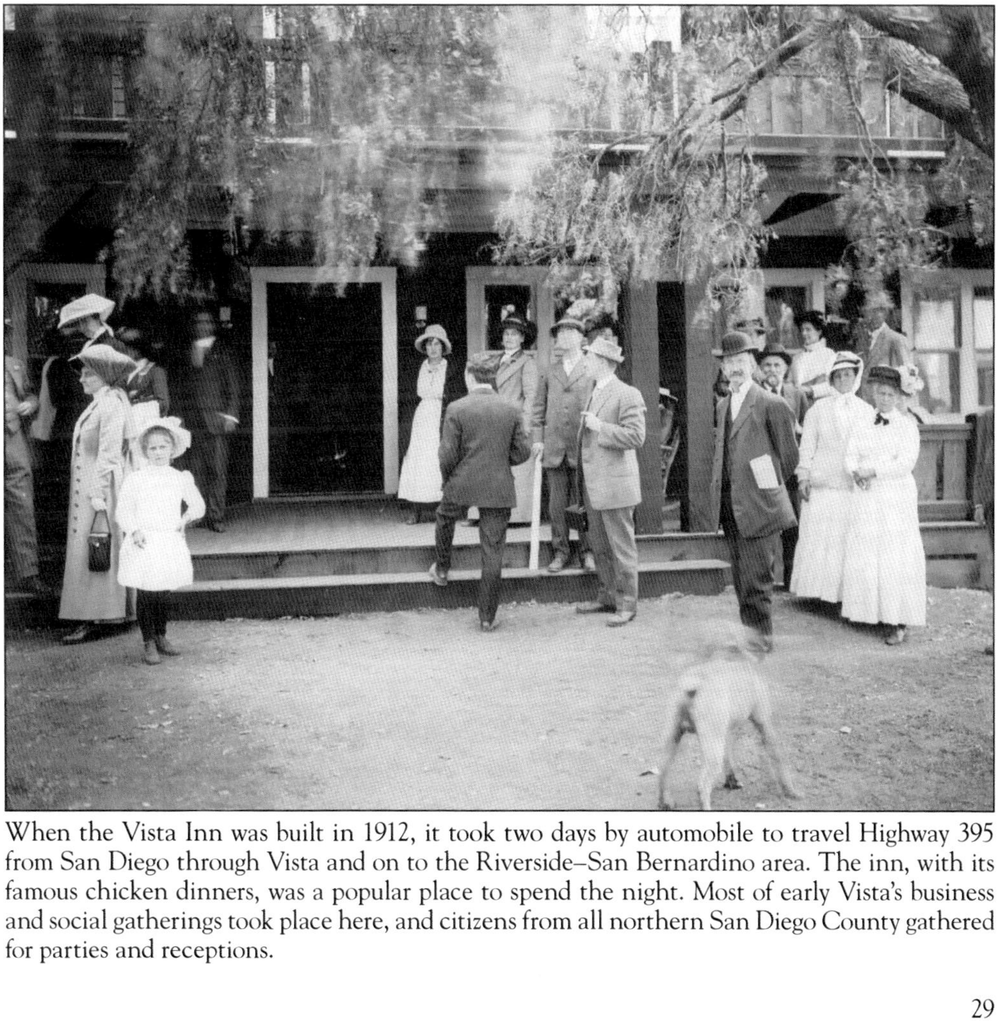

When the Vista Inn was built in 1912, it took two days by automobile to travel Highway 395 from San Diego through Vista and on to the Riverside–San Bernardino area. The inn, with its famous chicken dinners, was a popular place to spend the night. Most of early Vista's business and social gatherings took place here, and citizens from all northern San Diego County gathered for parties and receptions.

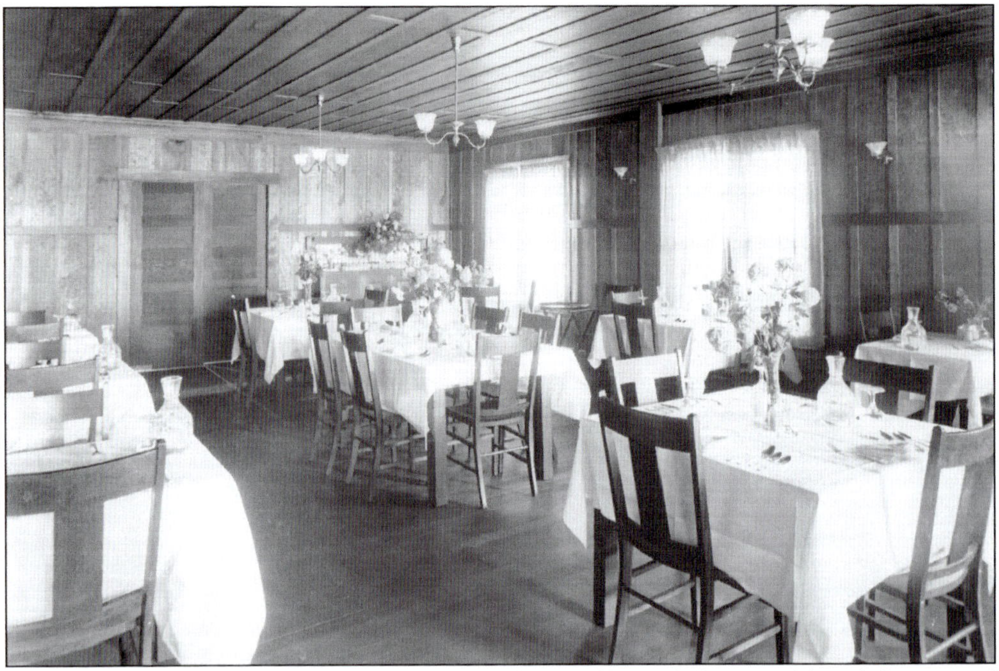

The dining room of the Vista Inn was a popular place. Tables and chairs could easily be grouped for large parties or moved aside following dinner to create a dance floor. After the inn was sold in 1941 and moved to South Santa Fe Avenue at Escondido Avenue, the knoll on which it sat was leveled for commercial use.

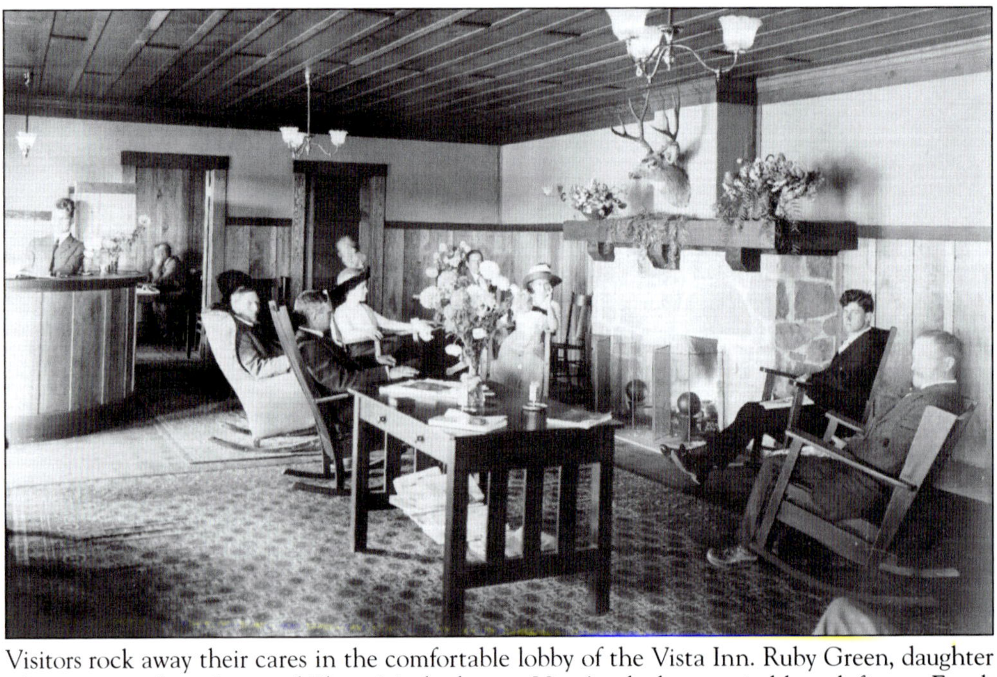

Visitors rock away their cares in the comfortable lobby of the Vista Inn. Ruby Green, daughter of pioneer residents Luis and Elvira Machado, ran Vista's telephone switchboard, first at Frank Nash's market and then in the lobby of the Vista Inn after it was moved here in the late 1920s. She also registered guests because there were not enough telephones in Vista to fill in her time.

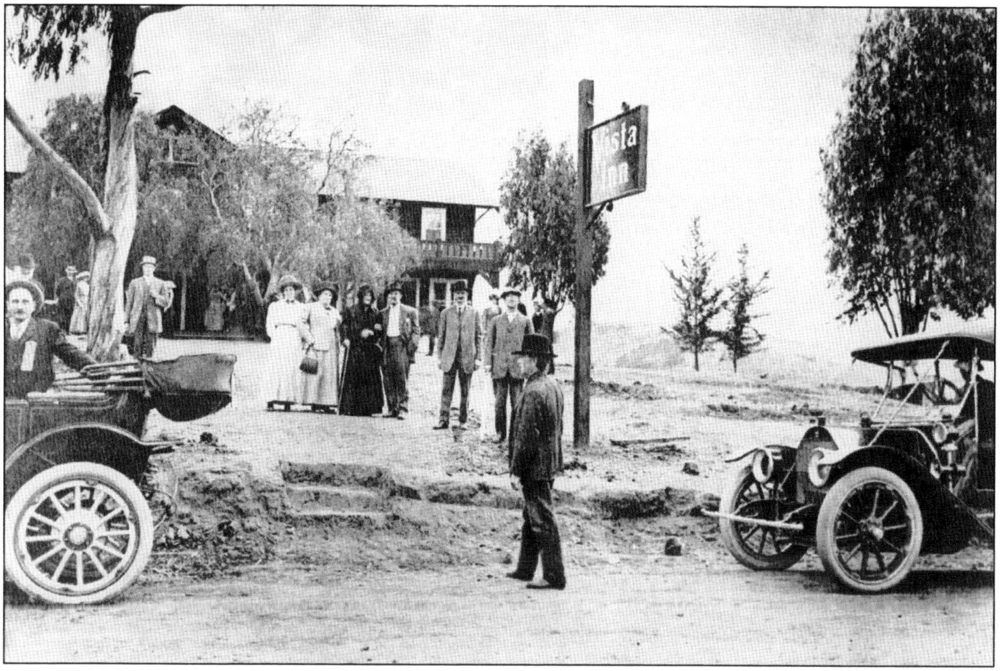

Most of Vista's organizations and businesses were formed during meetings held at the Vista Inn in the 1920s and early 1930s. The chamber of commerce was formally instituted here on June 13, 1923, and such groups as the Woman's Club of Vista, American Legion, and Vista Community Church also held their initial meetings here.

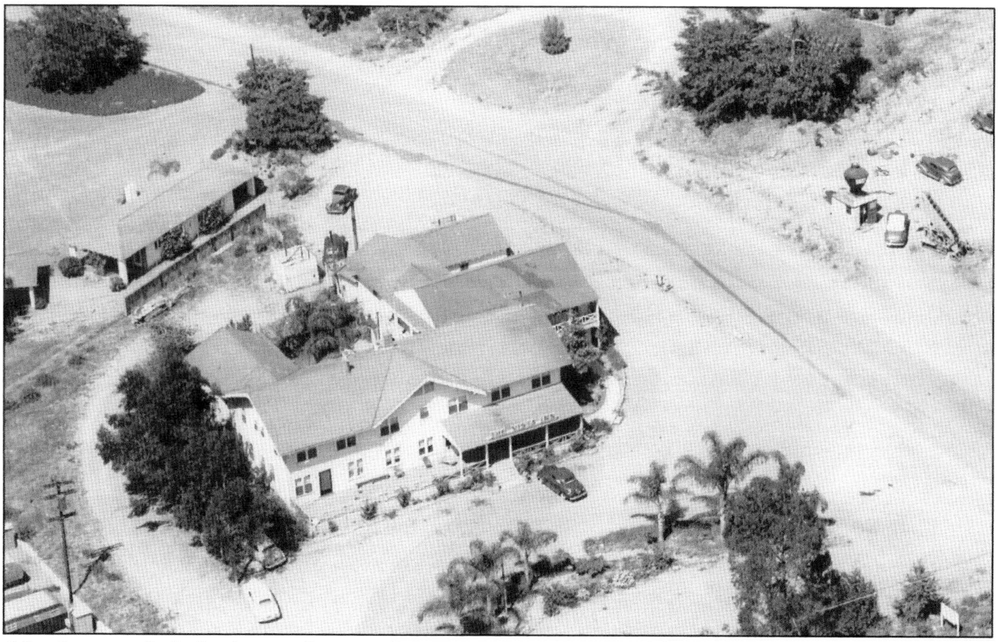

After being refurbished several times, the Vista Inn was again sold. In August 1941, it was moved to this site on South Santa Fe Avenue at Escondido Avenue. The inn regained its popularity for a time and then was briefly a department store and private home. In 1960, the building was demolished by two high school teachers and the lumber and other materials were used in shop classes.

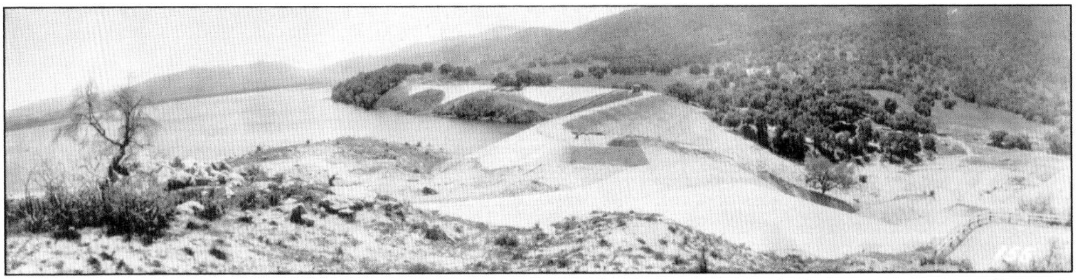

Pictured here are Lake Henshaw and Henshaw Dam, which have provided a major source of Vista's water supply since 1926. At the formation of Vista Irrigation District in 1923, negotiations began with then–Lake Henshaw owners San Diego County Water Company and Escondido Mutual Water Company to access lake water. The very first Vista Water Company was organized in 1911, using wells along Buena Vista Creek.

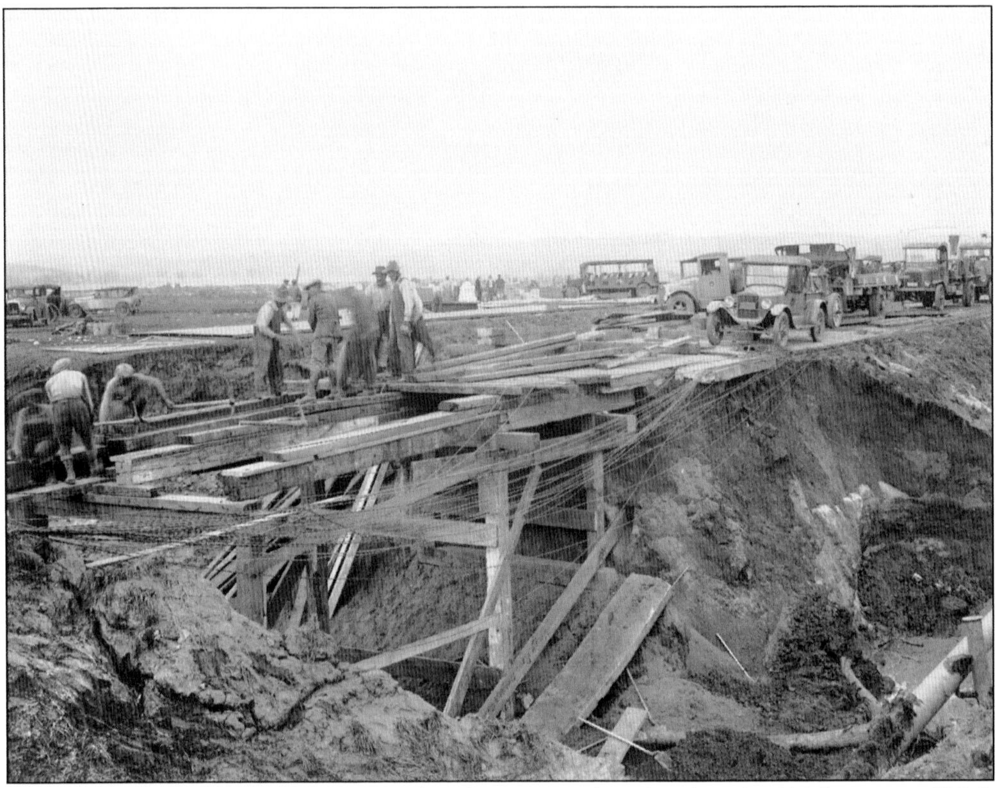

The $1.7-million Vista Irrigation District bond issue passed on October 10, 1924, by a vote of 96-0, which included all eligible voters but the six who were ill or absent. Soon afterward, workers began to enlarge the Escondido Canal and build the flume from Lake Wohlford and on to Pechstein Reservoir in Vista. The long and often hazardous labor that lay ahead is demonstrated in this 1925 photograph.

Vista Irrigation District officials held a ground-breaking ceremony on May 16, 1925, to begin this project, which would ultimately bring water to Vista from Lake Henshaw, 40 miles away. Using what was then the most modern equipment, two workmen are pictured moving some of the tons of rock that needed to be displaced along the route of the pipeline.

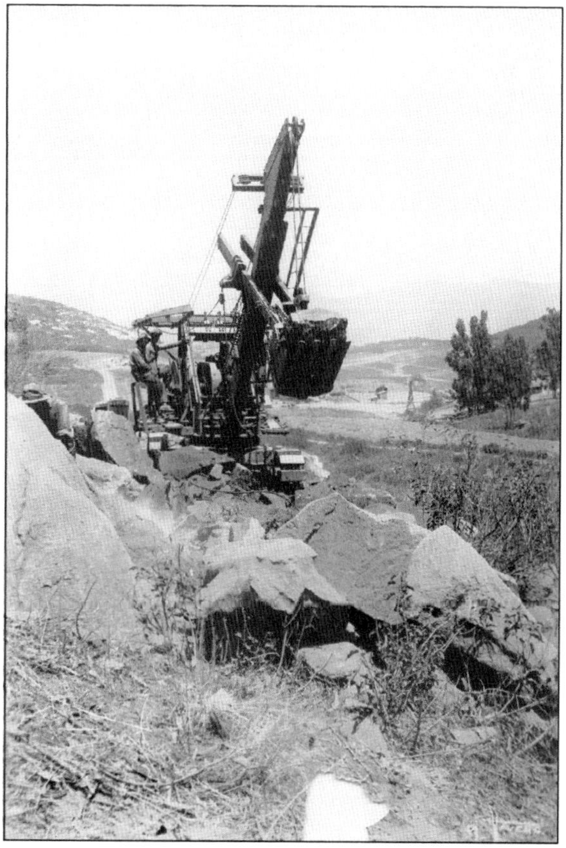

A group of laborers prepares a trench for the laying of concrete pipeline. At a May 1925 meeting of the Vista Irrigation District board of directors, final contracts were awarded to the Escondido Cement Products Company for approximately 60 miles of the concrete pipe. It was the largest cement pipe job in Southern California at that time, and the *Oceanside Blade* noted that "it speaks well for the ability of a local concern."

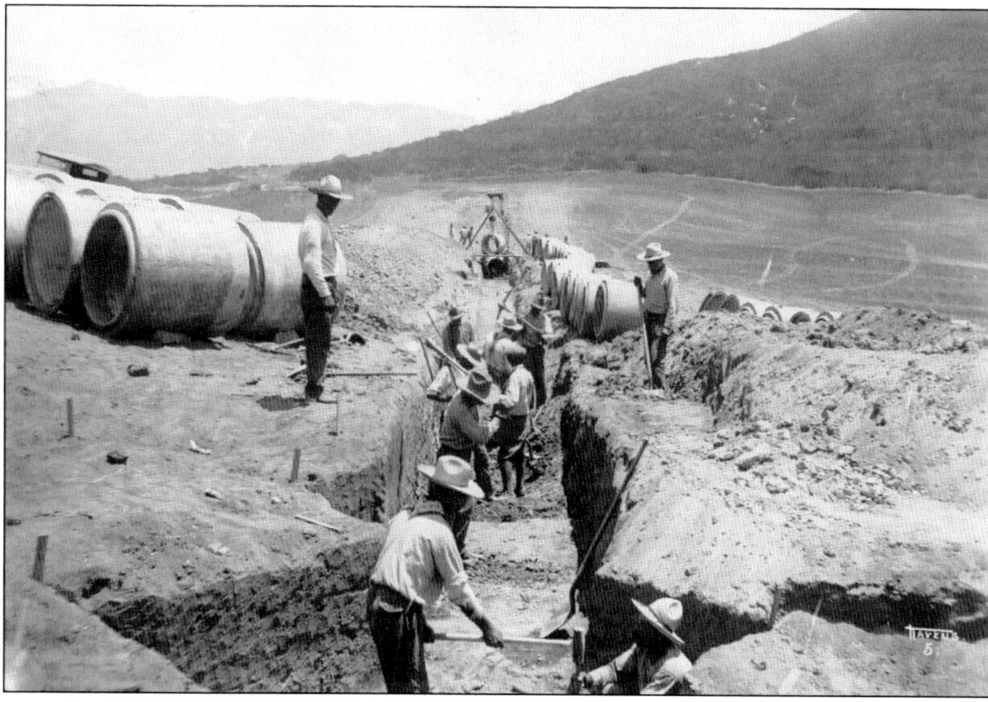

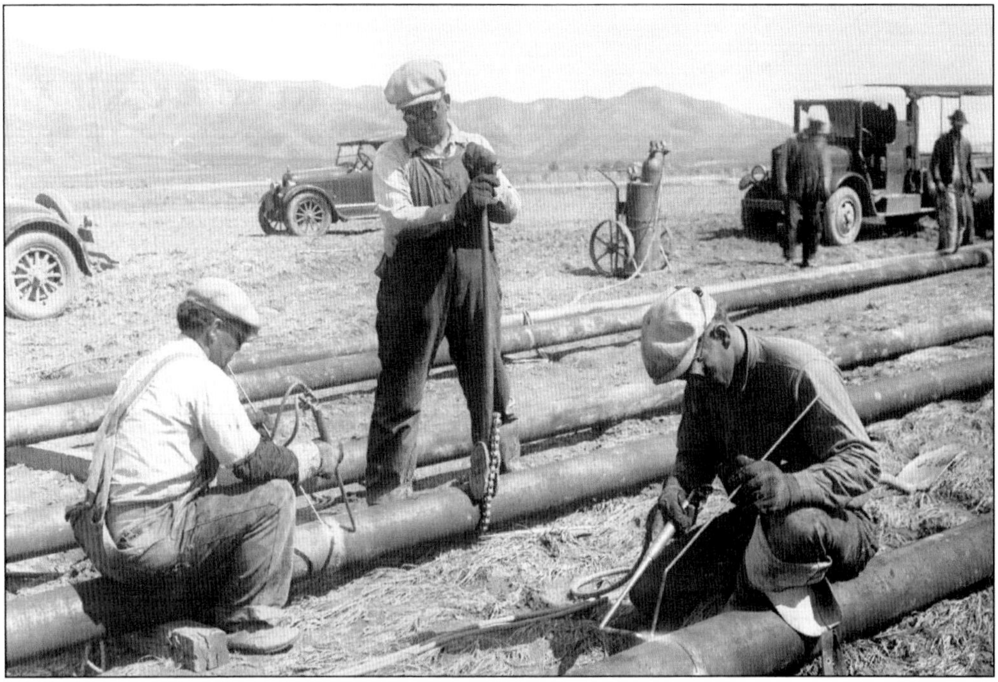

Workers weld sections of pipe as the project moves across bare, sometimes desert-like land in the spring and summer of 1925. At the celebration of the completion of this project on February 27, 1926, the population of Vista was 350. The *Vista Press* noted on February 17, 1928, just two years later, "It is conservatively estimated that there are 1,200 persons residing in the district."

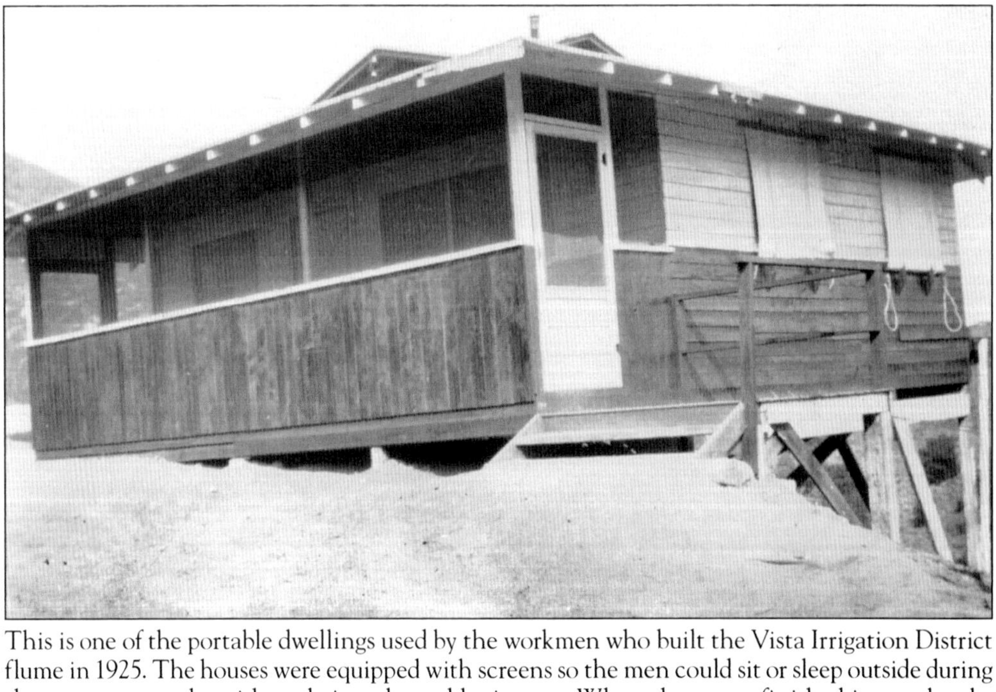

This is one of the portable dwellings used by the workmen who built the Vista Irrigation District flume in 1925. The houses were equipped with screens so the men could sit or sleep outside during the summer months without being plagued by insects. When they were finished in one locale, they simply took their portable village apart and moved it to a new site.

Three

Water Arrives, Everyone Thrives

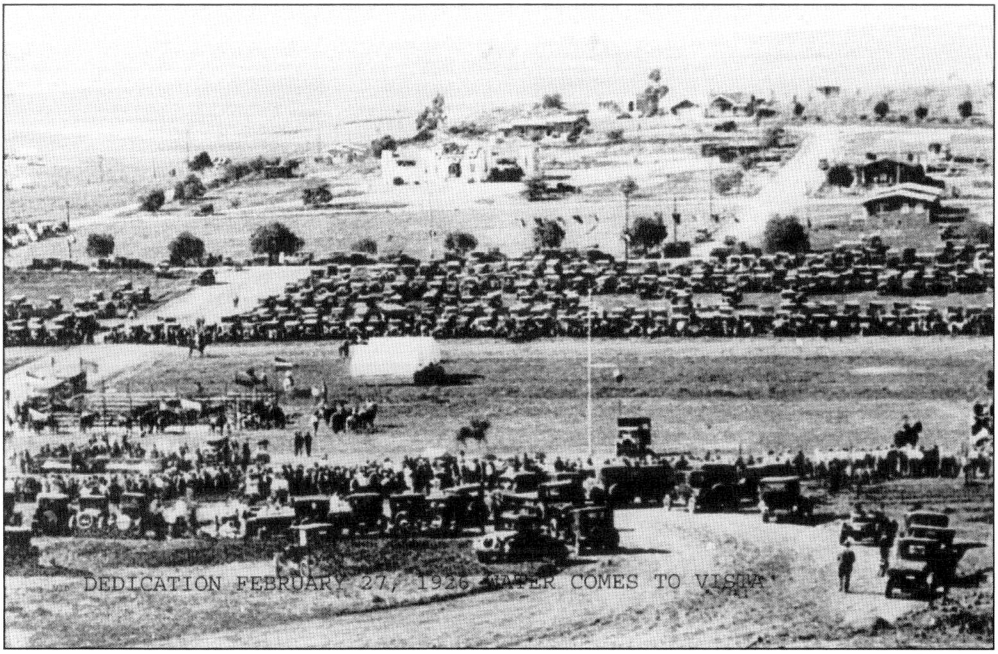

This view of the celebration of the coming of ample water to Vista on February 27, 1926, is indicative of the importance of the newly built flume and reservoir that conveyed Vista's water supply the 40 miles from Lake Henshaw. Thousands of dignitaries and citizens from all over northern San Diego County joined in the gala ceremonies, which were held on land that would soon be a thriving downtown. Vista Union School, later Jefferson Elementary School, can be seen in the background. Within a few short years, the surrounding barren fields and hillsides were covered with homes and groves, and Vista was the avocado capital of the world.

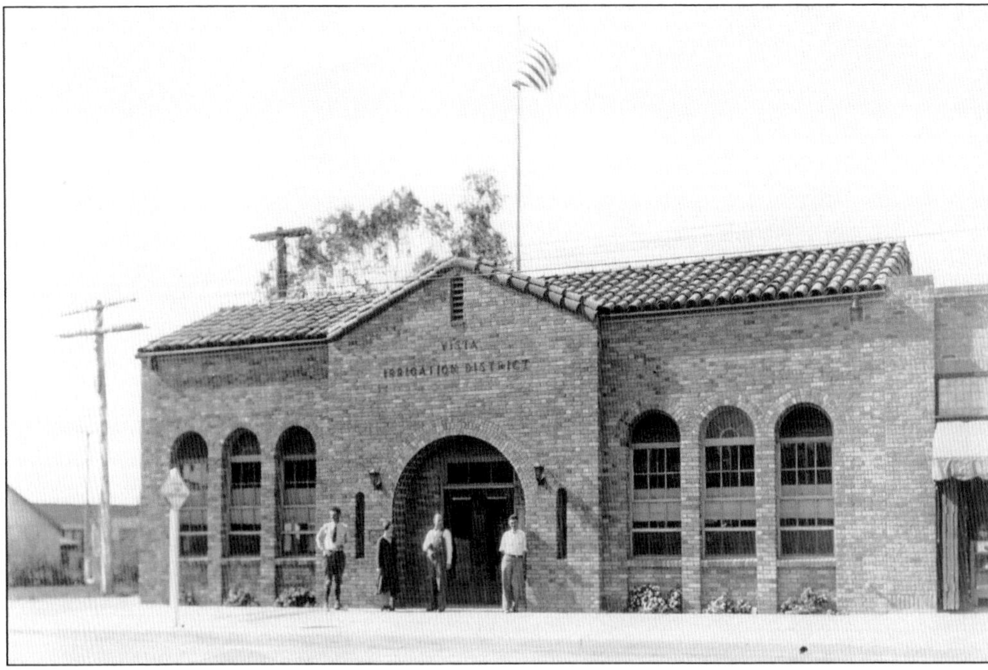

This was the first permanent Vista Irrigation District building, located adjacent to the Pechstein Building in the 100 block of what is now Main Street. It was noted in the *Oceanside Blade* on August 7, 1924, that previously the newly formed district's board of directors "held their regular meeting Tuesday for the first time in the district's new office in the former El Camino Garage of Mr. William B. Pechstein."

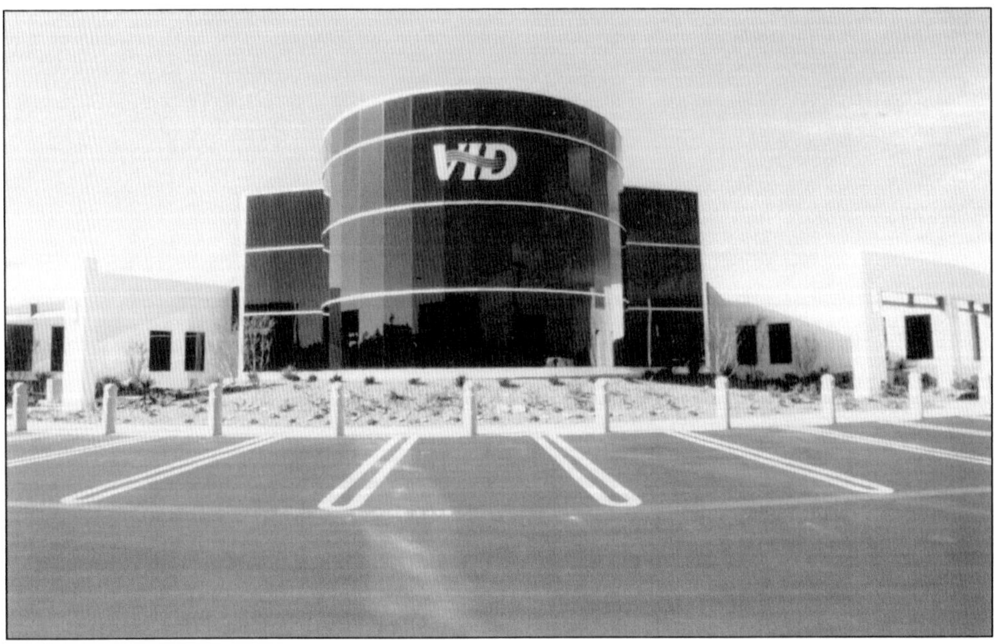

The Vista Irrigation District had its second headquarters office on Connecticut Avenue and in June 2001 moved to this striking new building at 1391 Engineer Street in the industrial area of south Vista.

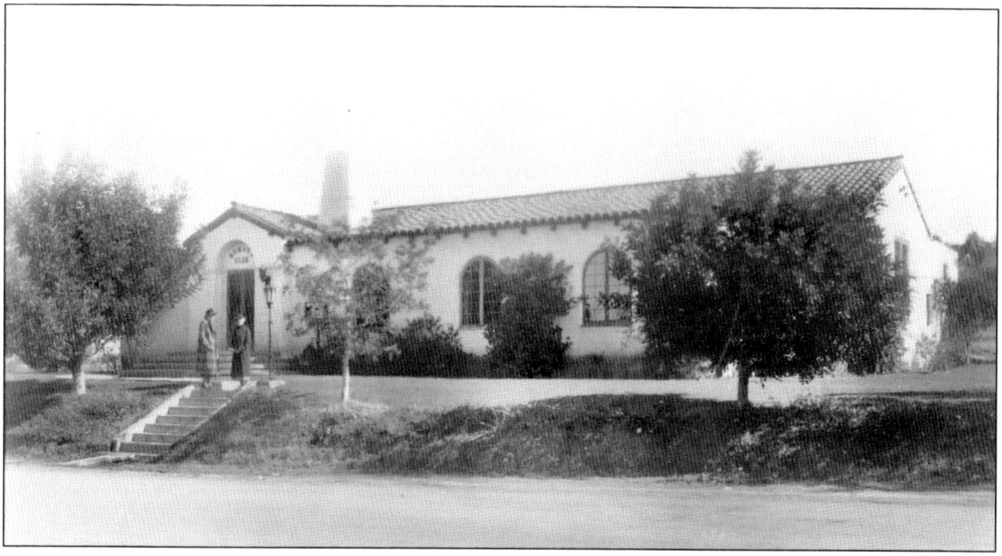

Seven Vista ladies organized the Women's Current Events Club in 1916. They paid $400 for Rennebec Hall on North Santa Fe Avenue near Jefferson Street, set up Vista's only public library there in 1921, and gave monetary assistance to nearby Vista Union School. In 1929, they changed their name to the Woman's Club of Vista and built this new clubhouse on Park Circle, next to Vista Community Church.

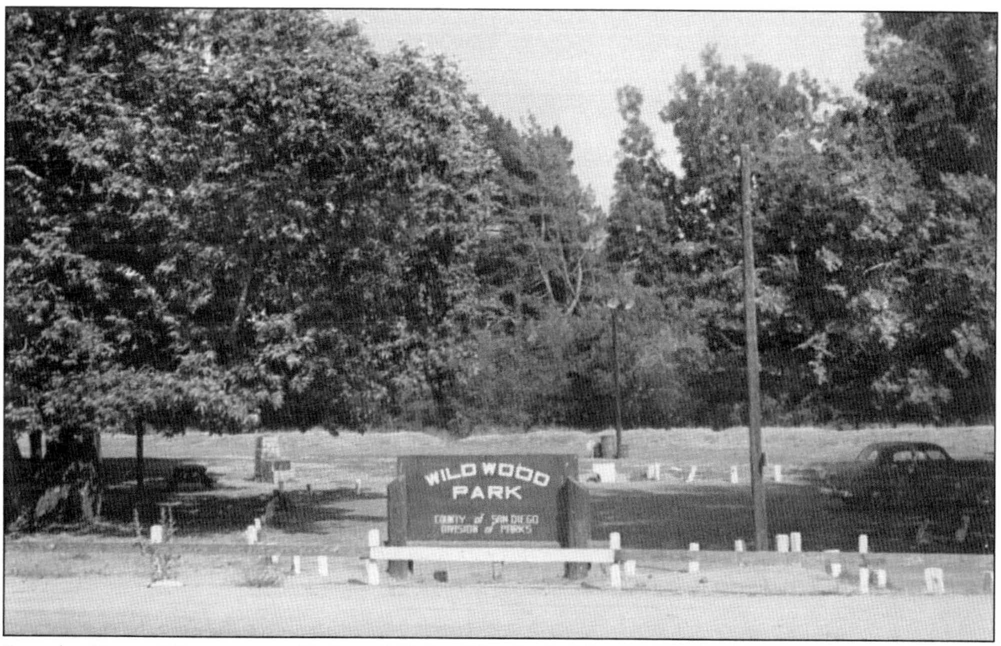

Rancho Buena Vista owners Jack and Helen Knight held a dinner for the chamber of commerce in 1923 and offered this parcel of land, at the corner of what is now Escondido Avenue and East Vista Way, for a park. The land was deeded in perpetuity in 1925 and formally dedicated in 1929. Lillie Remsburg won the Vista Garden Club contest to choose a name, and it has been Wildwood Park ever since.

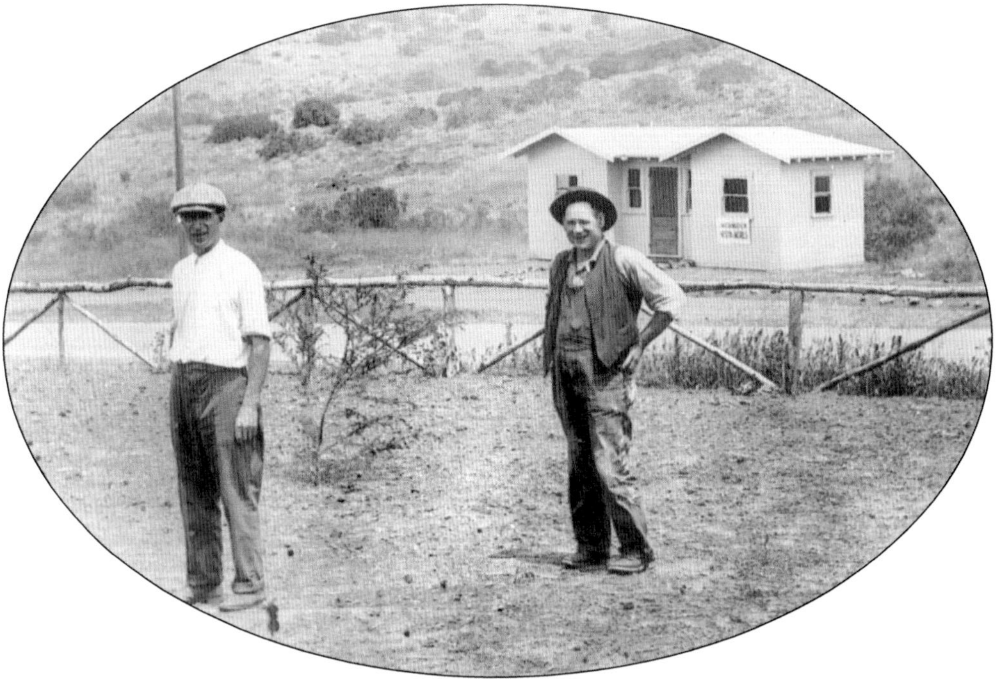

When A. B. Ormsby came to Vista from Toronto, Canada, in October 1925, he was joined by his associate, horticulturist George Cosh, and his family. The two set up Ormsby Plantations in the Vista Grande area. Cosh (left) is pictured here with Ormsby in front of the latter's real estate office in 1929.

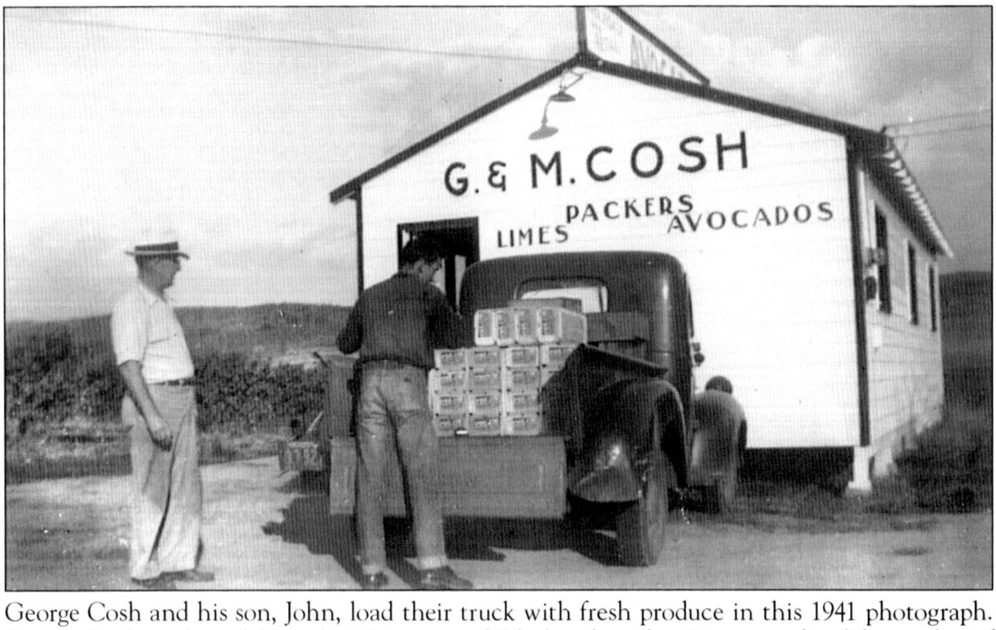

George Cosh and his son, John, load their truck with fresh produce in this 1941 photograph. George Cosh graduated from the University of Edinburgh and at 18 was made a life member of the Royal Botanical Gardens. He taught horticulture at Cornell University and then went to Canada before coming to Vista in 1925 with his wife, Margaret, and son John. The Cosh family has been involved with community activities ever since.

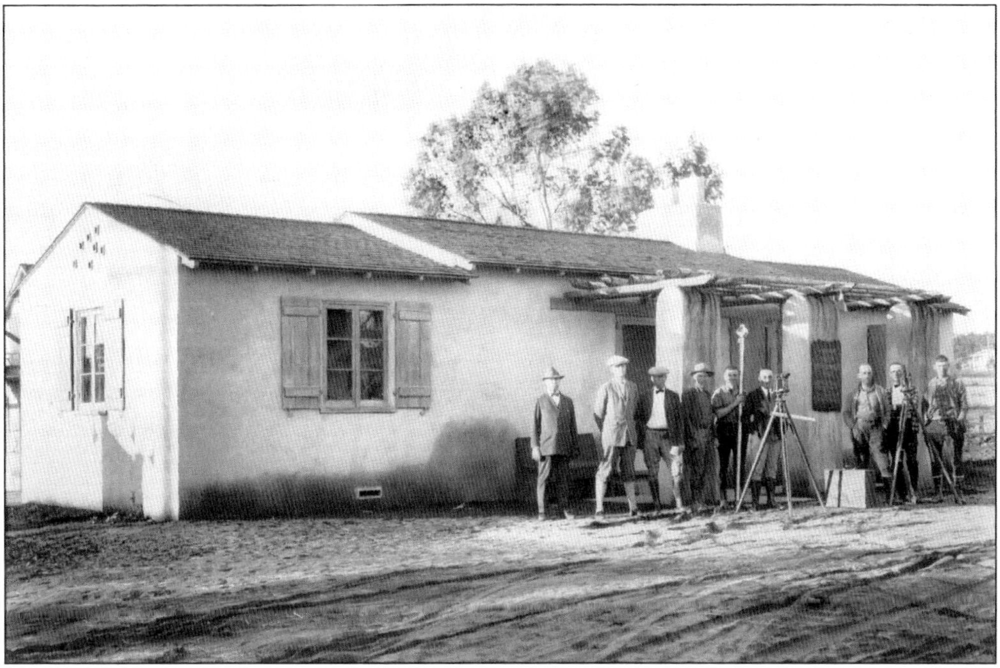

Already well established in Los Angeles, real estate developer Edwin G. Hart came to Vista in 1925, saw the potential, and organized the Vista Development Association. He bought Vista Land Company, plotted out the downtown area, and purchased 2,200 acres of land to subdivide for groves and commercial enterprises. Hart was an organizer of First National Bank and was instrumental in financing construction of the commercial building that housed it. Pictured above are employees of Vista Development Association in front of Hart's first sales office on what is now Main Street. Below is another view of the busy office, with a sign referring to Hart as general manager and offering lots, homesites, and farms for sale. Down the street to the right is the first office of Vista Irrigation District, before the new quarters were built.

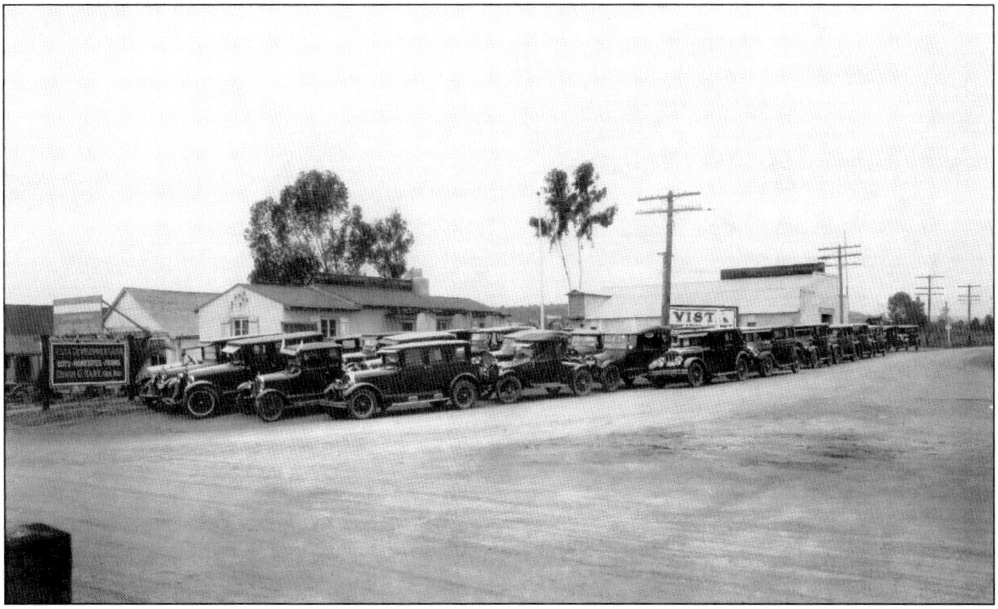

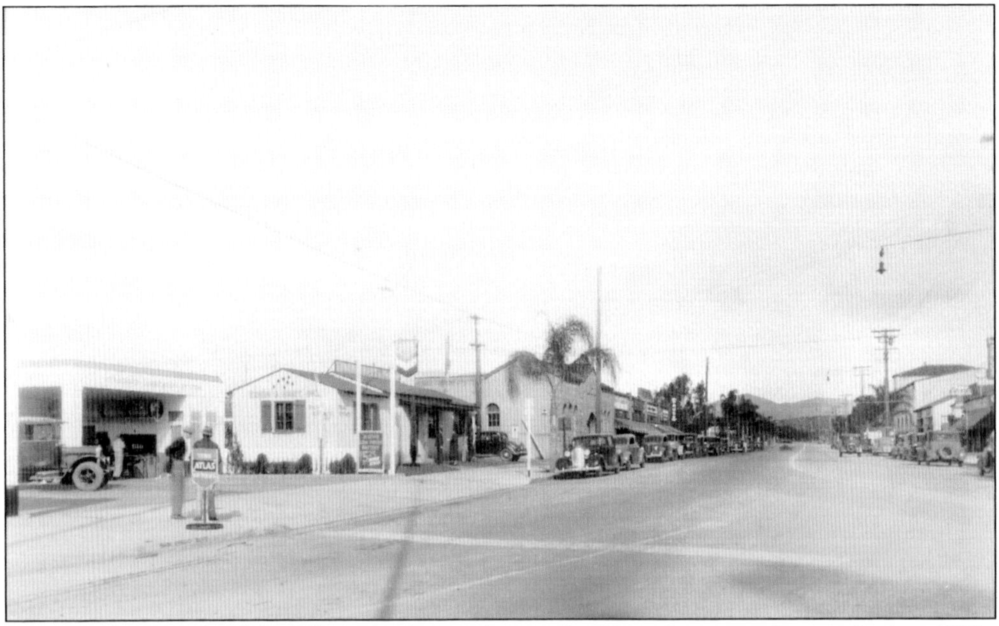

This is a photograph of the Edwin G. Hart real estate building that was taken in the late 1930s, with a service station now on the corner and the Vista Irrigation District and Pechstein buildings to the right. Hart was tragically killed in an automobile accident on November 23, 1939. Until the early 1940s, what is now Main Street was San Diego Boulevard; it was later renamed East Vista Way.

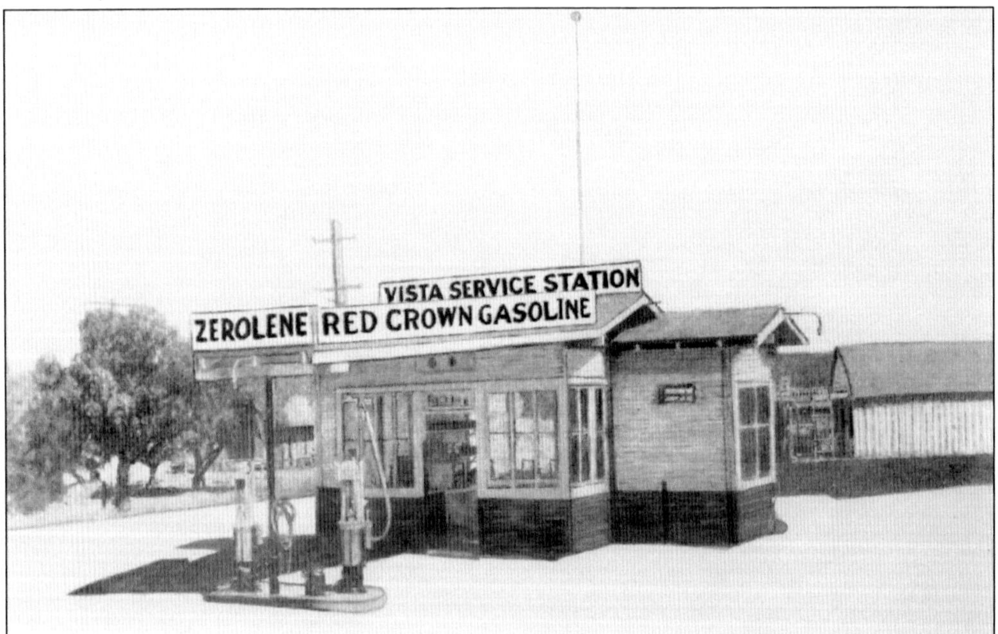

Robert Douglas came to Vista in 1925 and started Vista's first service station. It was located in what is now the 700 block of South Santa Fe Avenue, on land that was later to become the Firestone Tire and Service Center. Douglas later renamed his business the Rancho Vista Service Station, and in mid-1928, he added a 3,500-square-foot automotive repair garage.

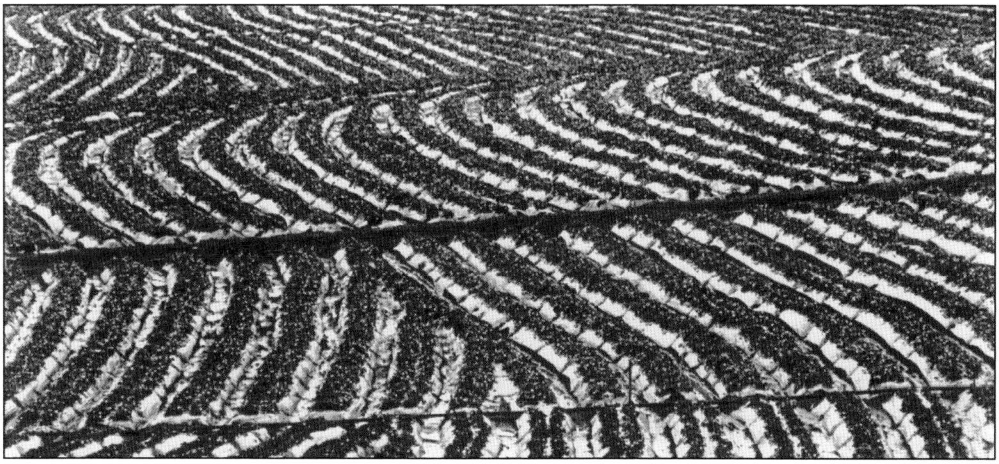

Rows of prime strawberry plants weave an intricate design onto Vista's landscape. John S. Webb had a large acreage of strawberries as early as 1926. The finest were shipped in the evening by way of Santa Fe Railway, with connections in Oceanside that would get them to Hall, Hass, and Vessey wholesalers in Los Angeles in time for the 1:00 a.m. market opening.

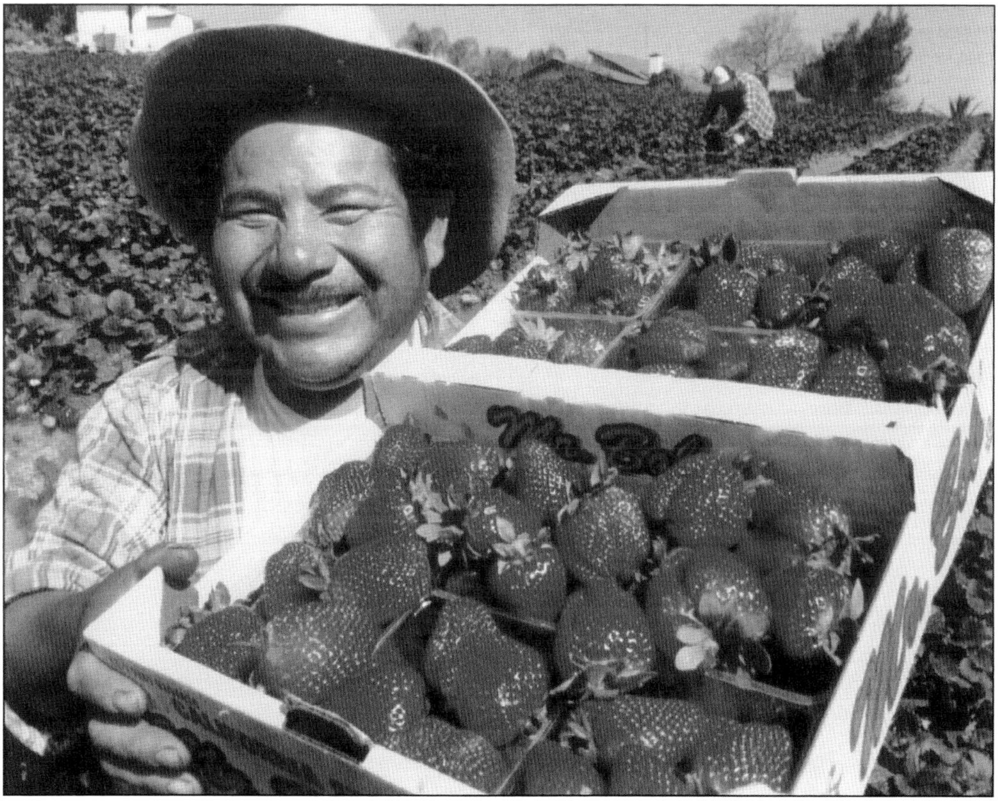

Strawberries are still grown at this East Vista Way site, and in late spring and summer, travelers stop at the roadside stand to buy their fill. In this 1991 photograph, a worker proudly displays the pick of the crop. Vista was for many years a major exporter of strawberries to European countries. (Courtesy of *Escondido Times-Advocate*.)

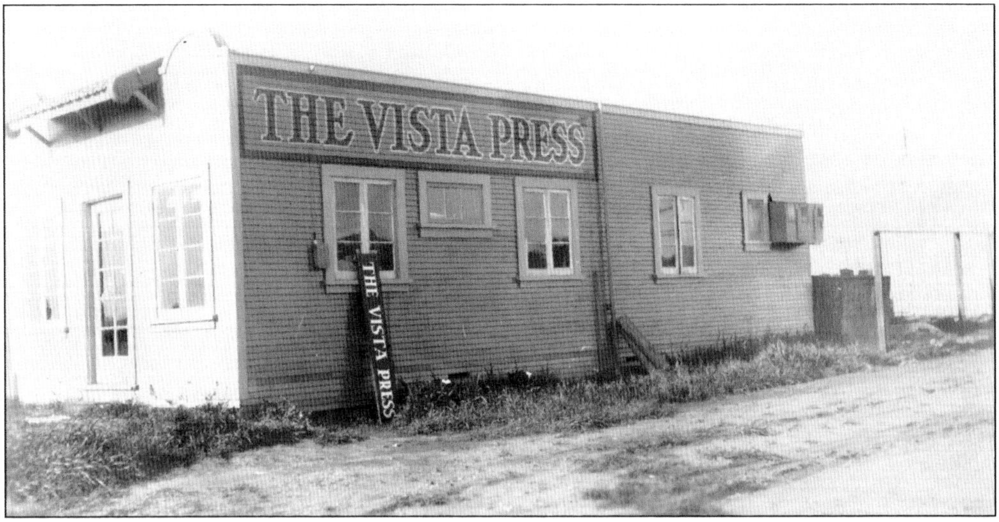

The inaugural issue of the *Vista Press*, dated September 24, 1926, was printed in San Diego. Publisher and founder Melvin Z. Remsburg, always known as "M. Z.," built this 16-by-32-foot building at Indiana and Jefferson Streets. It was the first of several plants as the community grew. On November 19, M. Z. and his son, Everett Remsburg, produced the first in-house issue with their own linotype and press.

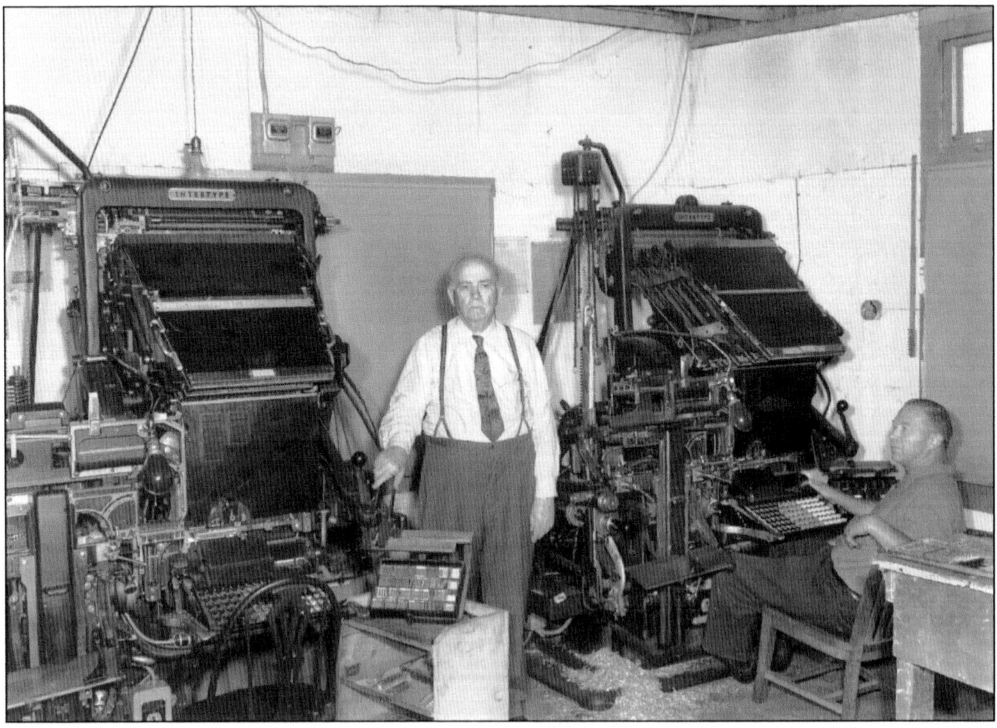

"It is the plan of the publisher to issue a paper that will be a credit to the town and district," wrote publisher M. Z. Remsburg in the October 8, 1926, issue of the *Vista Press*. He is shown here with his son, Everett Remsburg, and two Intertype linotypes, updates from their first Mergenthaler typesetter. Everett Remsburg worked alongside his father from the first issue of the *Vista Press* in September 1926.

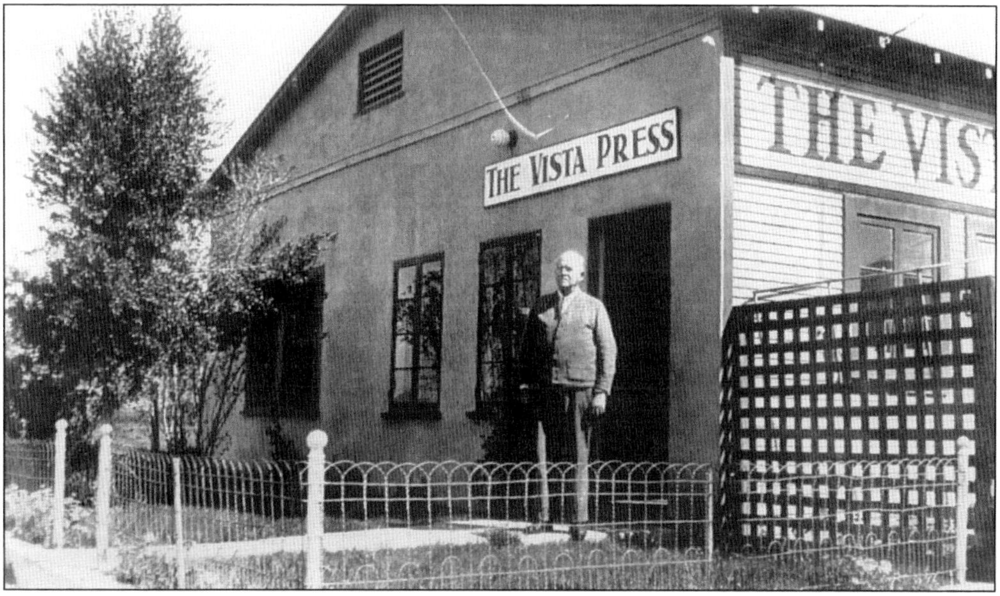

Publisher M. Z. Remsburg stands proudly in front of his first building, which was remodeled 11 times as the paper grew with the community. The publisher of Vista's first newspaper brought a wealth of experience to his chosen community in 1926 and with his family spent the rest of his life promoting, chronicling, and participating in life in Vista.

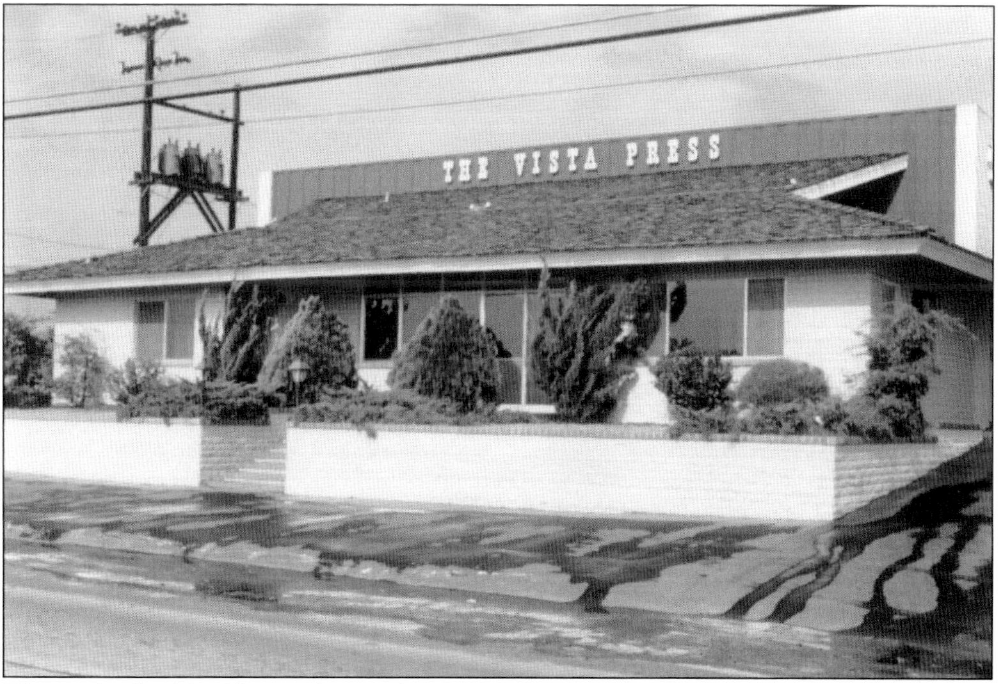

This is the final building to house the *Vista Press*. Built in 1960 at 425 West Vista Way, it boasted a 48-page Hoe press with color capabilities, a modern composing room, a newsroom, and advertising offices. Publication went from once to twice a week in 1955 and to tri-weekly in 1964. The newspaper modernized from hot-type to photo-offset printing in 1970 and became a daily in 1973.

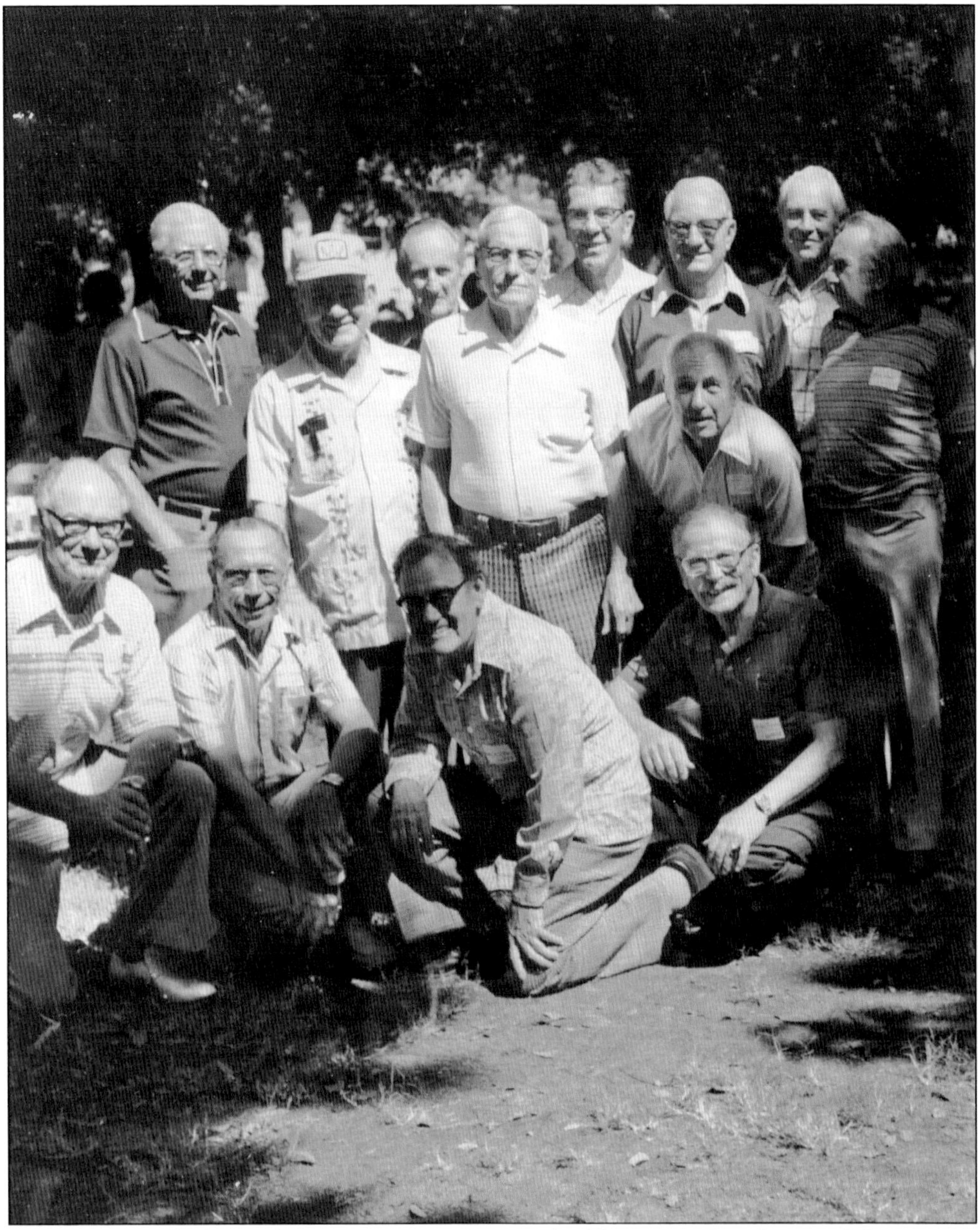

A fire in a wastebasket at the Vista Irrigation District building in 1927 underscored the growing need for a local fire department, and the Vista Volunteer Fire Department was promptly organized. The department operated for almost three decades on a strictly volunteer basis. Early-day stories are rampant about the firefighters' dedication to their community and how they would hear the siren and dash from their nearby jobs to board the engine at the first firehouse on Indiana Avenue. Pictured here are early members of the Vista Volunteer Fire Department, who gathered at Wildwood Park on September 30, 1979, to reminisce about their many years of service to the community. From left to right are (first row) Charles Mull Sr., Burnoit Hayden, Luther Wallace, and Dr. Frederick Spiegel; (second row) Lew Fields, Chet Lawrence, George Sexsmith, and Bruce Brown; (third row) Alex McDougall, Harvey Itzaina, Al Stanbro, Joe Barnes, and Glenn Hayden.

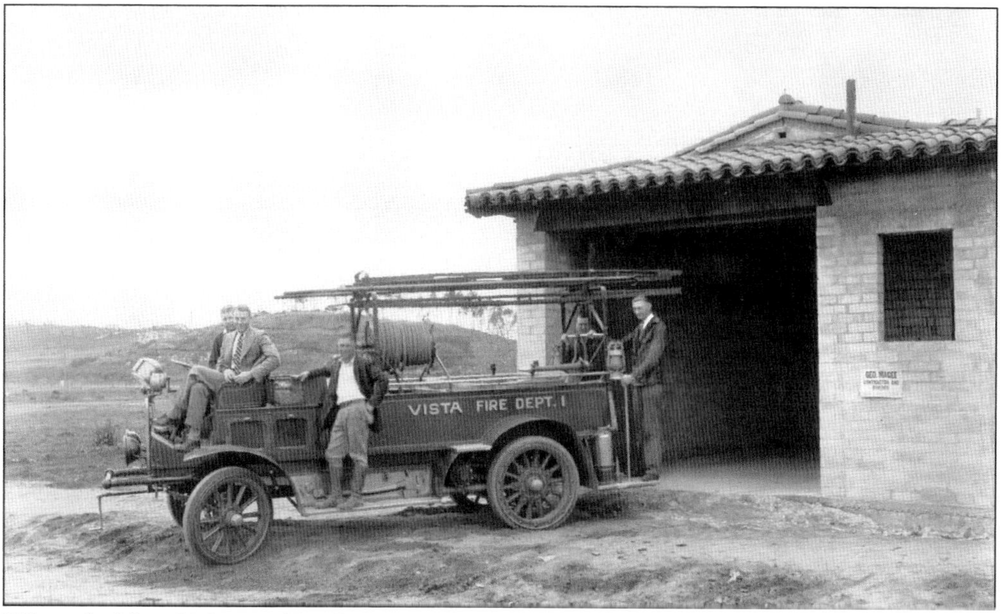

When the Vista Volunteer Fire Department was organized in 1928, the first piece of equipment was a hose cart that had to be pulled by hand. If there was a long distance to go, a volunteer would pull the cart behind his truck or mules from the Hart Company would be conscripted. In 1928, the department acquired a red 1911 Seagrave chemical and hose engine from the Orange Fire Department. By May 1930, Vista volunteers were converting their own Model A Ford fire truck, shown above, at a total cost of $1,200, and in June, they were honored as the best equipped rural firefighting unit in the county by the San Diego County Firemen's Association. In June 1945, the department acquired a resuscitator/suction machine and a large Mack fire engine.

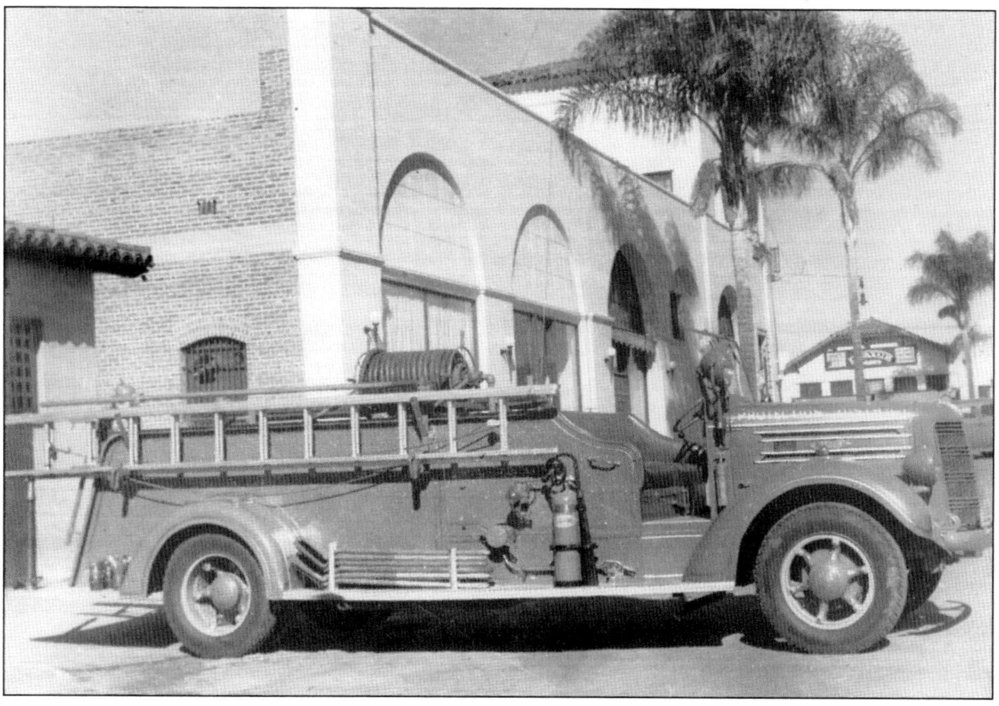

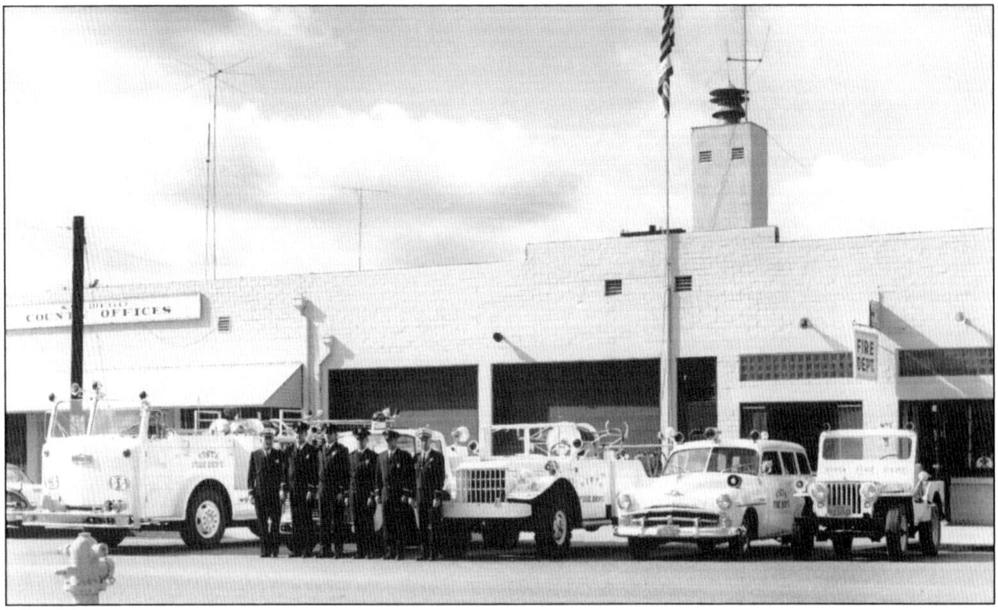

William Elder, Vista's first paid full-time fire chief, was a battalion chief with the Arcadia, California, fire department when he signed on with Vista in 1957 for an annual salary of $6,300. He is credited with bringing true progress to the department until his retirement in 1971. Chief Elder (right) is pictured in 1963 with firefighters and equipment at the first fire station on Indiana Avenue.

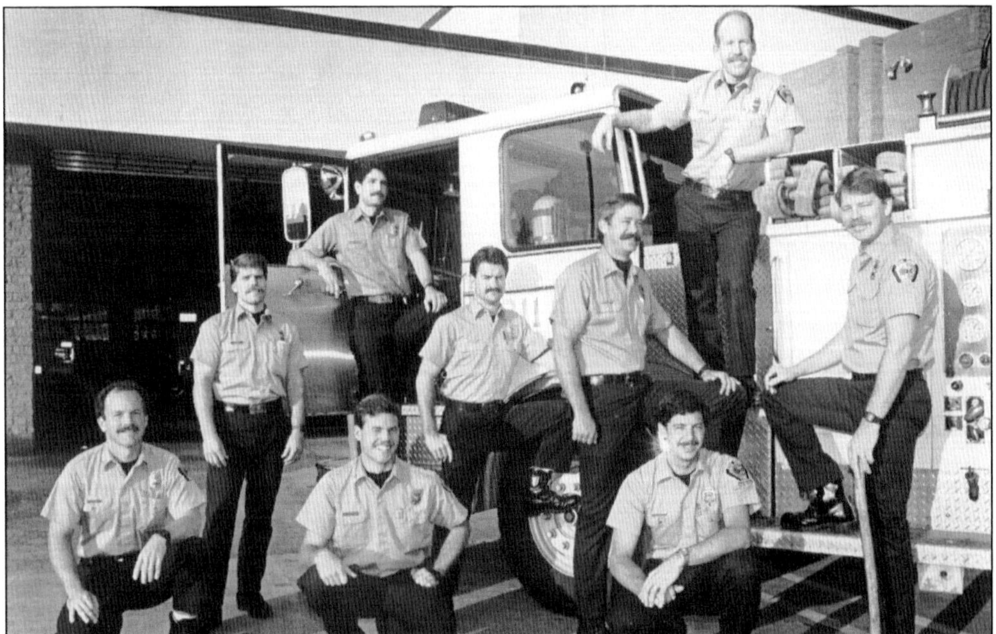

It appears that 1988 was the year for moustaches at Vista Fire Department headquarters on Melrose Drive. Firefighters pictured are, from left to right, (kneeling) Tom Day, Mike Brown, and Kevin Magoon; (standing) Jim Chumbley, John Greenstone, Bill Conover, Bill Reagan, Jerry Ormond, and Randy Terich. Headquarters station dedication ceremonies on May 24, 1974, honored early volunteers and current firefighters. (Courtesy of *Escondido Times-Advocate*.)

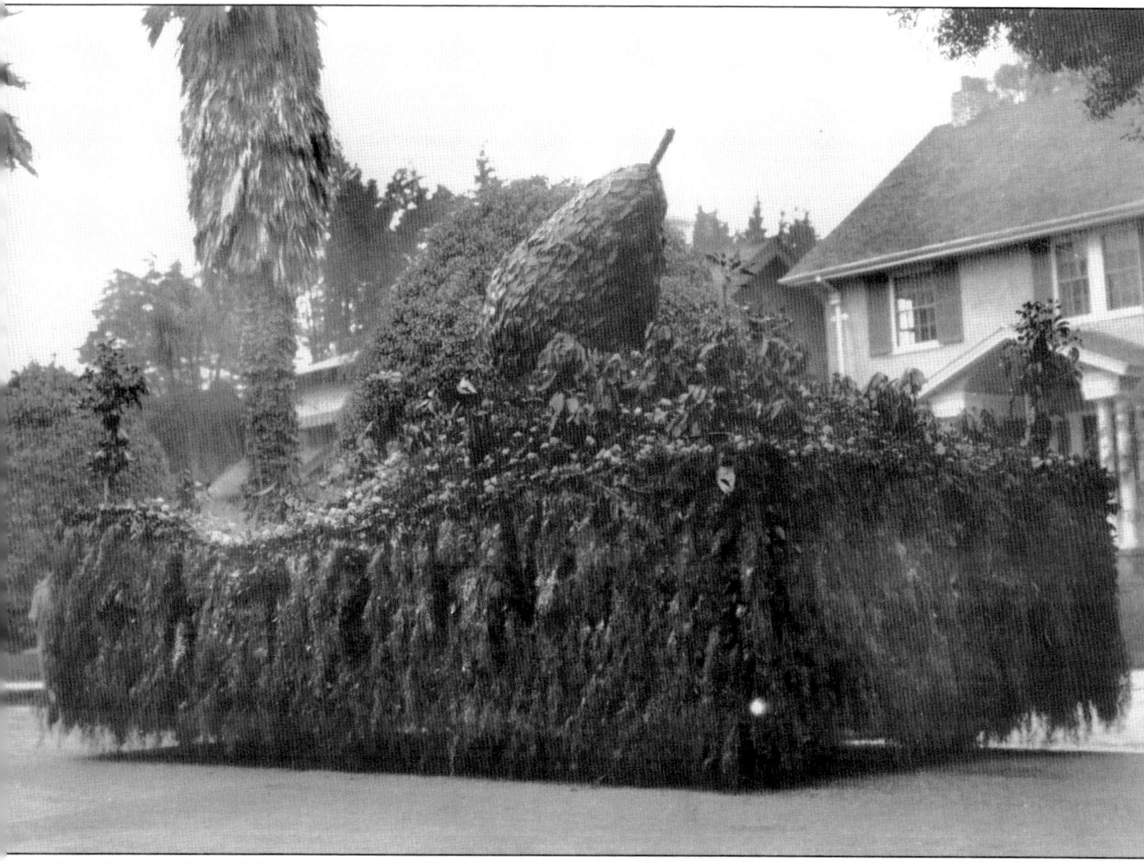

This float in the 1928 Tournament of Roses Parade in Pasadena was the pride of Vista and a major outreach by the newly burgeoning community. Sponsored by the chamber of commerce and the Horticultural Society of Vista and Vicinity, the 10-by-27-foot float was designed to represent the rolling hills of the Vista district. It was topped by a 5-foot-tall avocado, with small avocado trees placed in grove formation and surrounded by white and pink carnations, pepper boughs, holly, poinsettias, and marigolds. According to the January 6, 1928, issue of the *Vista Press*, "The avocado leaves were pinned on in such a manner that the large imitation of a fruit was very realistic and attracted undivided attention while it was passing the countless thousands who lined the route of the great parade." The float was awarded a special prize, a loving cup that is still on display at the Vista Historical Society Museum, alongside the silver bowl and ribbon from the 1932 parade.

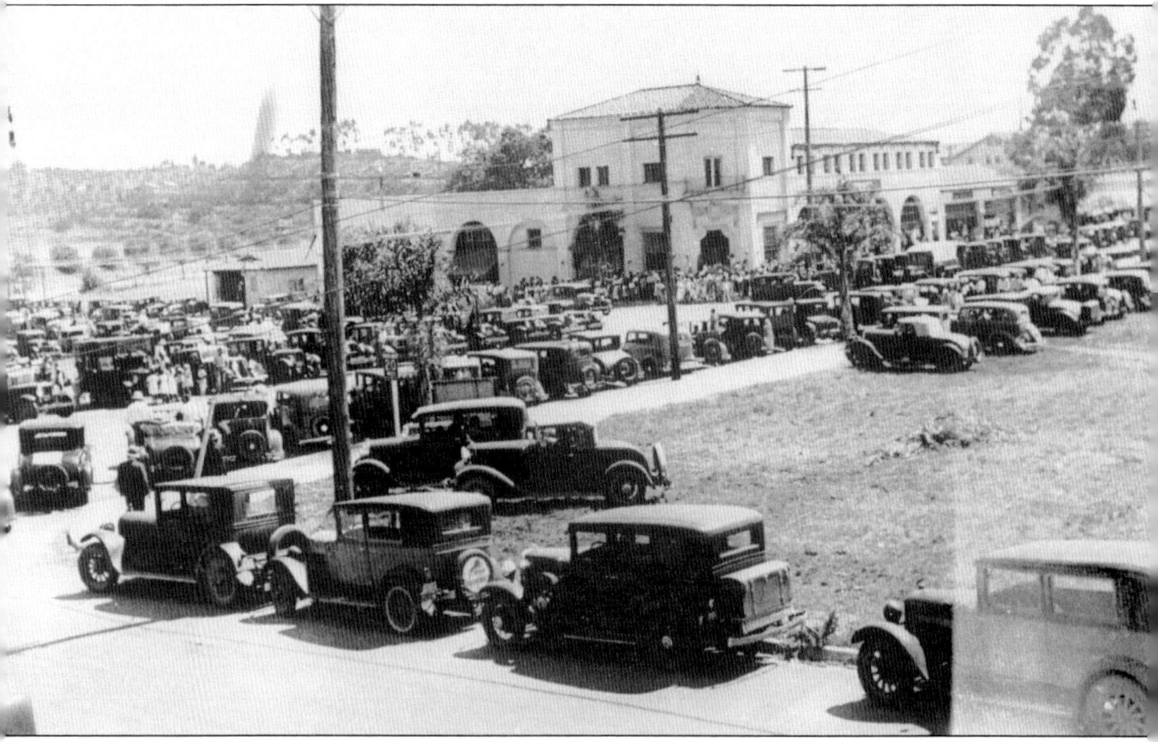

The all-day, all-evening reception honoring the opening of the First National Bank building on September 14, 1928, drew a huge crowd from all over northern San Diego County. The bank had opened on February 18 of the same year in temporary quarters in the Pechstein Building down the street while Edwin G. Hart, Inc., financed the construction of this imposing complex at a cost of $40,000. The building featured four stores and 13 offices arranged in suites. The charter for the bank was granted in April 1927, and the application for the name First National Bank was approved the following August. A February 17, 1928, editorial in the *Vista Press* noted that with the new bank, "This district will make faster strides than ever in growth." First National Bank was started with a capital stock of $25,000.

The Renaissance Revival–style architecture of the First National Bank building, with its wrought-iron railing, mosaic tile, and ornate facade, is shown up close in this photograph. The fascia has been modified several times over the years, but the building remains the cornerstone downtown structure. In later years, it was Union Bank. The building sat empty for several years until it reopened as offices for Vista orthodontist Ronald M. Roncone.

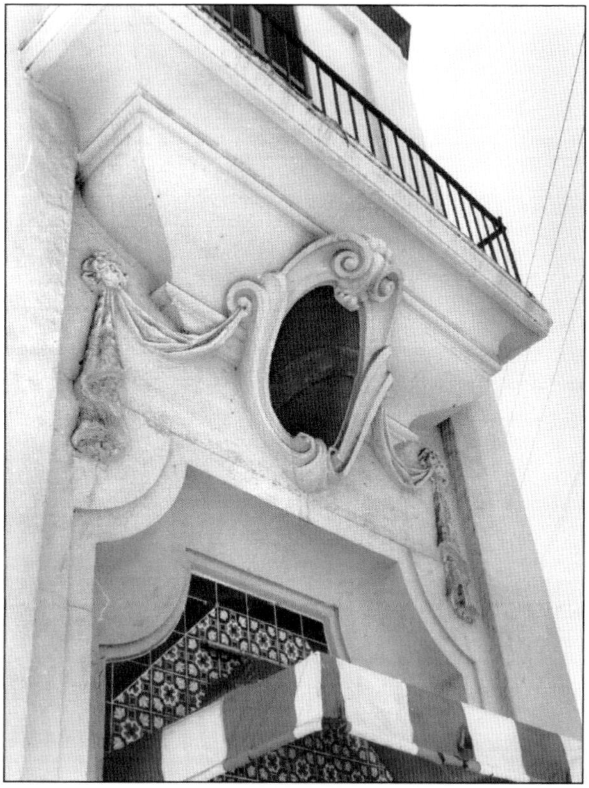

Downtown Vista is pictured in this 1928 aerial photograph, just after the First National Bank building was completed. There is virtually no development beyond the bank except a few young groves. The circle, laid out by Vista Development Association, is shown clearly to the right. Santa Fe Avenue runs across the bottom of the photograph, and the Vista Inn can be seen through the trees at the intersection.

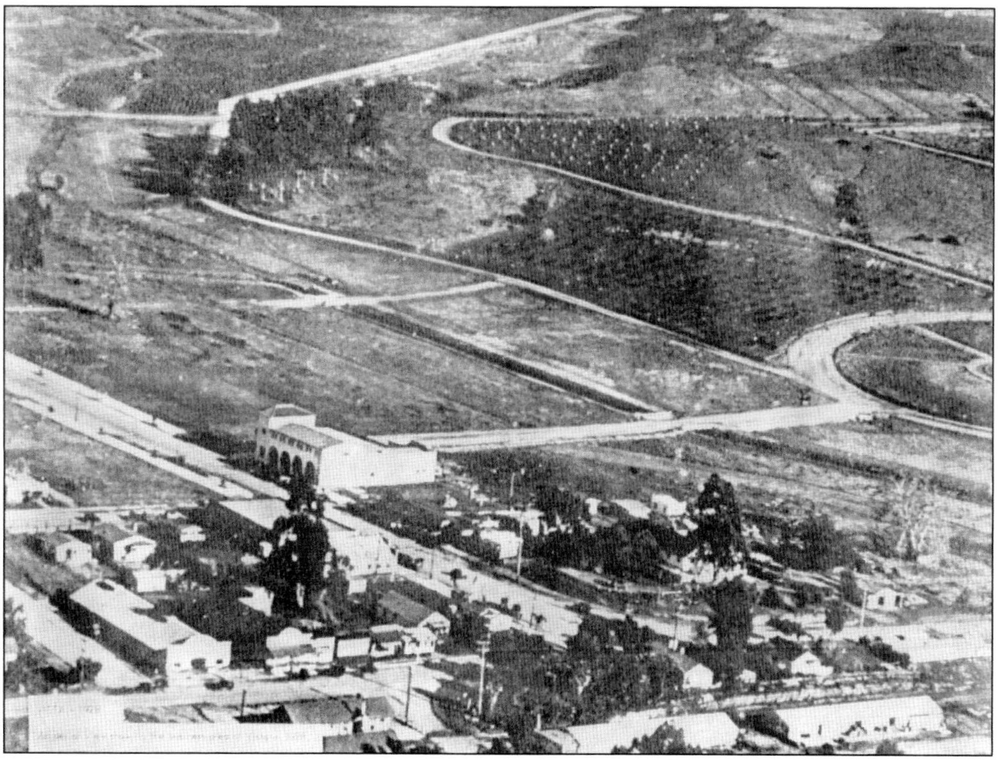

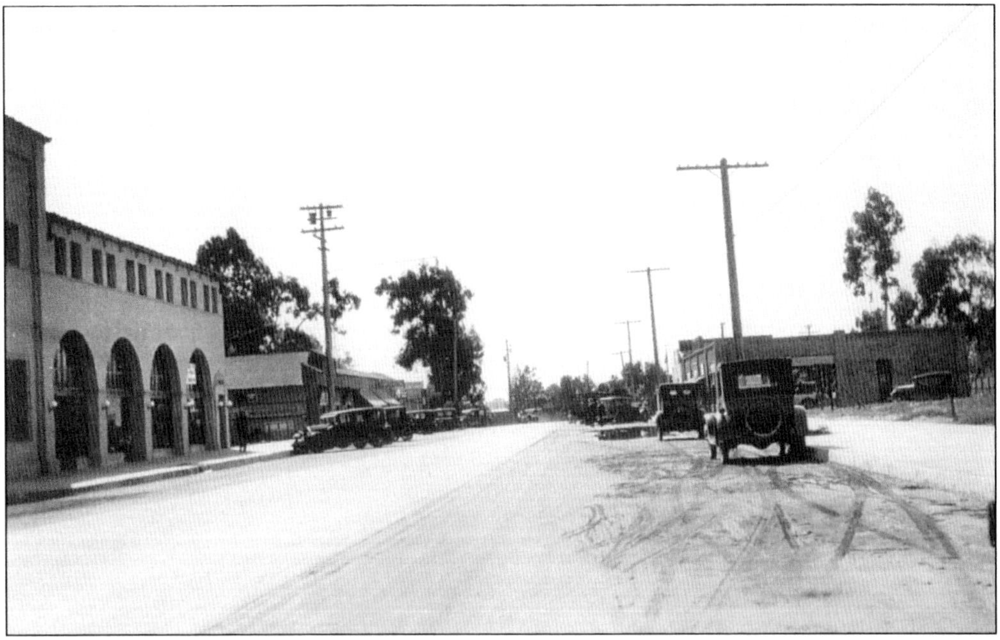

This 1928 view looks west on what is now Main Street toward Santa Fe Avenue. The new First National Bank is at left, and the Pechstein Building can be seen just past the automobiles on the right. The center of the roadway has been macadamized, but the sides are still unpaved.

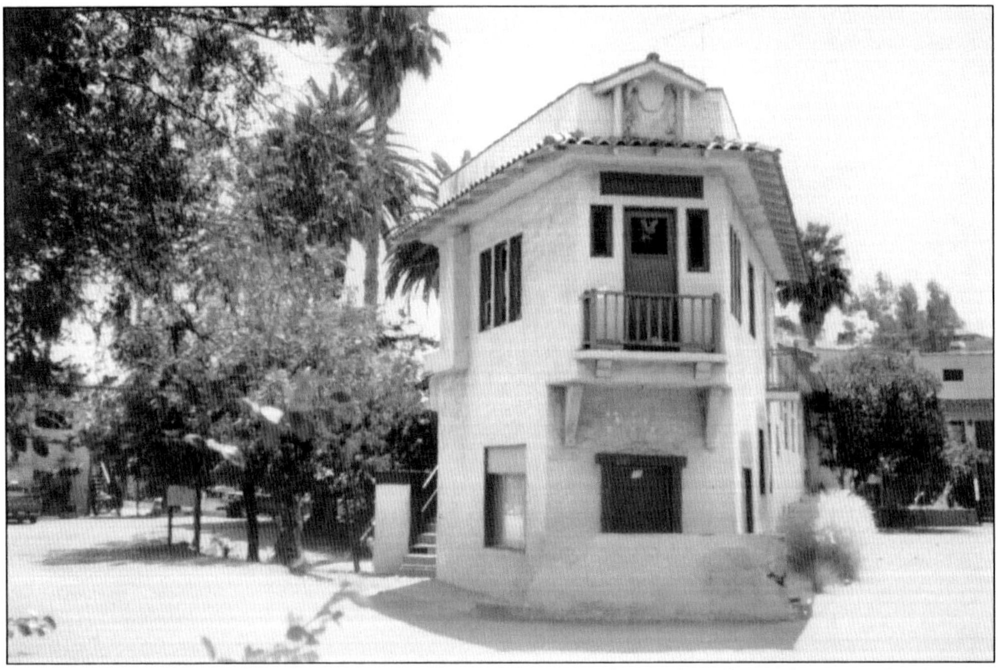

The "Crazy House," located at the corner of Buena Creek Road and South Santa Fe Avenue near the railroad tracks, earned its name because of the multitude of odd architectural angles used in its construction. Rumors persisted that it was built in 1927 as a house of prostitution. The building was abandoned in the late 1930s, remodeled into apartments and refurbished several times before it was demolished in 1999.

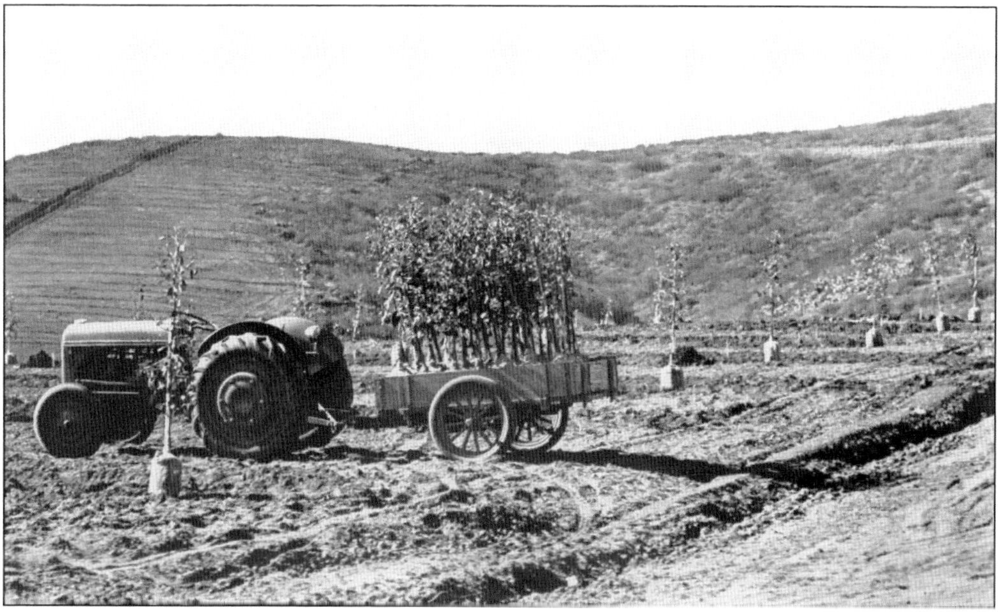

The hillside is terraced, cultivation is completed on the level ground, and the rich Vista soil is ready for another new grove. In this 1928 photograph, seedling trees are being hauled to the site a few at a time by tractor and cart and then carefully placed at correct intervals for planting.

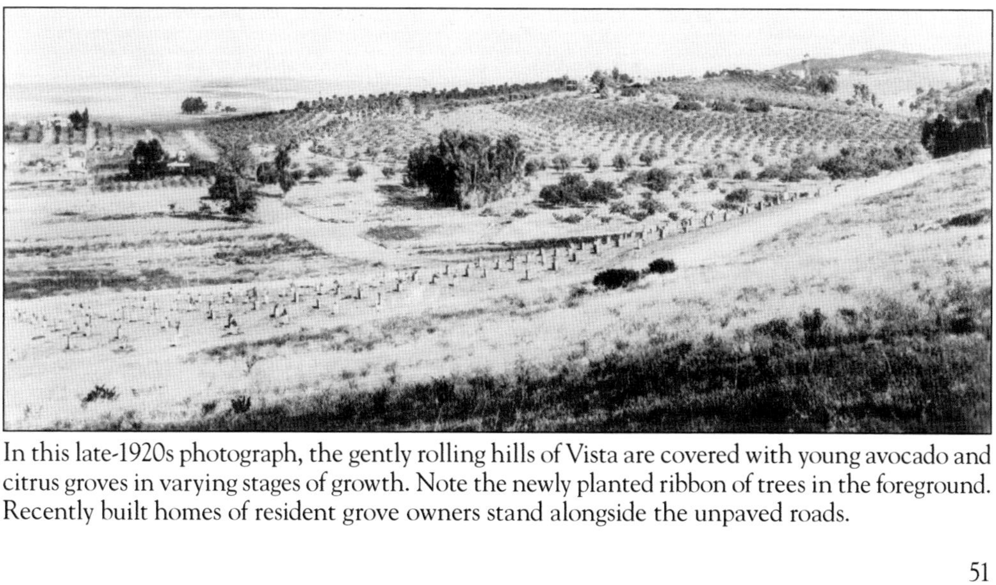

In this late-1920s photograph, the gently rolling hills of Vista are covered with young avocado and citrus groves in varying stages of growth. Note the newly planted ribbon of trees in the foreground. Recently built homes of resident grove owners stand alongside the unpaved roads.

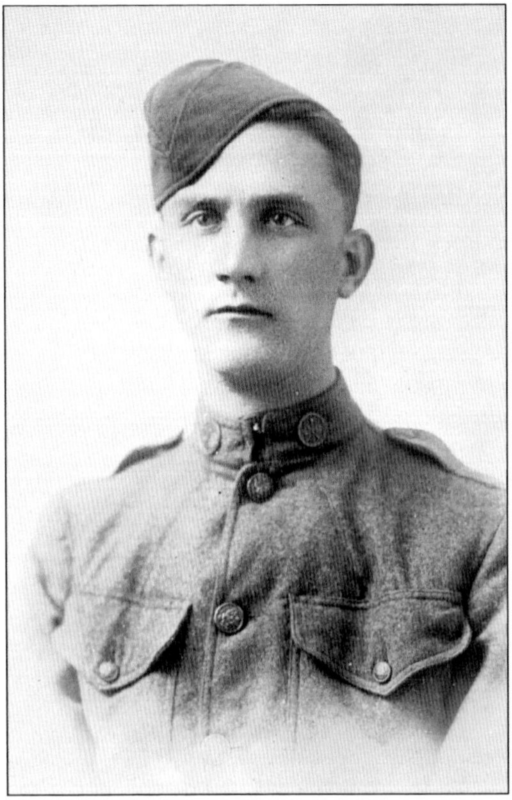

After serving in the military, Royal Elwood Bobier moved to Los Angeles and married Amye Anderson in December 1922. They came to Vista in the late 1920s and stayed on the same property for the rest of their lives. Bobier is pictured here in his World War I uniform.

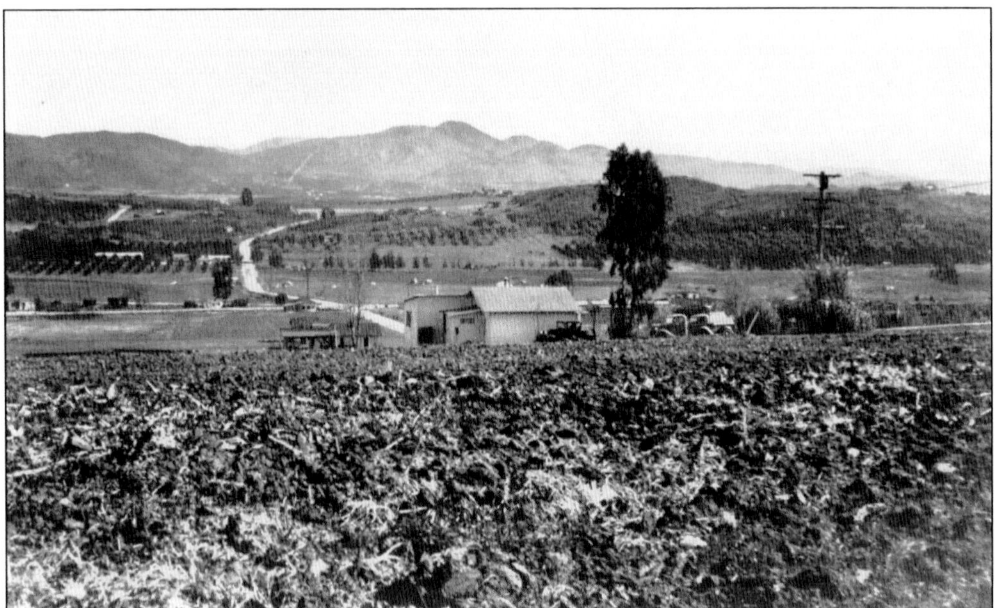

Bobier Drive, one of Vista's main east-west arteries, was named for Royal Elwood Bobier, who was born July 6, 1891, in Pennington County, South Dakota, and came to Vista in 1928 or 1929 with his wife, Amye. This 1945 view of their home and orchard, at center left, looks east along Bobier Drive from North Santa Fe Avenue toward East Vista Way.

Royal Bobier, at left, poses for a 1935 photograph with his father (first name unknown), who was the mayor of Twin Falls, Idaho, at the time. They pronounced their name Bo-beer, not with the French pronunciation that often has Vistans and visitors unsure if it is Bo-bee-ay. Royal Bobier was always known in Vista as Roy.

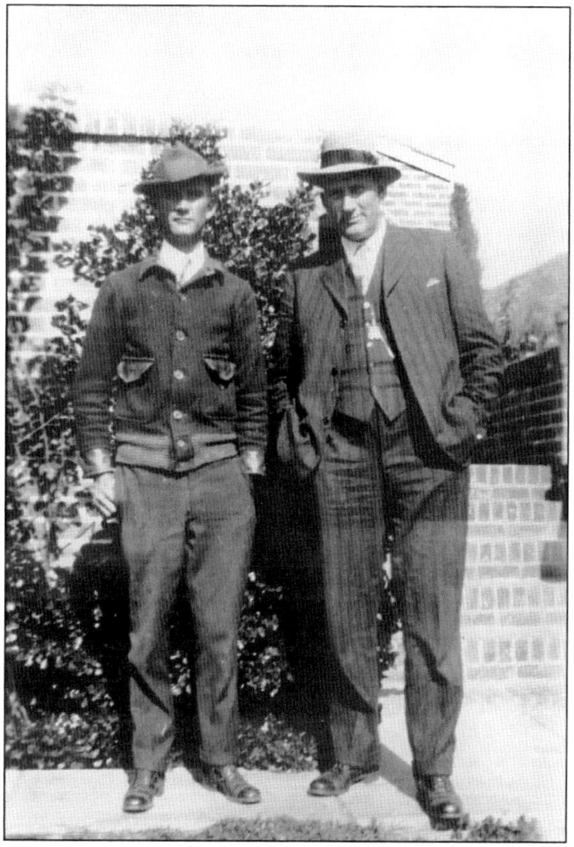

Esther and Lois Bobier, in the wagon, and their brother, Jim, have fun while they help with the planting on Roy and Amye Bobier's ranch in this 1931 photograph. The three children were nieces and nephew of the couple, who had no children of their own.

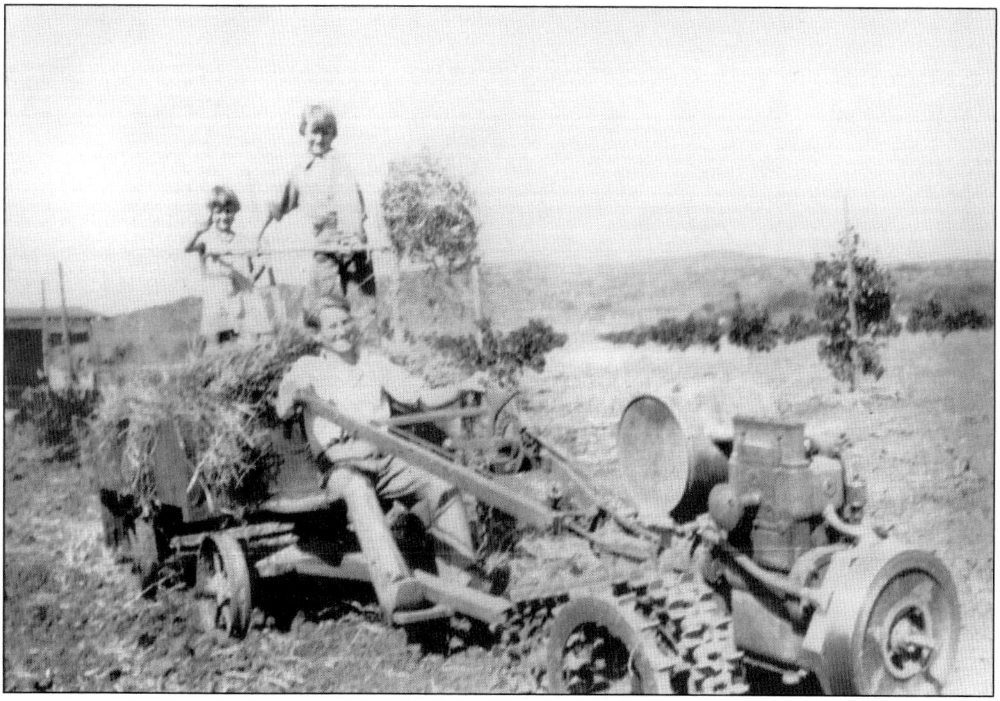

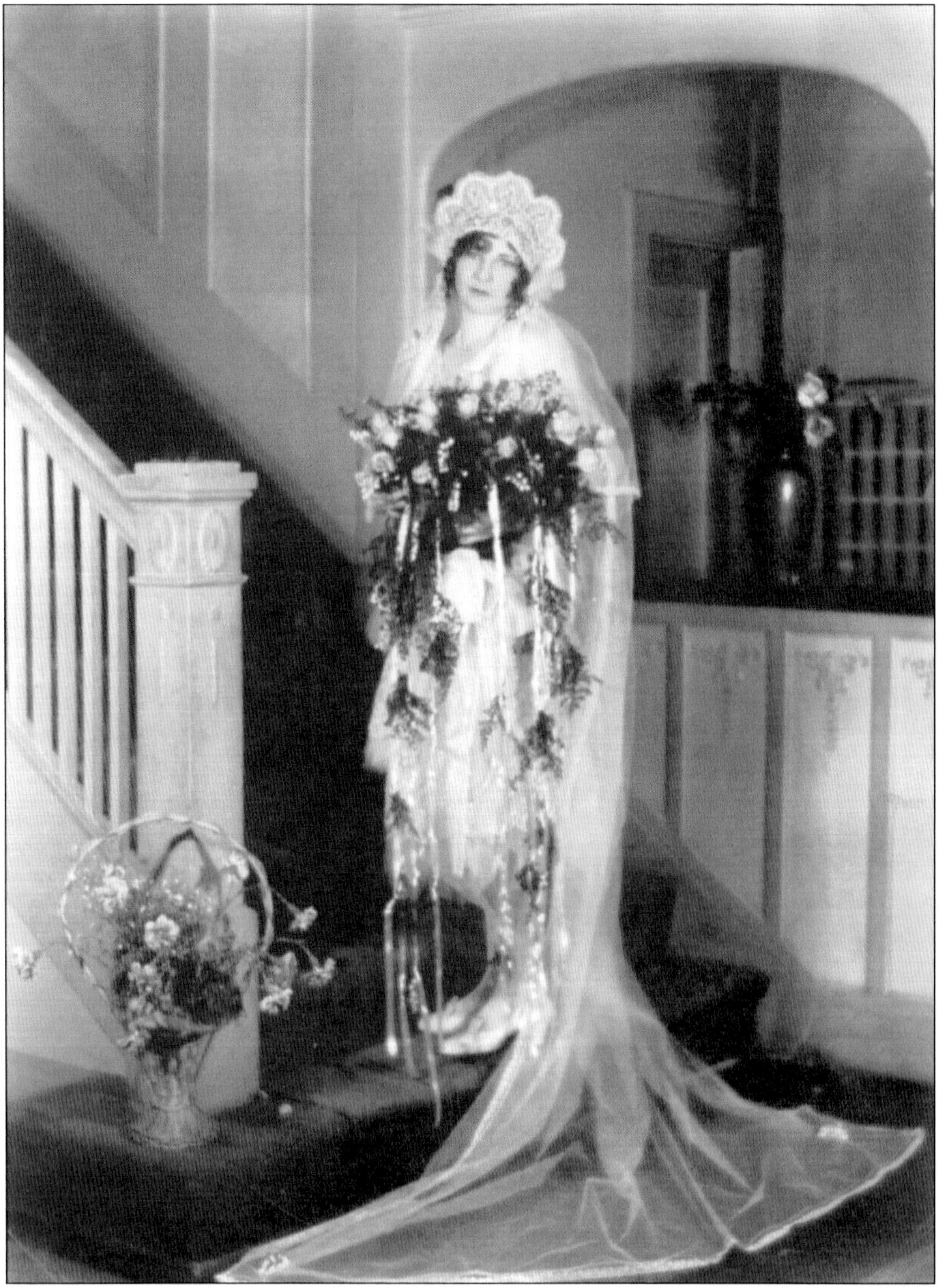

Theodosia Mary Taber carries a bridal bouquet of roses and ribbons as she poses regally for her wedding portrait on the day of her marriage to Joseph V. Clement in 1929. The couple, always known as Joe and Ted, moved in 1931 to family-owned property on East Vale View, now Beaumont Drive. Both were active in local agricultural, social, and civic affairs for the rest of their lives.

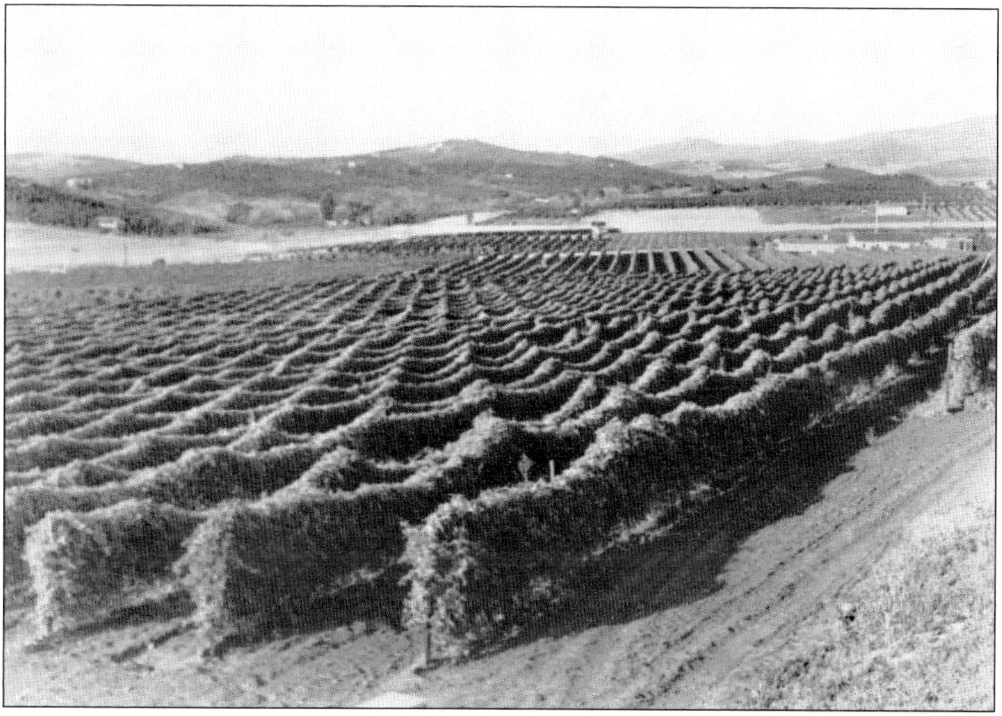

The three-generation Clement family planted avocados in 1931, but by 1933, it was passion fruit that literally became their passion. They built a processing building and made and sold gourmet jelly and pure juice. Unable to keep up with the nationwide demand, they planted 50 additional acres. In 1937, a severe frost killed the young vines and damaged the rest. The Clements went back to raising avocados.

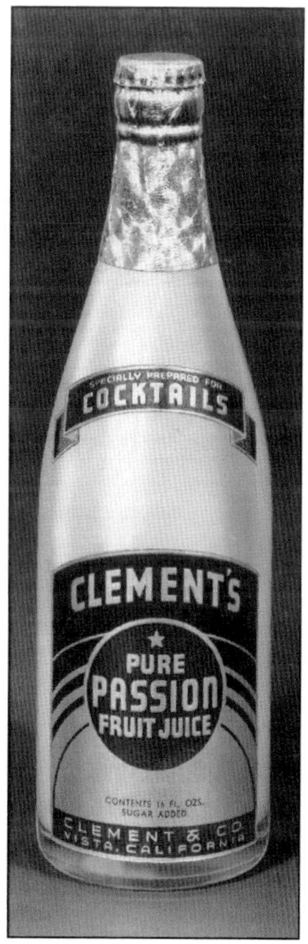

Even the Queen of England ordered some of Vista's passion fruit juice. The Clements formed Clement and Company and prepared specialty products like this pure passion fruit juice that was specially formulated for cocktails. They even strung passion fruit vines from the branches of their avocado grove in an attempt to keep up with the orders.

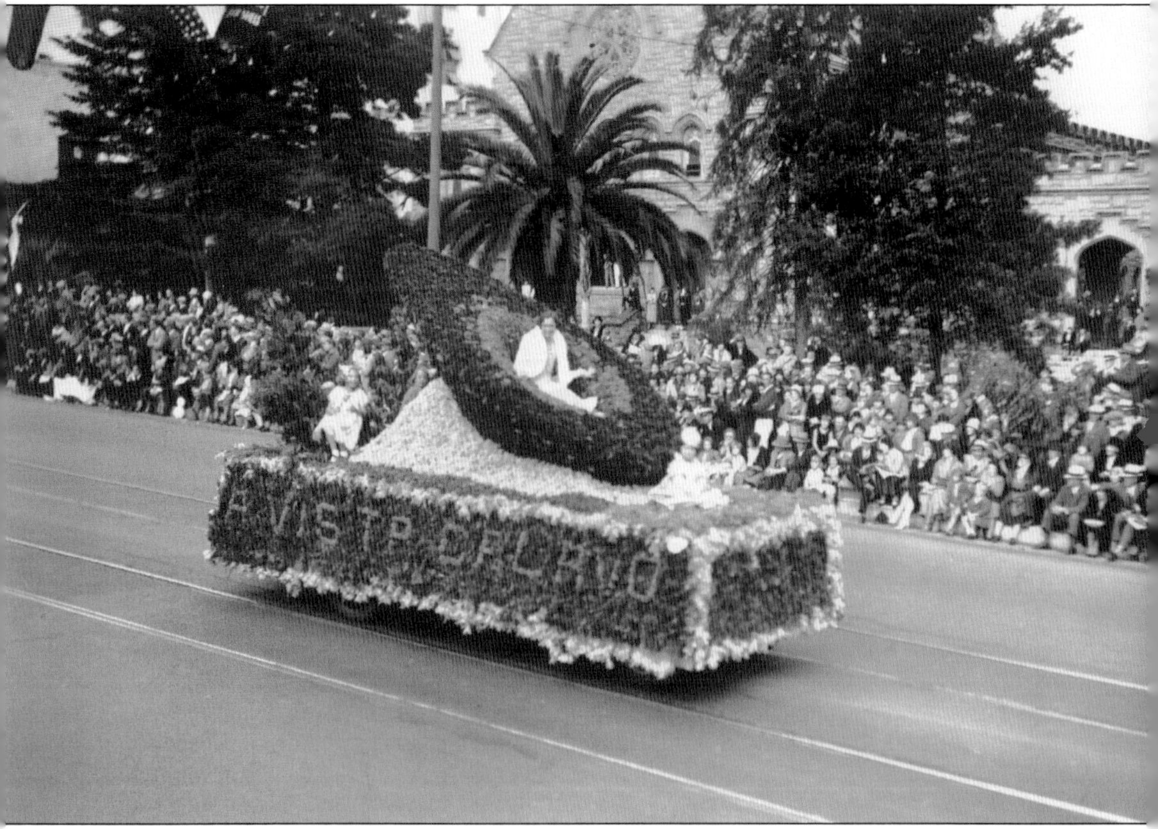

"From Sagebrush to Calavos in Five Years" was the theme of Vista's entry in the 1932 Tournament of Roses Parade, symbolizing the community's dynamic business and agricultural rise. The float was sponsored by Vista Chamber of Commerce with the cooperation of local Calavo growers, using their trade name for avocados. It featured Marjorie Harmon, a grower's daughter selected by 2,800 junior college girls as queen of the 1931 Pasadena Flower Show, as "Miss Calavo." She was seated in the center of an 8-foot-tall avocado half, resting against a base of sagebrush and a hillside of orchid-colored chrysanthemums. Attendants included little Donna Lee Hoskins of Vista, seated in front. The avocado leaves covering the outside of the avocado were individually hand-sewn by Vista volunteers. The January 7, 1932, edition of the *Vista Press* stated that pictures of the float in many newspapers brought both the Vista district and the Calavo association "a great deal of favorable and valuable publicity."

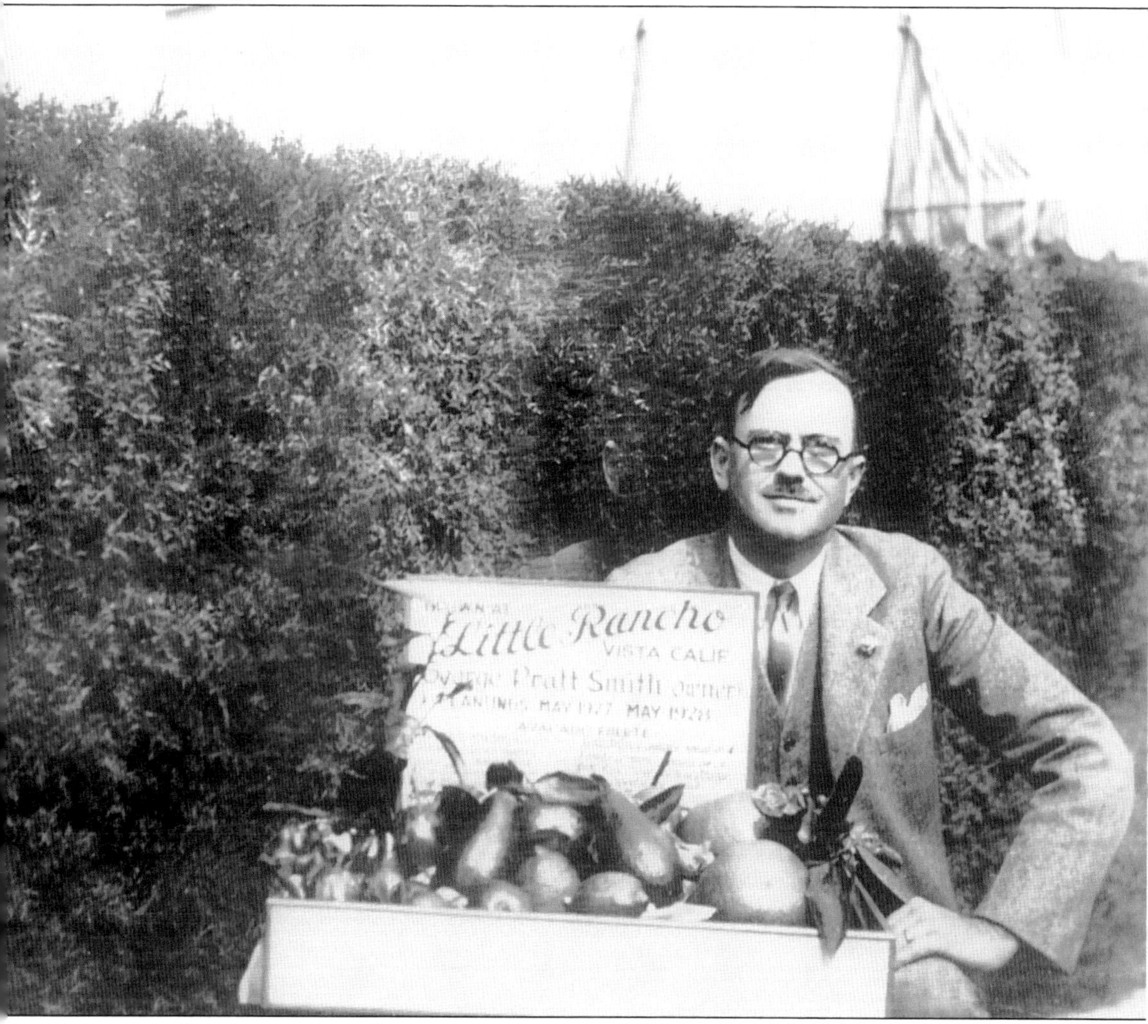

George Pratt Smith was a land salesman, grove owner, and dedicated member of the Vista Chamber of Commerce board of directors in the early 1930s. In January 1932, his fellow board members appointed him as Vista's representative to the Tournament of Roses Association awards dinner in Pasadena, where he accepted a silver bowl and ribbon for Vista's entry in the Rose Parade. Along with Giles Hart of the publicity department of Calavo Growers, Smith was largely credited with the success of the float project and its resultant far-reaching and effective publicity through reprints of photographs and float details in various publications. He is shown with samples of avocados and citrus fruit from groves planted in 1927 and 1928 on his Little Rancho property. Smith was the grandfather of Lance Vollmer, who for many years was active in Vista civic and service projects.

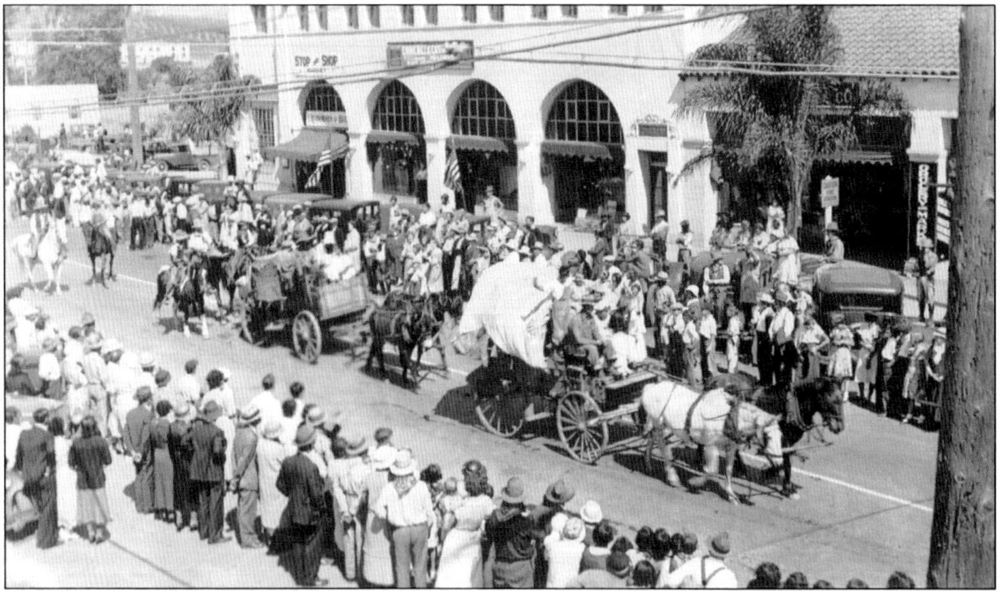

The "Days of '49" parade, named to honor California's heritage, was sponsored by the American Legion as a fund-raiser each spring from 1932 to 1939. Vista became Grizzly Gulch for the day, and the event quickly became so popular that there were often four or five times more spectators than the population. Up to 10,000 people, mostly wearing Western garb, lined the streets to view homemade floats, horses and riders, covered wagons pulled by mules, and an assortment of local organizations and children's groups. Film actor Leo Carrillo, who owned a ranch in Carlsbad, was unanimously elected honorary mayor by the 1937 parade committee. A beard contest, bronco-busting, and other events added to the festivities. As the 1940 parade approached, the American Legion's first building was almost completed. Post members agreed that they were overwhelmed by their own success and discontinued the event.

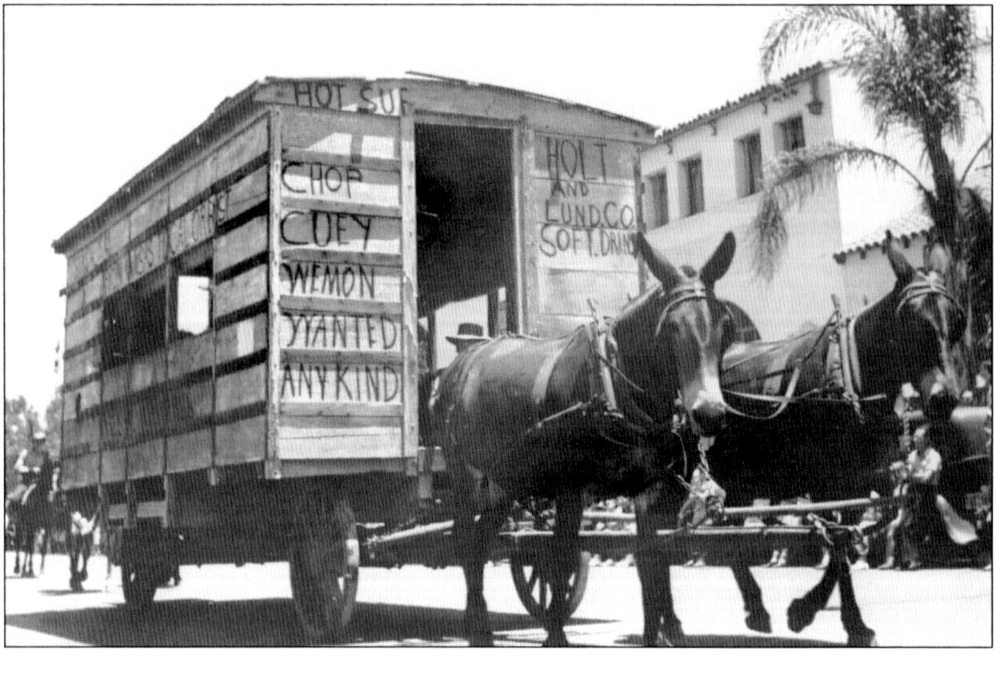

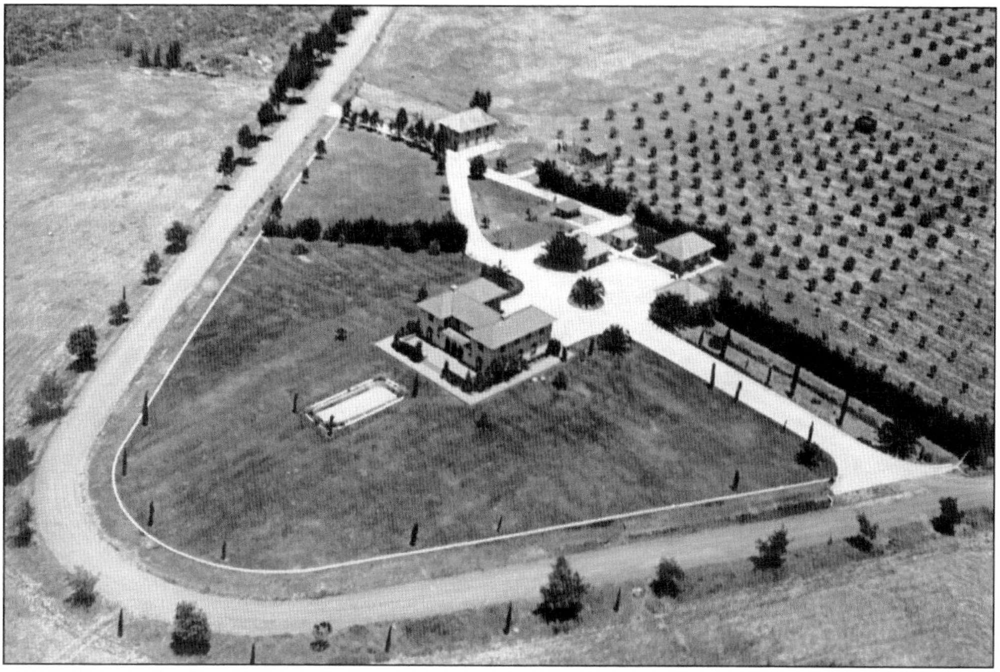

Mr. and Mrs. Charles Brawn built this stately home on Vale View Drive in late 1920s. The pristine property includes a newly planted grove, the barn and other outbuildings, and the ultimate luxury of the time, a swimming pool behind the house. Mrs. Brawn (first name unknown) was a charter member of the Vista Garden Club, which formed in February 1930. The elegant front of the home features arched doorways, wrought-iron railings, and a tile roof. Dale E. Wood, who came to Vista in 1926 as a representative of the Edwin G. Hart Company and later had a successful real estate career as well as serving on the Vista Irrigation District board of directors, later lived in the house with his wife, Gene.

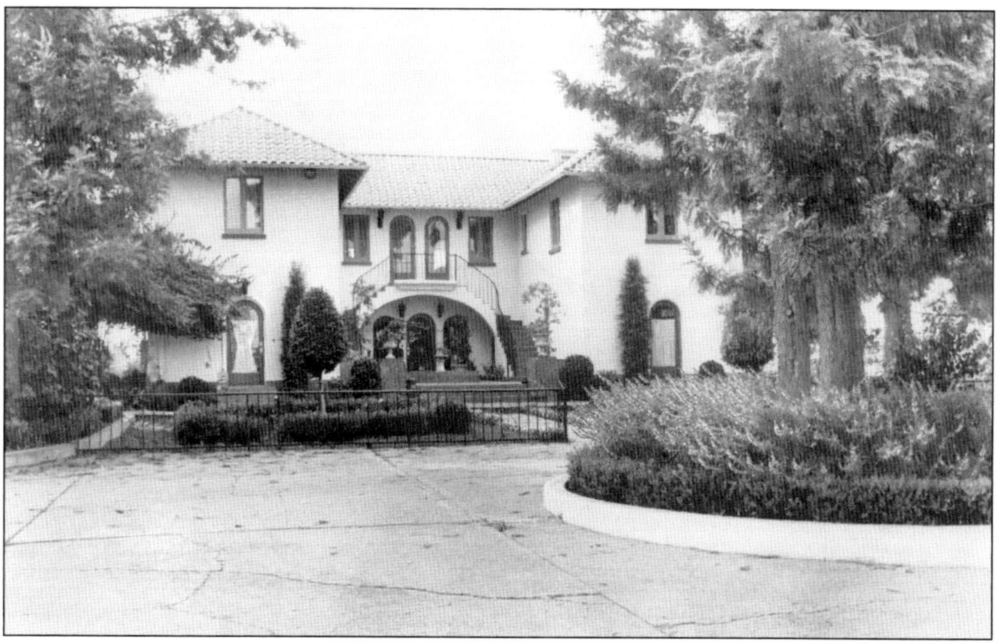

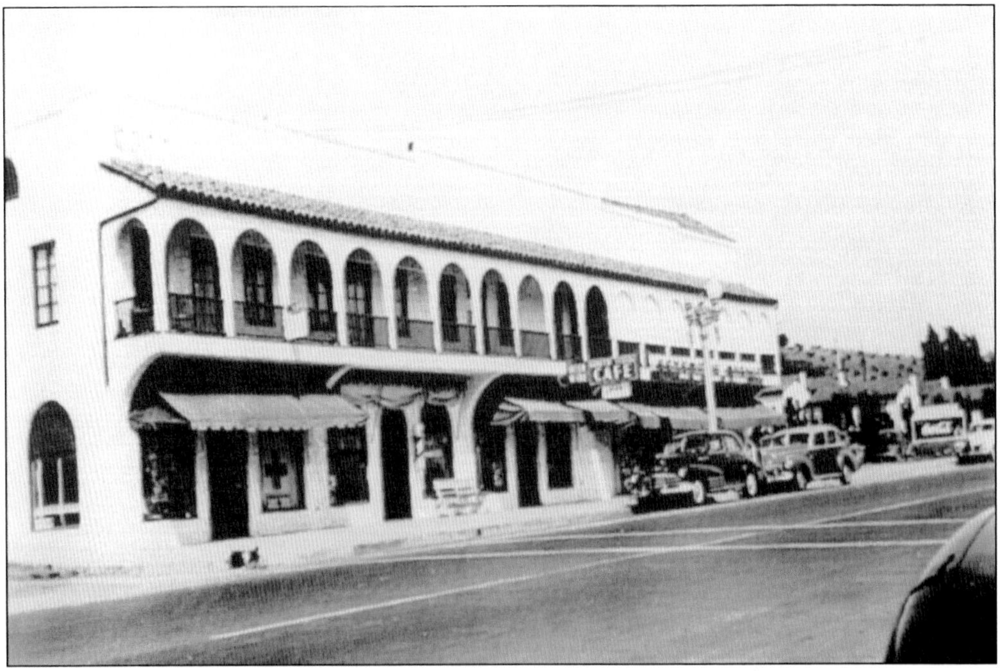

The *Vista Press* edition of December 2, 1927, announced the beginning of construction on a two-story, 100-foot-long building on South Santa Fe Avenue. Financed by Rancho Vista Development Company, the Spanish-style structure featured nine office rooms upstairs and a lodge hall with anteroom and kitchen. Named the Granada Building, the structure housed Sexsmith's Market for three decades. New churches and organizations held their first meetings in the hall.

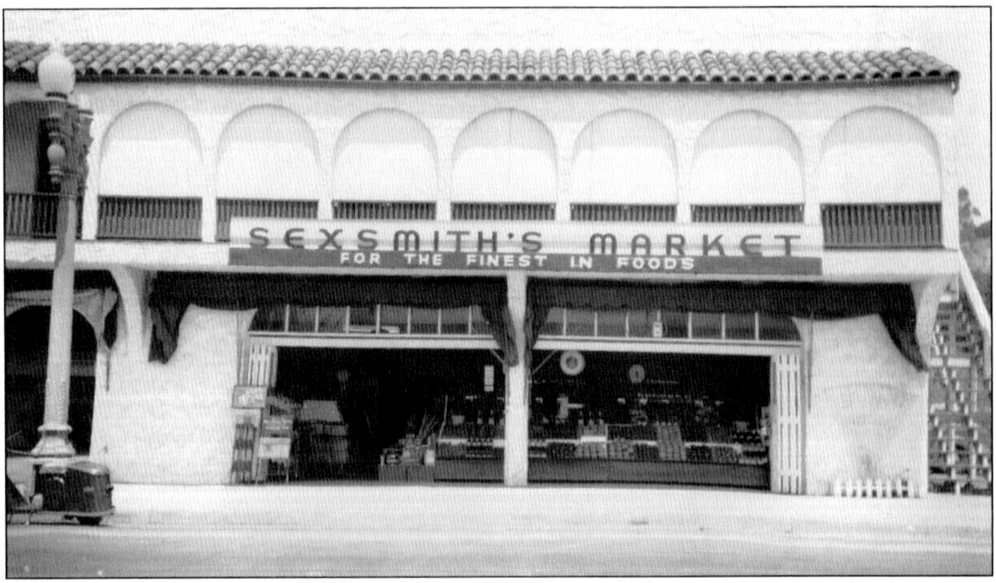

In 1929, George Sexsmith and his father, Charles B. Sexsmith, opened the popular Sexsmith's Market in the Granada Building on South Santa Fe Avenue. The full-service market continued to serve area residents until it closed in 1958. The Sexsmiths came to be revered over the years by many local citizens, who were given groceries on credit during the Depression and other difficult financial times.

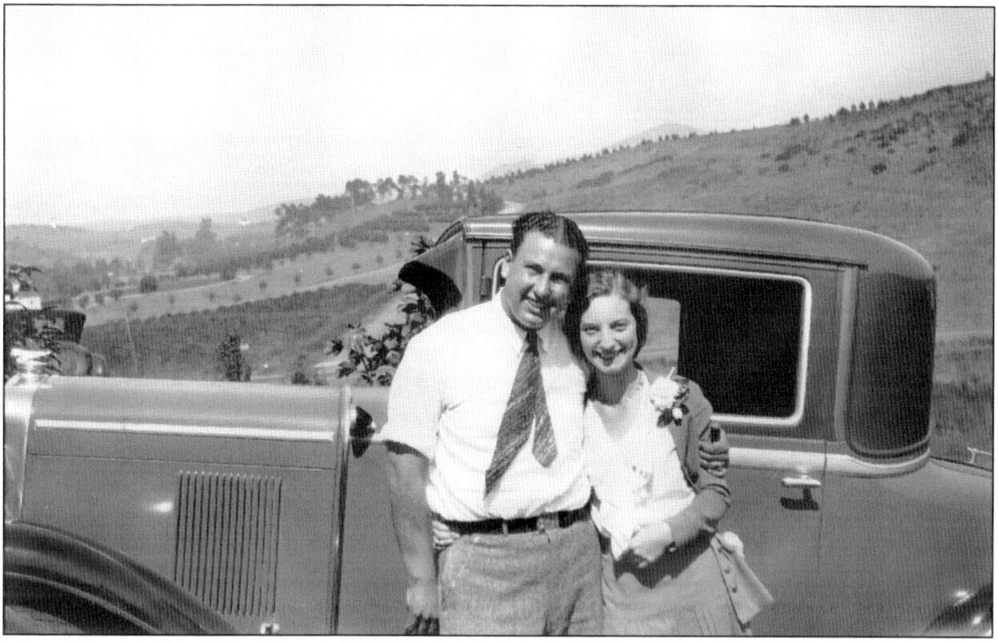

This photograph of George and Emily Sexsmith was taken as they arrived in Vista after their wedding in Glendale on September 25, 1932. Emily soon took an active part in running the family business, Sexsmith's Market. The couple is pictured with their new car against a hillside recently planted with groves. They spent the rest of their lives actively involved in philanthropic endeavors for the community they loved.

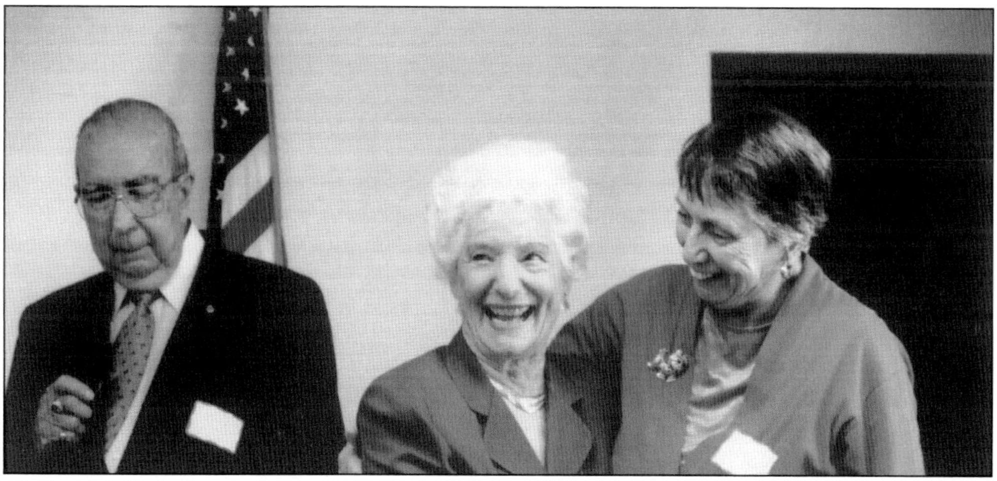

Wildwood Community Center was packed with well-wishers at a surprise 90th birthday party for Emily Sexsmith (center) in 2001. John Cosh, whose family arrived in Vista in 1925, mans the microphone to extol her exemplary service to the community from her arrival in Vista in 1932. Sexsmith, known for always being stylishly dressed, shares a laugh with her longtime friend Eve Cole.

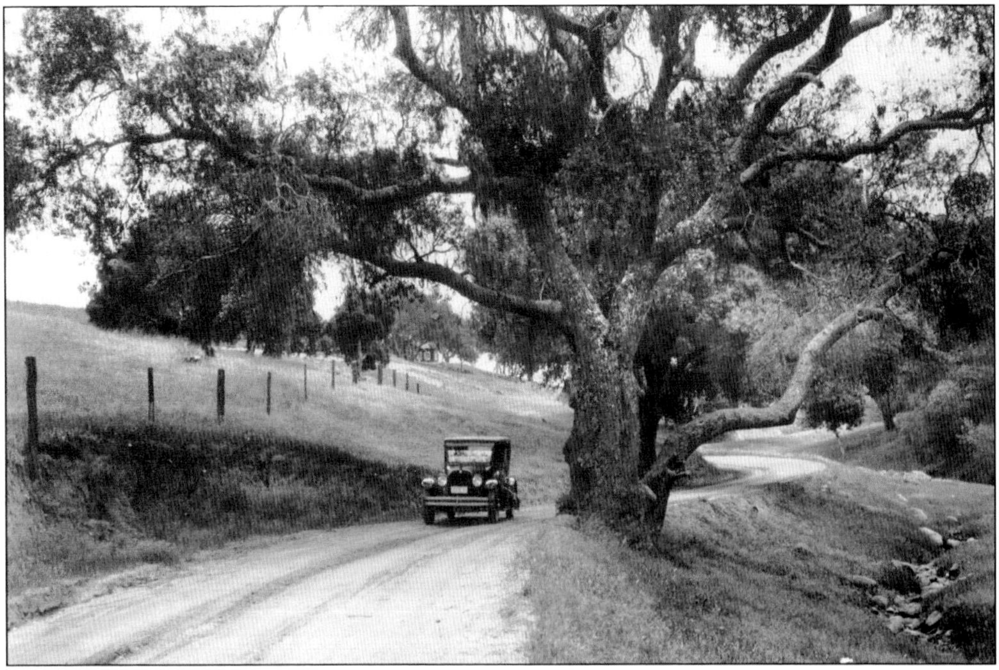

A traveler winds along one of Vista's back roads, past formidable old trees, fenced acreage, and a dry creek bed. Such scenes would soon give way to avocado and citrus groves. This photograph was donated to the Vista Historical Society by Harrison Doyle, one of the society's founding members.

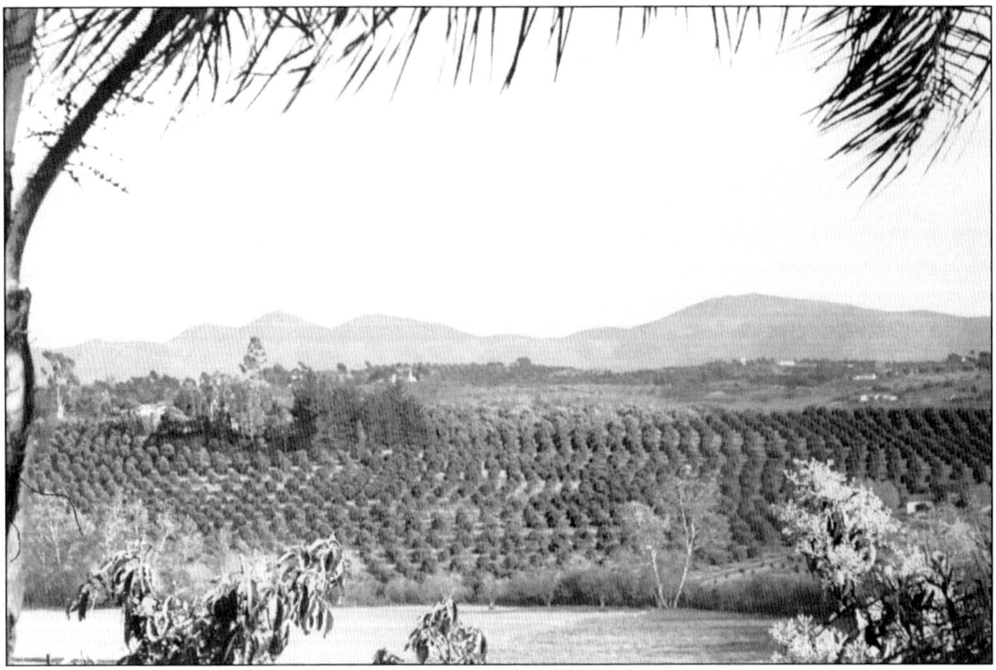

Artistically framed by a palm tree, this 1930s photograph shows Vista's gently rolling terrain, dotted with new homes and some of the maturing groves that were among the first planted when water arrived in 1926.

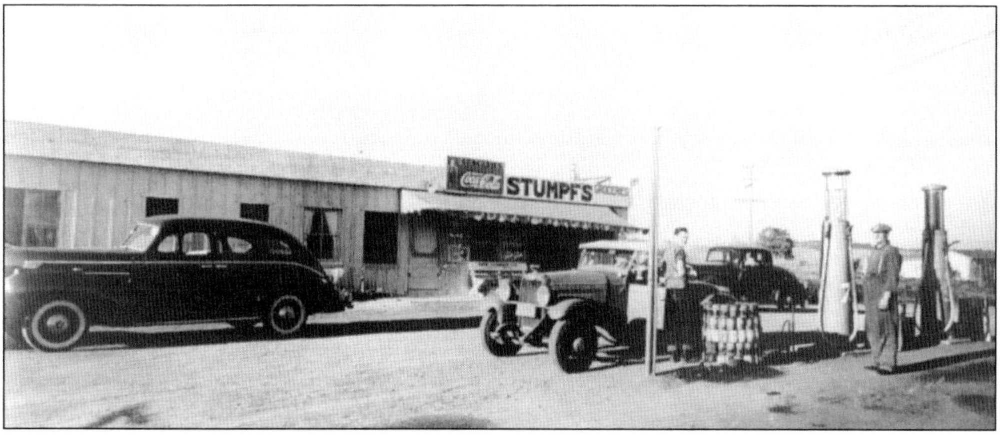

Stumpfs Groceries, at Emerald Drive and West Vista Way in the western area of town, was a favorite stopping place for supplies and gasoline in Vista's early years. The corner is now part of a heavily traveled intersection near on and off ramps for the Highway 78 freeway.

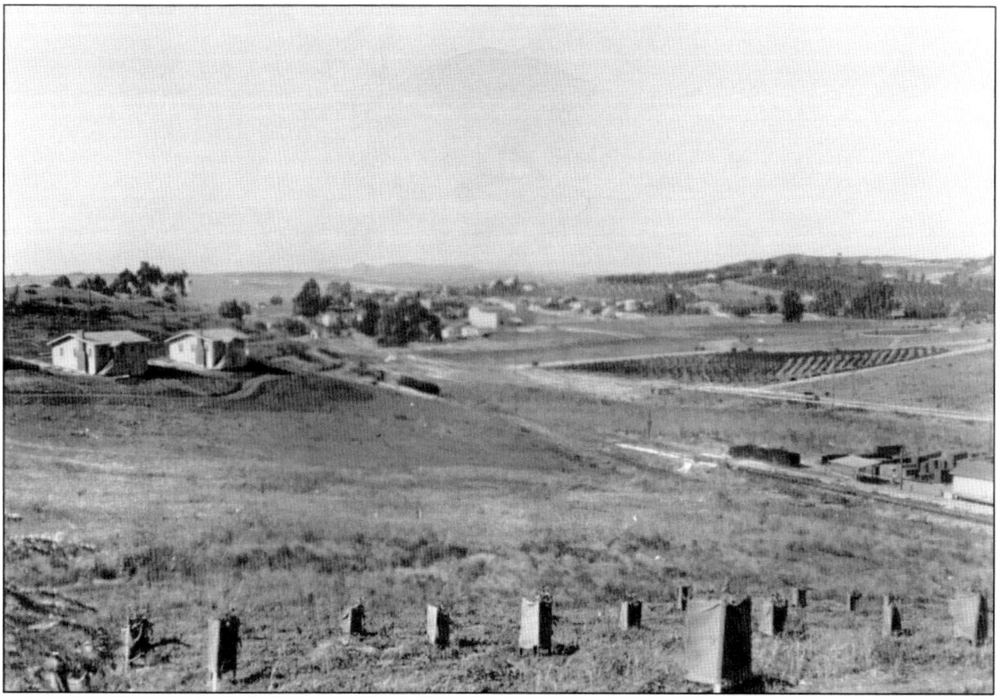

This 1929 photograph was taken from Lado de Loma Drive and Guajome Street, looking past the two new homes on the left and across the railroad tracks to South Santa Fe Avenue. The Vista Inn is on the knoll at left center, and the newly built First National Bank building is to the hotel's right.

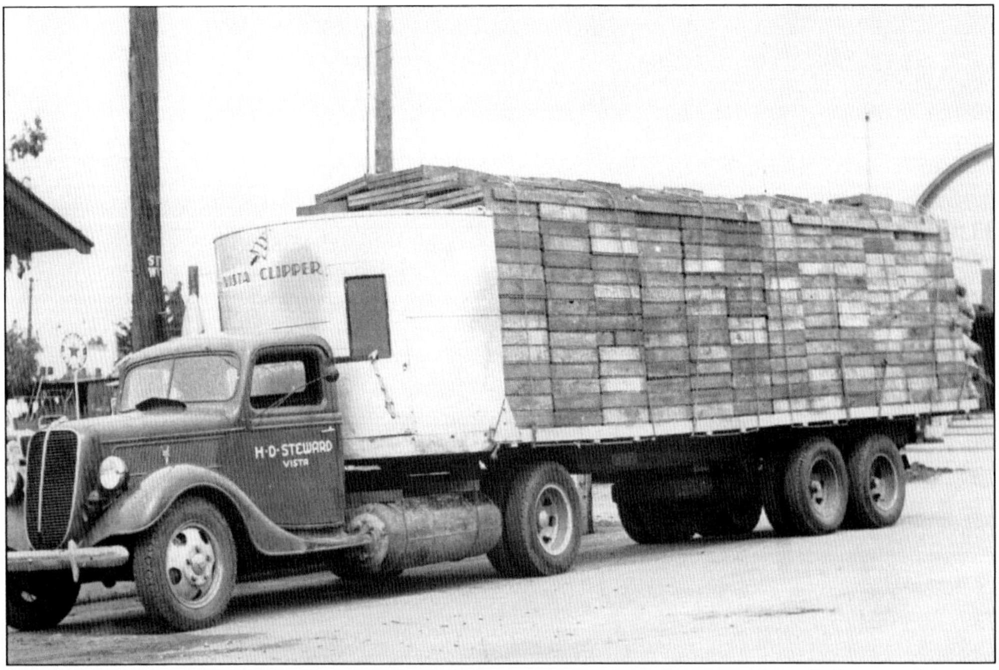

The "Vista Clipper," an H. D. Steward Company truck, is ready to transport Vista's first truckload of gladiolus bulbs. The bulbs were grown by Arville Williams, who came to Vista in 1927 and was one of the area's first gladiolus farmers. Steward's trucking company was located on Olive Avenue.

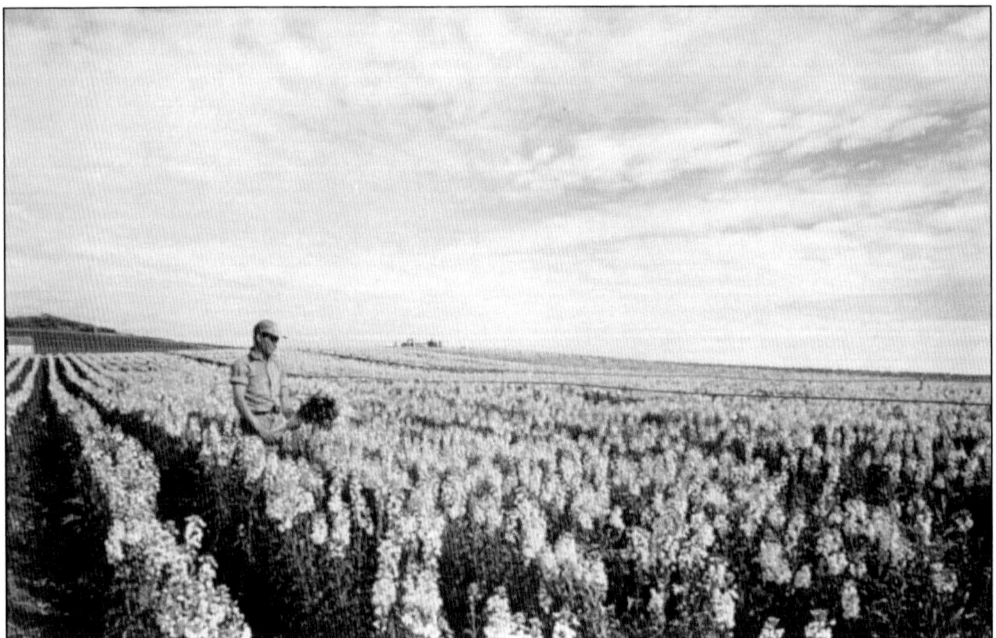
In 1939, Wilson "Vinnie" Vinson Jr. joined with Sam Fortiner to grow and ship gladiola under the name Vinson and Fortiner, Inc., at 315 North Santa Fe Avenue. They became the pioneer Southern California shippers of such delicate fresh flowers as the double-column stock shown in this photograph. They specialized in air-shipping flowers for San Diego County growers.

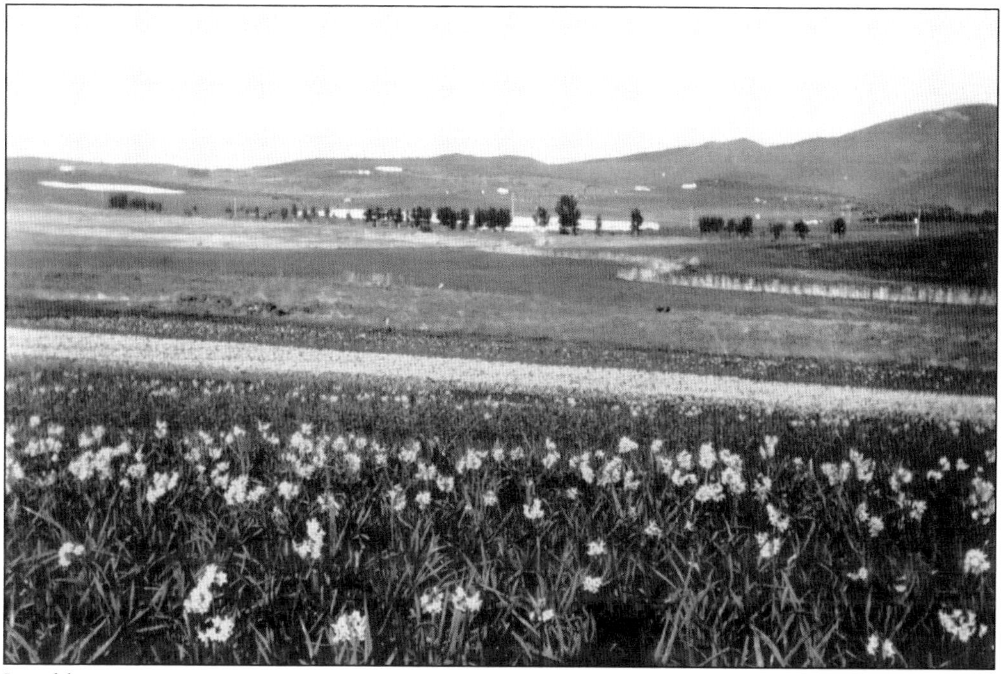

In addition to serving as Vista's postmaster from April 1, 1943, to October 13, 1955, Howard Skinner had a successful business as a flower grower. This view of his extensive Vista flower fields was photographed in February 1932.

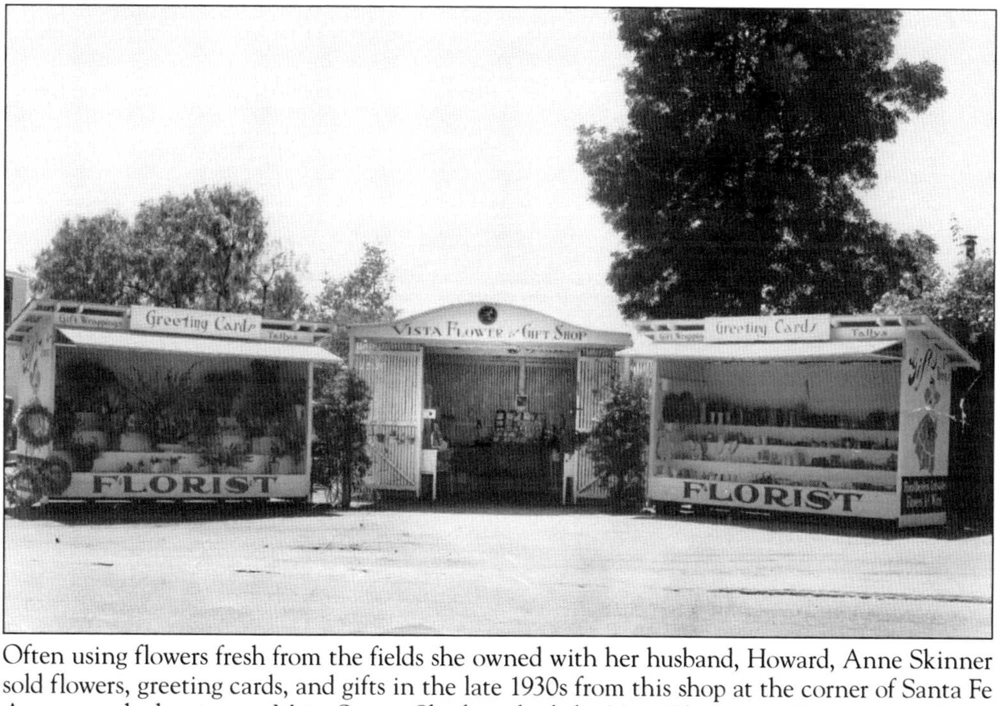

Often using flowers fresh from the fields she owned with her husband, Howard, Anne Skinner sold flowers, greeting cards, and gifts in the late 1930s from this shop at the corner of Santa Fe Avenue and what is now Main Street. She later had the Vista Flower and Gift Shop building constructed on West Vista Way. It was purchased by Harold Mitts in 1946 and later had several other owners.

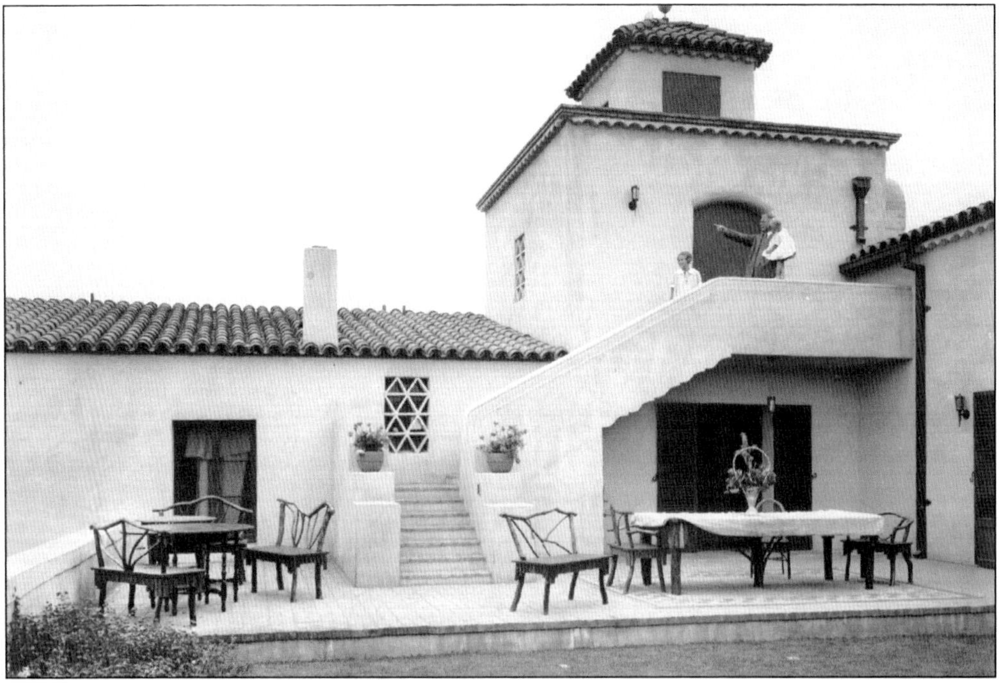

The McCurdy-Morton house was constructed in the early 1920s in the Spanish style, as were many of Vista's first homes.S. Charlton McCurdy and Robert N. Morton were contractors who built the home on Alta Vista Drive jointly with the idea that they would use some rooms in common and some privately. Andy Canellis, a Chicago candy maker, next owned the 44-acre ranch, followed by Gordon Dean, who sold the property to Arthur Viault in December 1949 and became chairman of the Atomic Energy Commission on July 13, 1950. Retired Air Force lieutenant colonel H. C. Muhlenberg, former commanding officer of Hickam Field in Hawaii, and his wife, Helen, bought land near Pechstein Dam before purchasing the Morton-McCurdy house in the early 1950s. The Muhlenbergs later moved to Joshua Tree. There have been several additional owners.

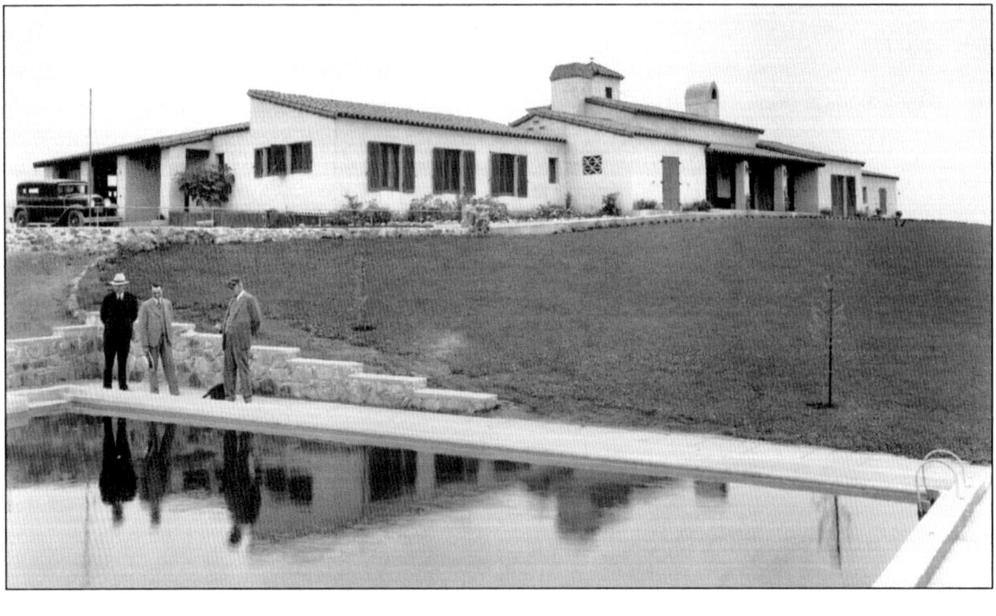

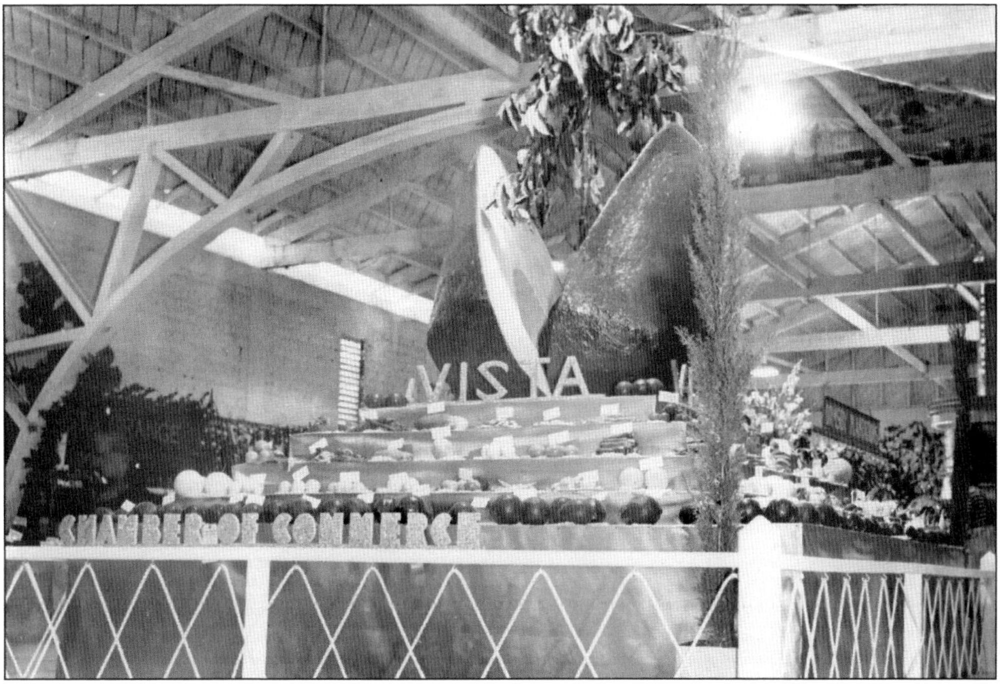

This Vista Chamber of Commerce exhibit won second prize of $100 at the 1937 Del Mar Fair and was later shown at the Los Angeles County Fair. Designed and constructed by Jules and Virginia Frels and George and Emily Sexsmith, the exhibit was made of papier-mâché and buckram, with light shining through the transparent "cut side" of the avocado. Local products were displayed around the base.

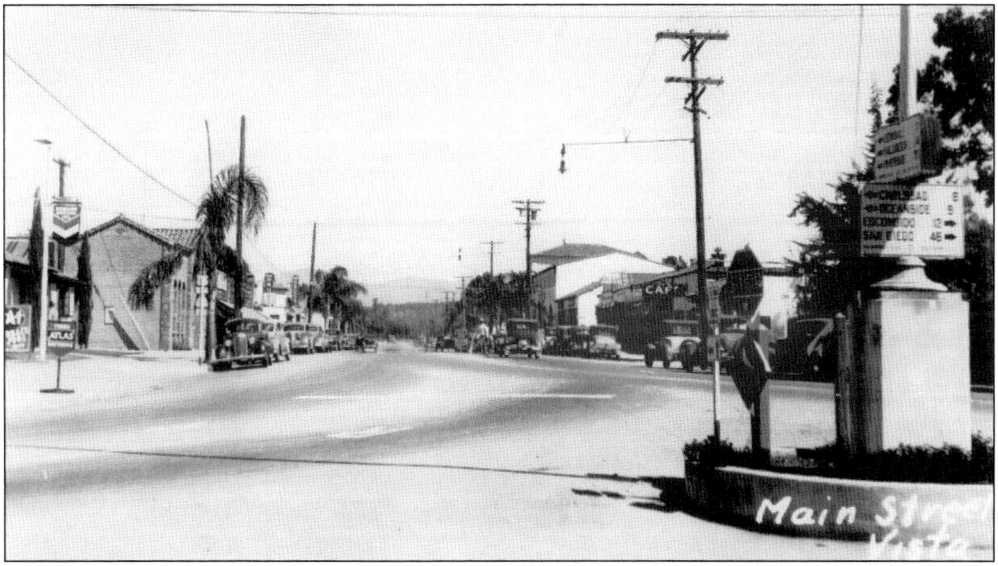

A late-1930s mileage sign at the corner of Vista's busiest downtown intersection, which was then San Diego Boulevard and Santa Fe Avenue, tells us that San Diego is 46 miles away, with Carlsbad just 8 and Oceanside 9. This view looks east along what is now Main Street, with the brick Vista Irrigation District building on the left and First National Bank building towering over other structures on the right.

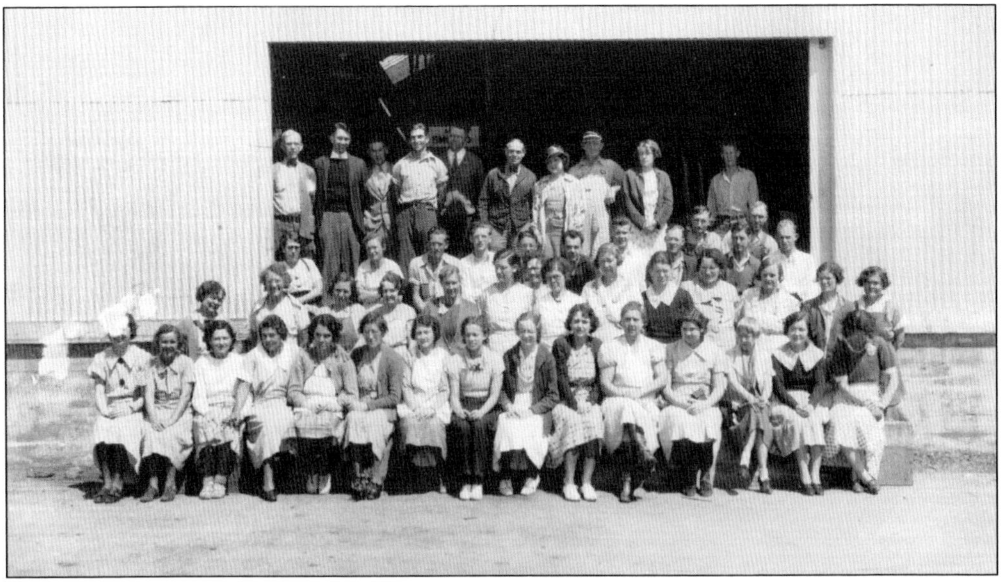

Managers and employees of the Vista Calavo packing plant took time out for a group photograph in December 1934, just one month after the opening of this first branch packinghouse of Calavo Growers of California. The plant was for 15 years one of the largest employers in Vista. Workers proclaimed it a "family place," and many wives of overseas service men worked there during World War II.

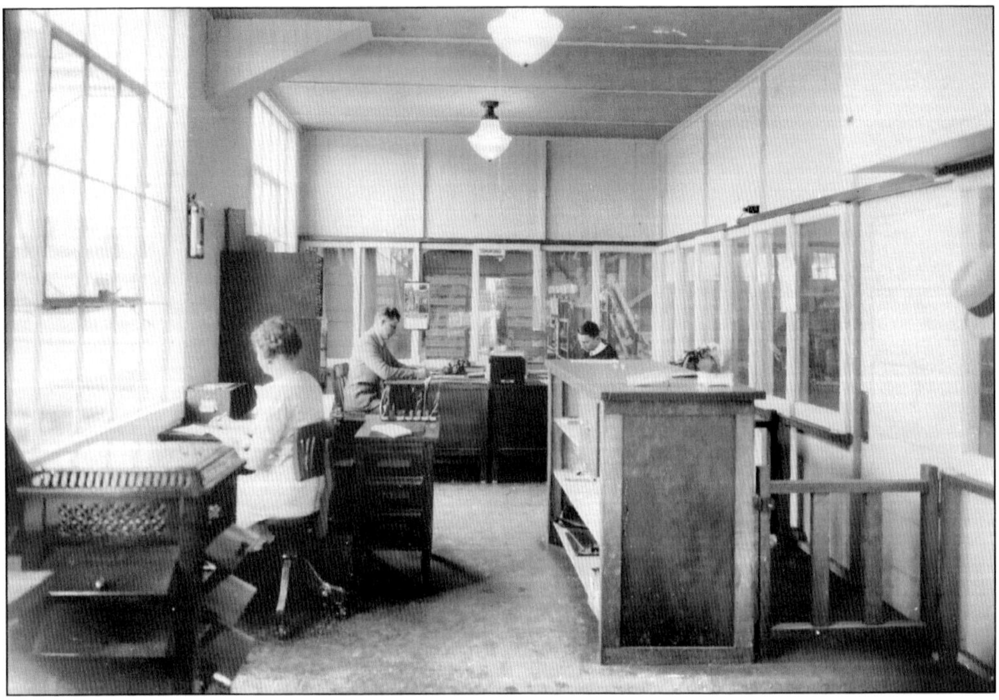

The office of the Vista Calavo plant was a busy place in January 1935, when Vista was the avocado capital of the world. Built on 2.7 acres of ground, the packinghouse was accessible to San Diego County growers and could easily be expanded to meet their needs. The woman in the foreground is identified as Mrs. Rabe and the man behind her (left) is J. Shepherd.

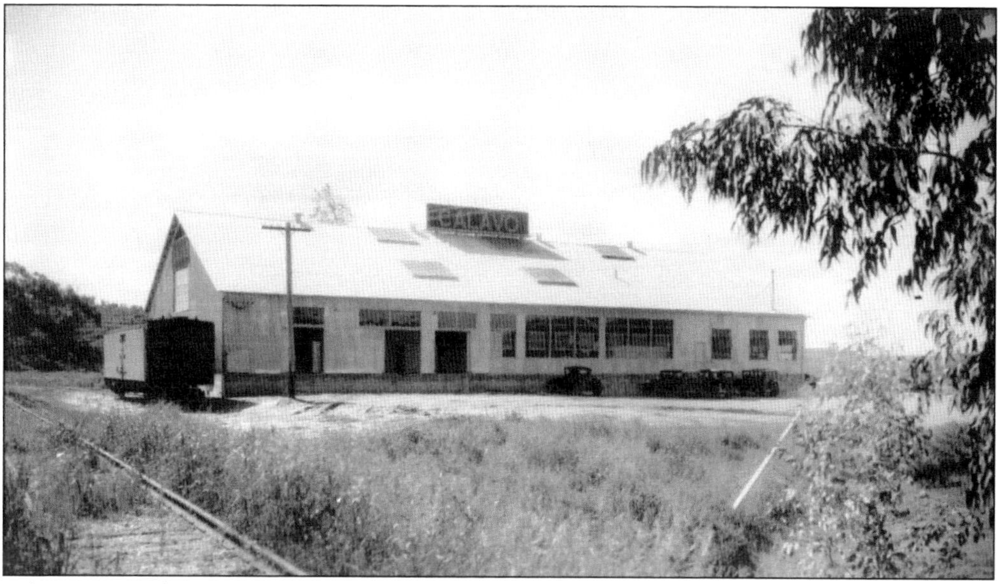

"The most modern of all time-savers and efficiencies are being incorporated in this first unit of an ultimate six-unit San Diego County plant," proclaimed the October 1934 issue of the *Calavo News*. This $11,000, 72-by-140-foot building was constructed with a cement floor at freight-car door level to ease loading. It had a packing capacity of two freight-car loads of avocados per day.

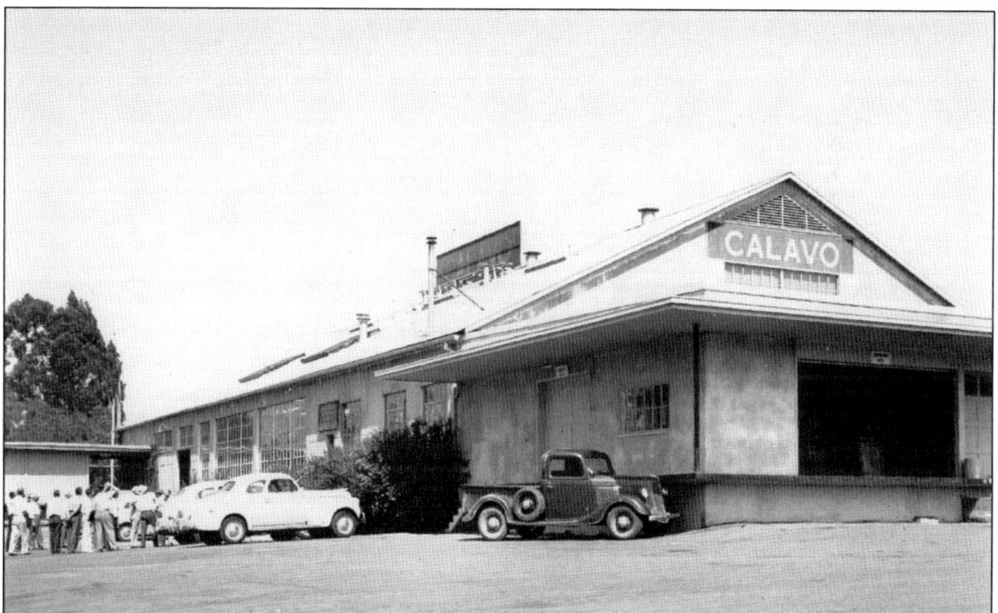

The first carload of 1,620 flats left the plant in mid-December 1934. Pictured here are additions that were made over the years to accommodate increasing demand by countywide avocado growers. After the plant burned in 1949, Peto's Farm Supply took over and restored the remaining structure. Robert Haymaker, a former state fruit inspector, moved to Vista to run the plant and remained as manager until the building burned in 1949.

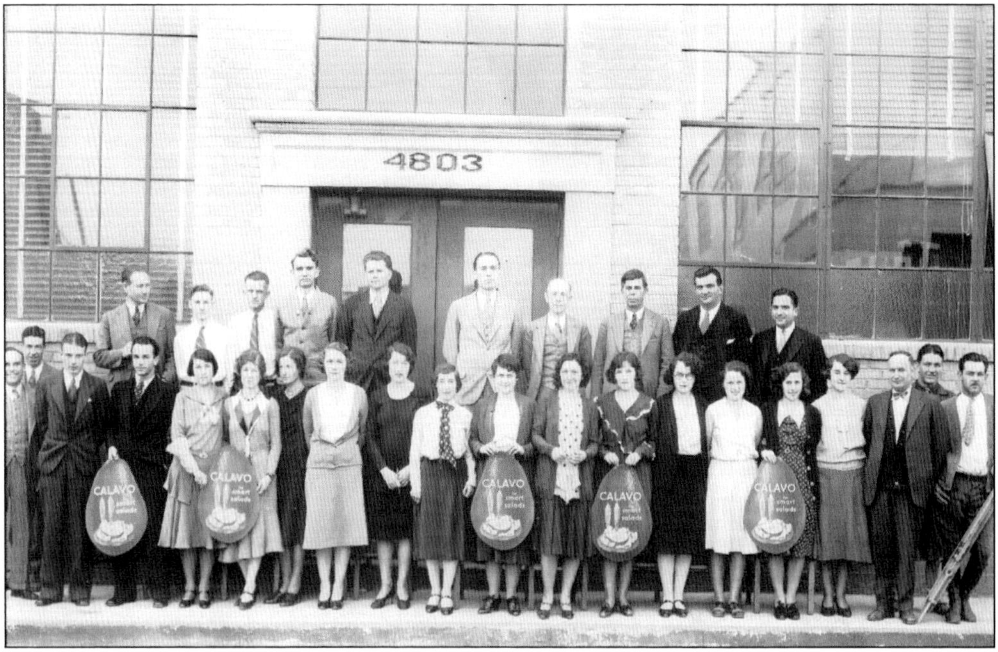

Area Calavo growers assembled for this photograph at a joint meeting in 1932. The avocado-shaped signs read, "CALAVO for smart salads." In an advertisement that appeared in one of the first editions of the *Vista Press* in late 1926, the Hart Company offered land at $400 an acre. The developer decreed "a guarantee of $4,000 a year for life on just one acre of avocados."

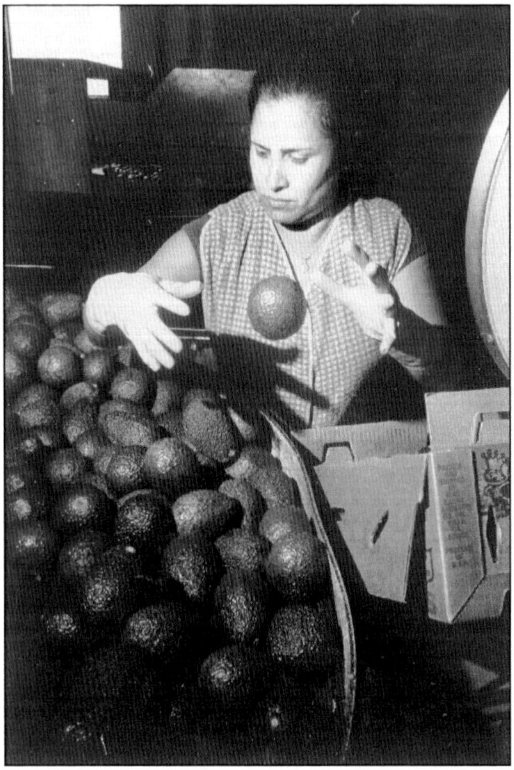

Although the Calavo plant was the largest, there were a number of other packing plants over the years for avocado, citrus, and field crops. Consuelo Moral Madrigal is pictured in November 1983 as she sorts avocados at the King Salad Avocado Company facility in Vista. (Courtesy of *Escondido Times-Advocate*.)

Four

HOMES REPLACE GROVES, AND A CITY EVOLVES

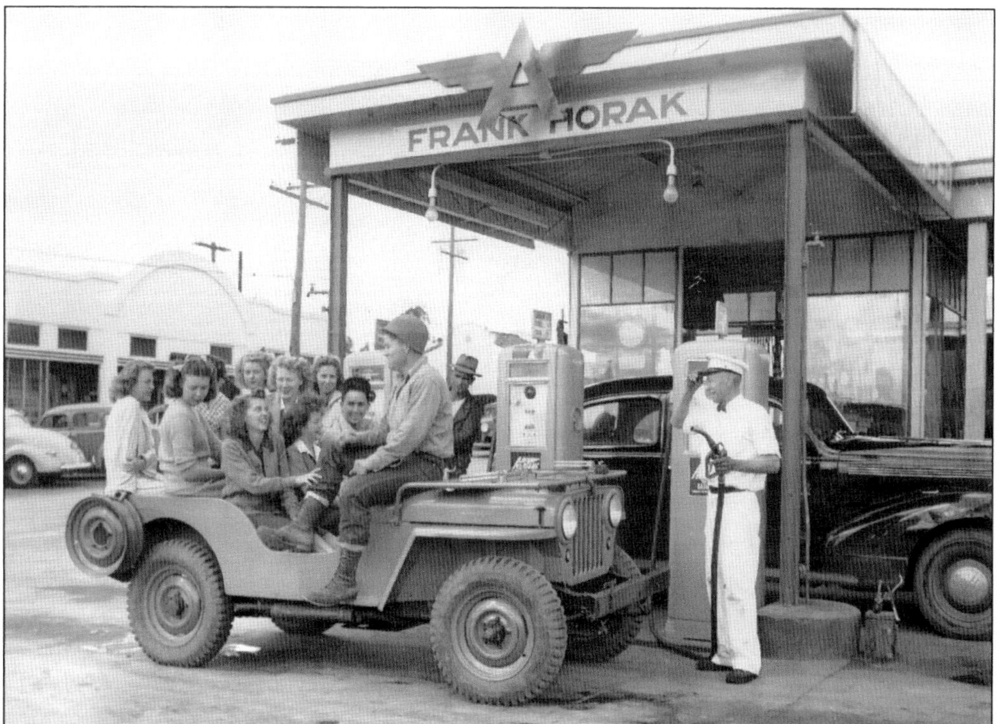

Frank Horak is ready to pump gasoline at 21¢ a gallon for a few of his friends in this 1946 photograph. There were free maps and Green Stamps, too. Horak's station was located at Michigan Avenue and what is now Main Street. The pretty girls, all from the Vista High School class of 1947, admire classmate Richard "Ole" Carlson, perched on the front of the Jeep.

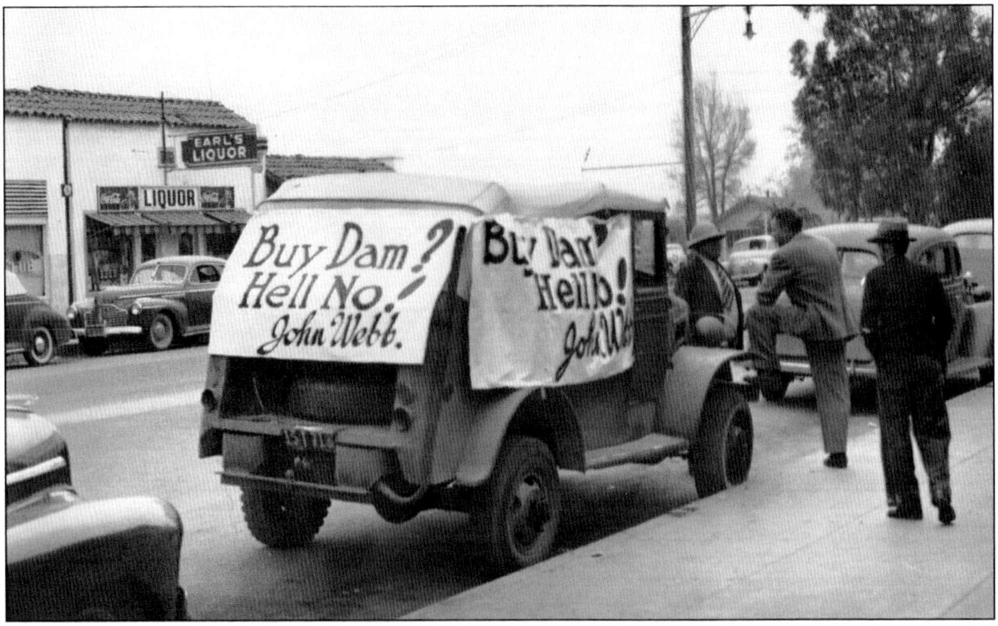

When voters passed a ballot proposal to buy Henshaw Dam by a 4-1 vote in May 1946, successful Vista businessman and grower John Webb made his stance on the issue clearly known. The $4.9-million purchase included Lake Henshaw, the dam, water rights, and the nearly 43,000 surrounding acres that constituted Warner Ranch. The extra land was leased for cattle grazing and specialty crops.

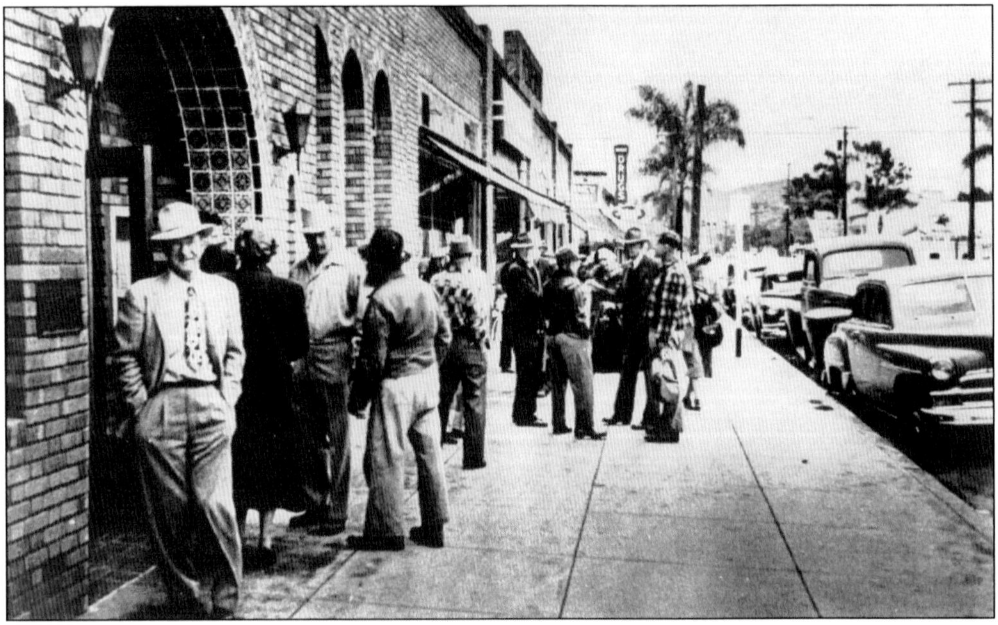

After World War II, the population surged and securing sufficient water was once again a priority. Anxious citizens are waiting outside the Vista Irrigation District building for the results of the May 1946 ballot measure that proposed the purchase of Henshaw Dam and surrounding property. Another successful election was held shortly thereafter, this time to join the San Diego County Water Authority to secure water from the Colorado River.

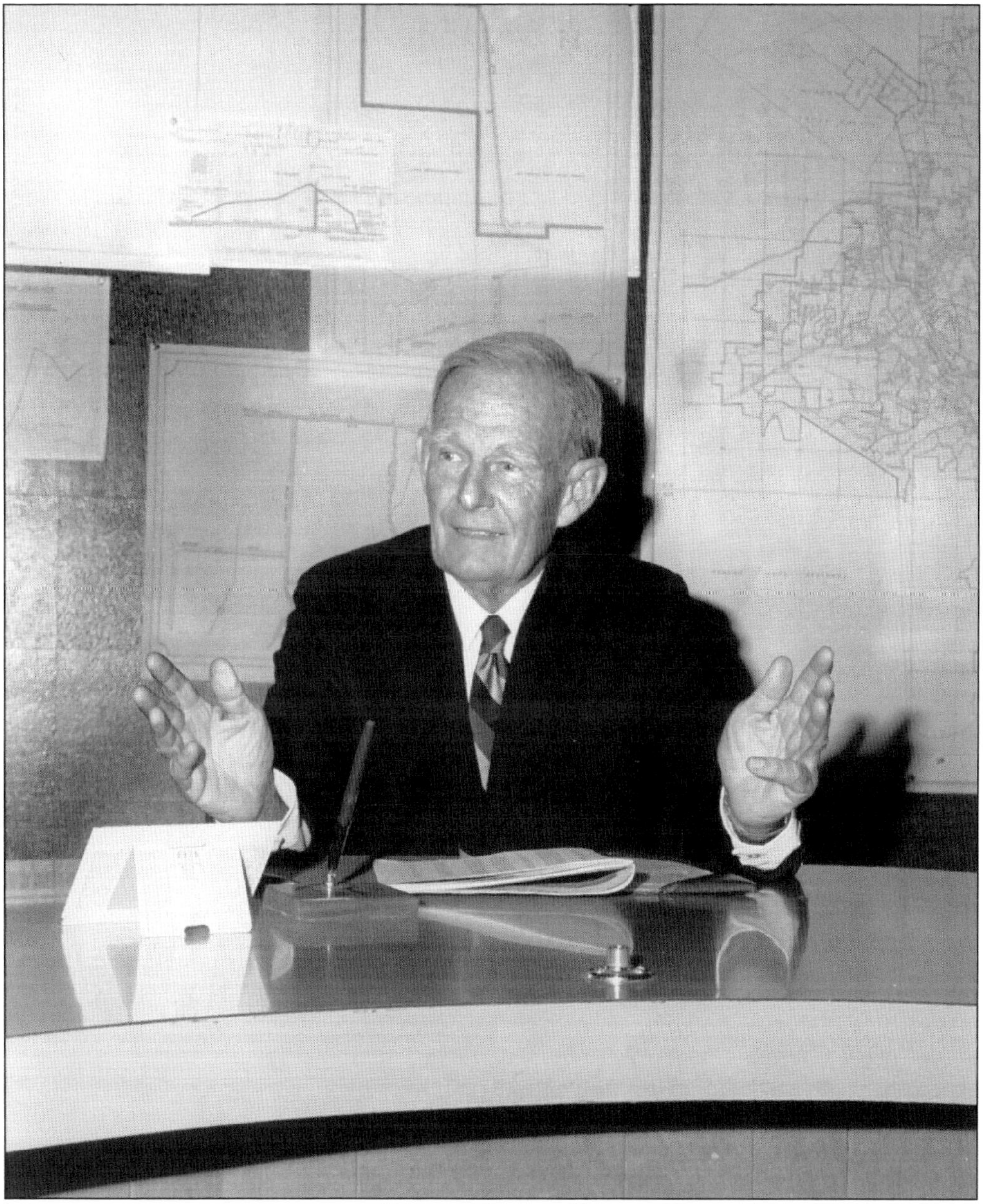

In the second half of the 20th century, water authorities throughout California had only one man they honored with the title "Mr. Water." Norwegian-born Hans Doe arrived in Vista from Milwaukee with his wife, Margaret, in 1946 with the plan of switching his career from engineer to grower of avocados and macadamia nuts. By 1951, he had been elected to the board of directors of Vista Irrigation District (VID), a post he held for 33 years. He had a rare understanding that many of the water issues facing Vista were impacted by decisions made beyond local jurisdictional boundaries. Doe was instrumental in the creation of the Bueno Colorado Municipal Water District and in having the VID join the San Diego County Water Authority. He served on both of those boards for 29 years as well as on the Metropolitan Water District of Southern California. It was said affectionately of Hans Doe that if anyone turned on a faucet in a room, he would deliver an hour-long, fact-filled speech on the importance of securing water.

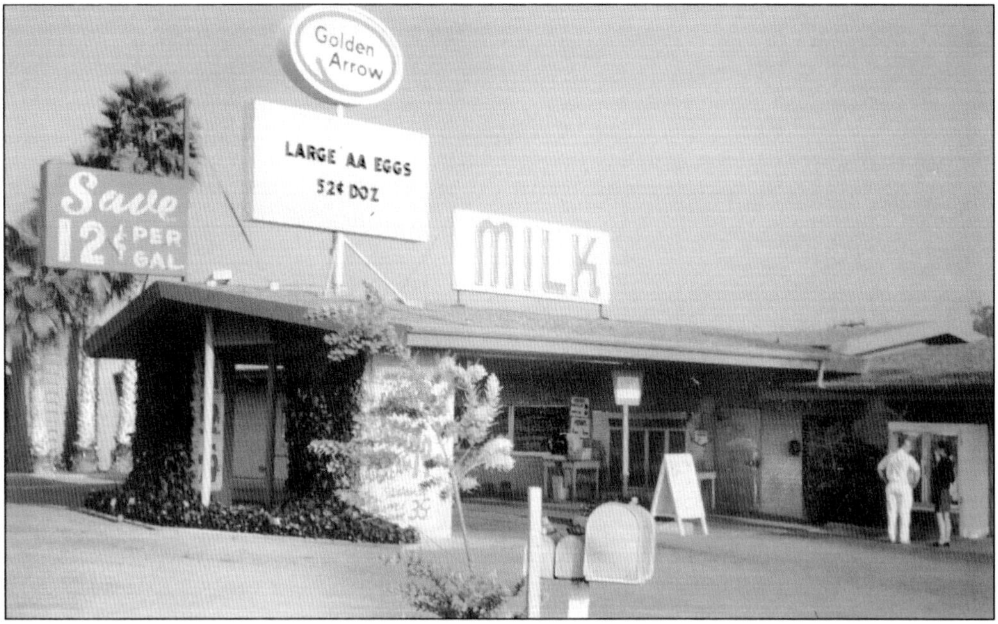

Longtime Vistans have favorite memories, and one of them is the regular trip to the drive-through at Golden Arrow Dairy for fresh dairy products and gasoline, all sold at discount prices. Located on the south side of Highway 78 west of Emerald Drive, the dairy was opened in 1955 and served Vistans for 25 years before being torn down for a $23-million shopping center and office complex.

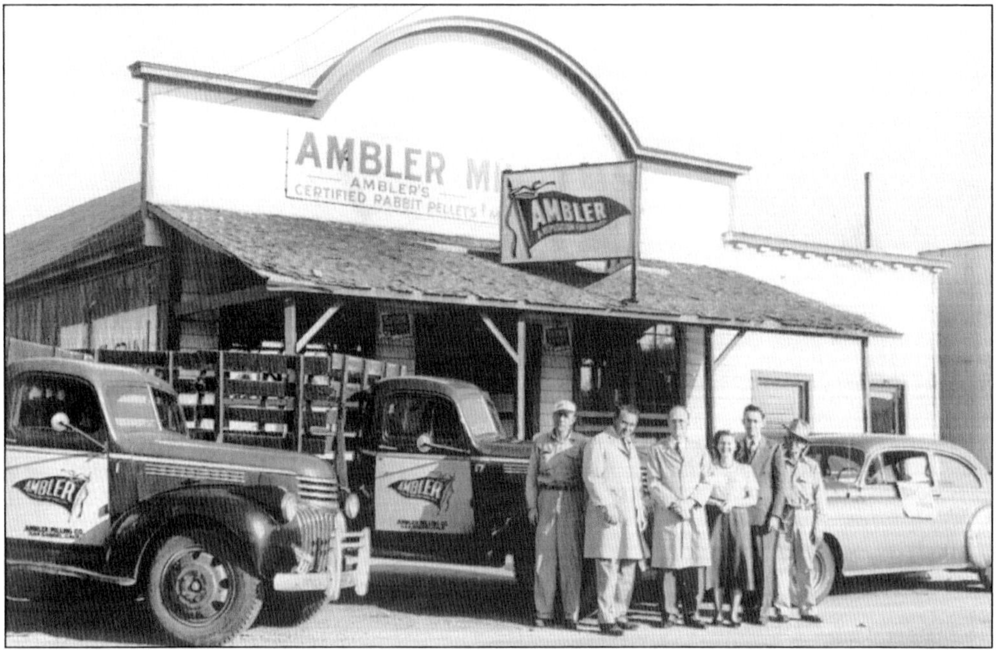

The Ambler Mining Company store was located on South Santa Fe Avenue for a number of years. Pictured in this 1940s photograph are, from left to right, Leland Card, Gordon Stotts, Raymond Ebersold, Frances Horak, Allen Burwell, and Anthony "Shorty" Landry. Ambler's was a popular place to buy feed.

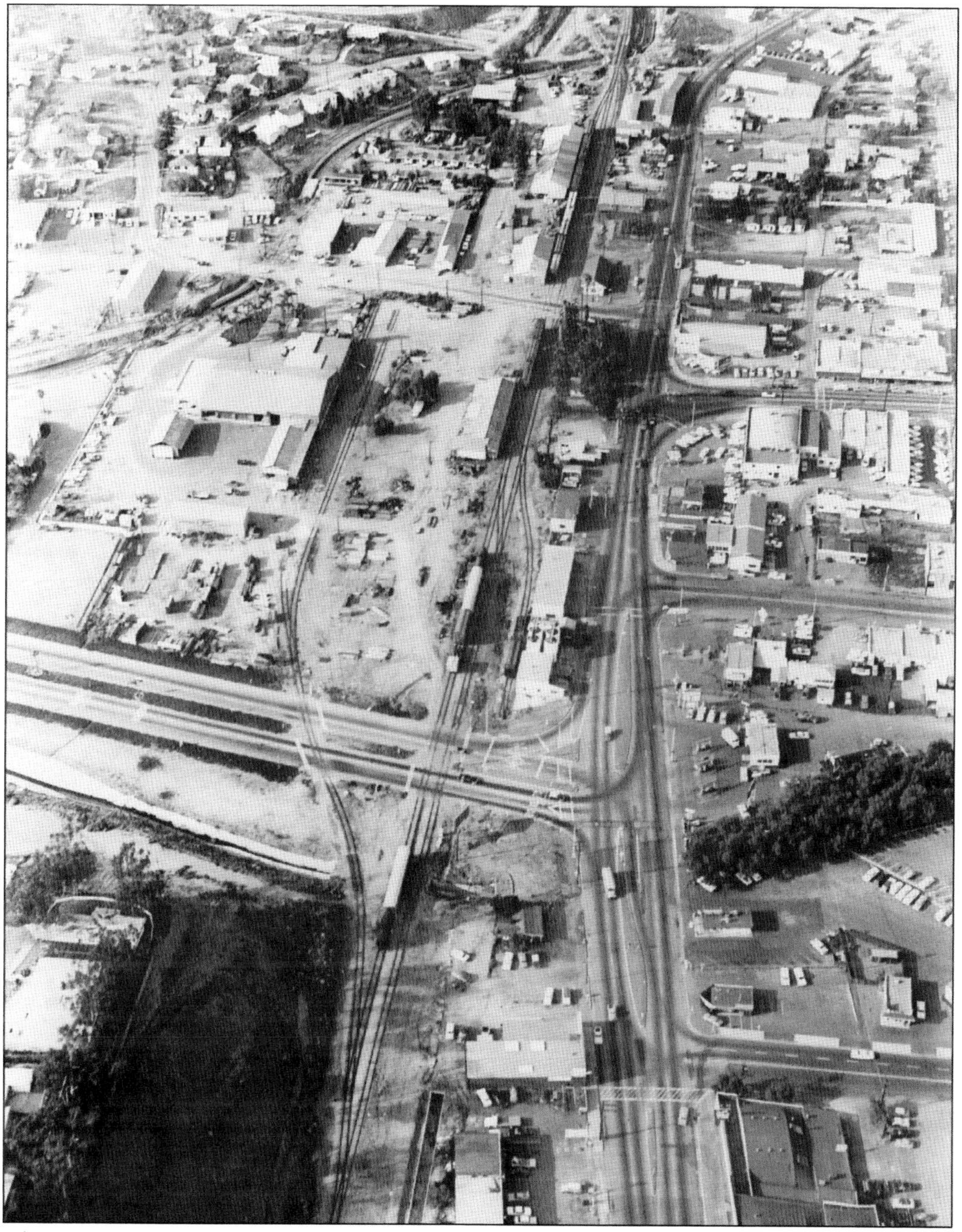

The importance of the Santa Fe Railroad to Vista in the 1940s is emphasized in this aerial photograph, which looks north along Santa Fe Avenue. The downtown area of Vista is at right center. Calavo Growers of California's first branch avocado packinghouse, built in Vista as a central location for county growers, was the largest such plant in town until it burned to the ground in 1949. Pictured here along the tracks are a number of other packing plants for avocado, citrus, and field and flower crops. As early as October 1927, it was announced in the *Vista Press* that the Union Fruit Company had already found that the packing shed it built that summer was too small and a 900-square-foot addition was underway at the south end.

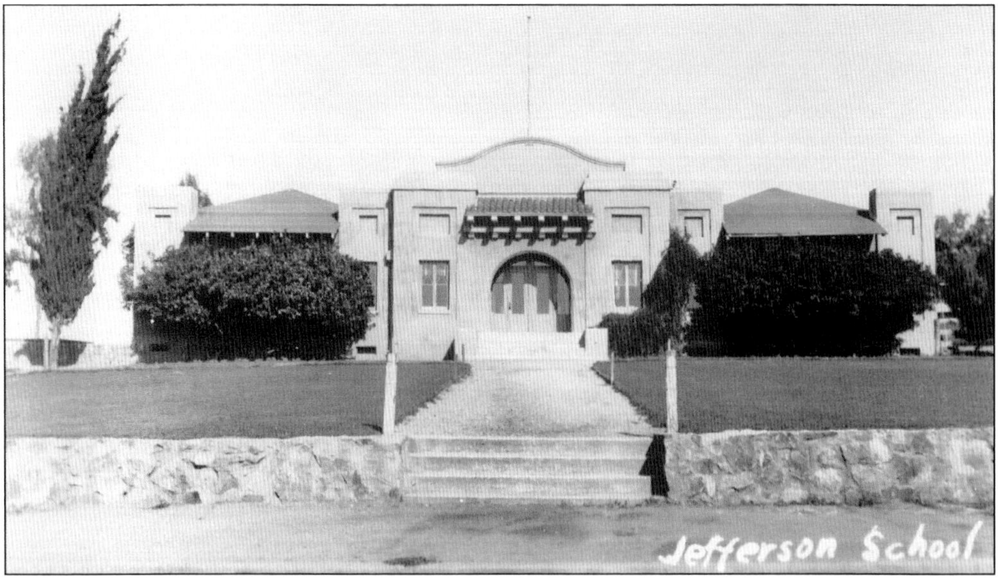

Pictured below is the Jefferson Elementary School fifth-grade class of 1938–1939. Vista Union School was dedicated in 1917 and renamed Jefferson Elementary School in 1930, later serving as Jefferson Senior Center for several decades. From left to right are (first row) Zoe Ann Bremmer, unidentified, Lavelle Murders, Bill Tracy, Bernard Dominguez, Richard Crouch, and Richard Daviscourt; (second row) Thelma Welcome, Jimmy Farmer, Gene Green, Richard Castellani, Ruth Shackleford, Carolyn Wood, and Joyce Landry; (third row) Jean McDaniel, Ardys Lawhead, Maxine Pascoe, Mary Lou Leak, Geraldine Leinert, Zelda Michael, and Stanley Foresman; (fourth row) Arnold Osland, Atsumi Sugita, Lorraine Lindeman, Tommy Irving, unidentified, Amparo Gonzales, and Robert Godwin.

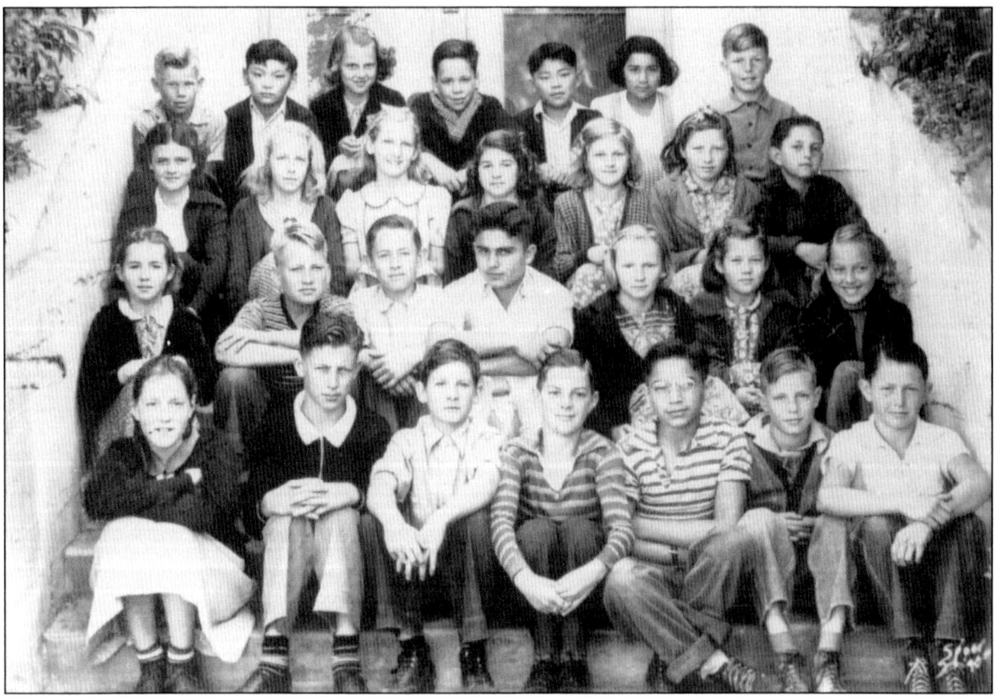

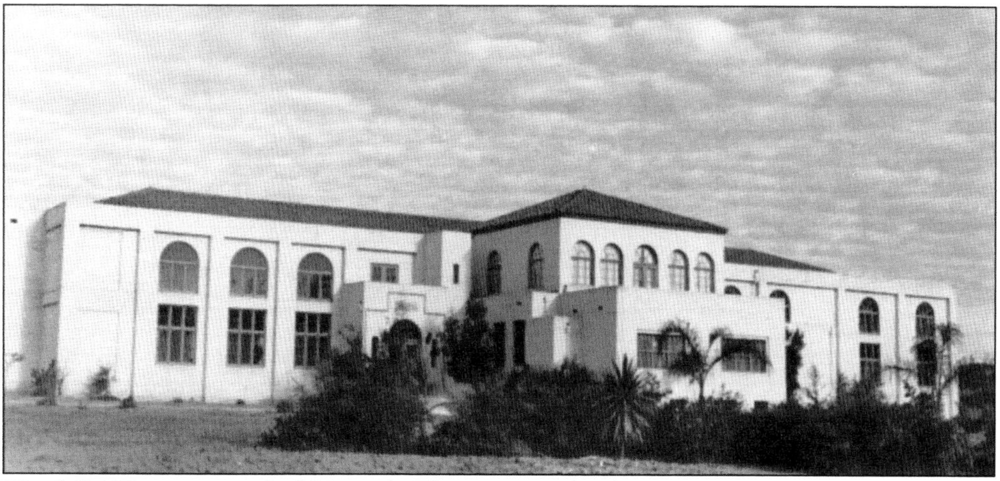

The $42,135 contract to build Lincoln Elementary School on Escondido Avenue was awarded in May 1930. Students were moved to the newly built Santa Fe Elementary School in 1950, and Lincoln became a junior high school. After the new Vista High School was built on Bobier Drive in 1972, the old site became Lincoln Middle School, and this building was used as district offices until it was razed in 1979.

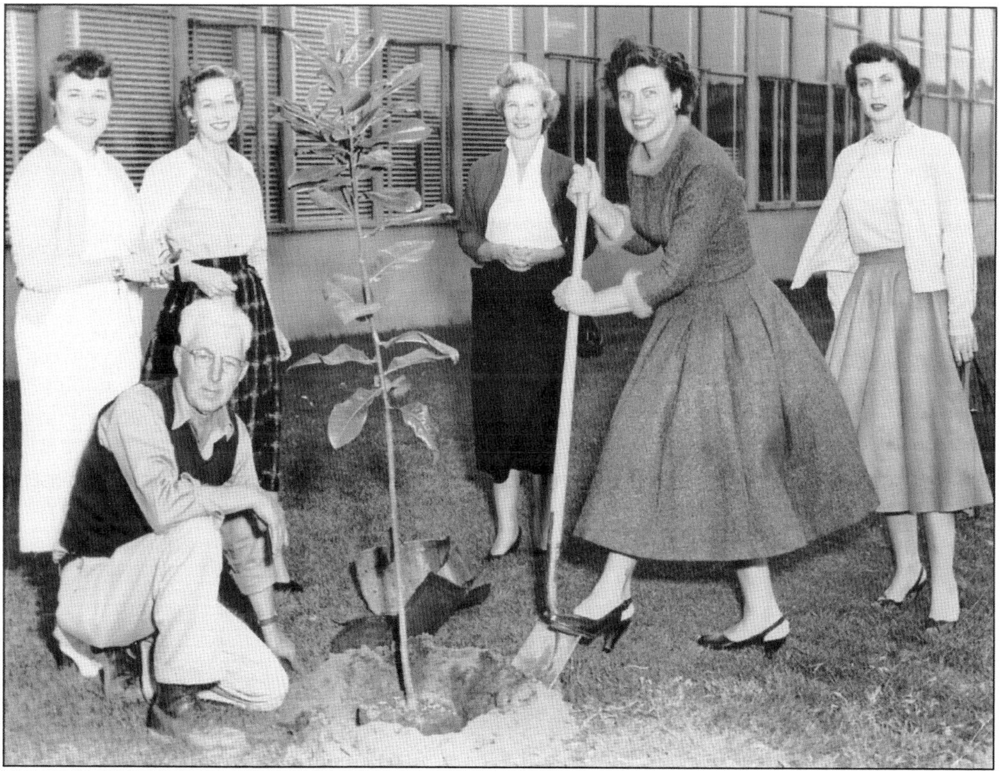

In this 1951 photograph, Mayme Barnes (left) watches as PTA mothers plant the first tree at the newly dedicated Santa Fe Elementary School. Kneeling is Dan Hinkle, head custodian. A revered Vista teacher and administrator, Barnes served as principal of Santa Fe and Olive Elementary Schools and then as director of elementary education for the Vista Unified School District. She passed away in May 2007 at age 96.

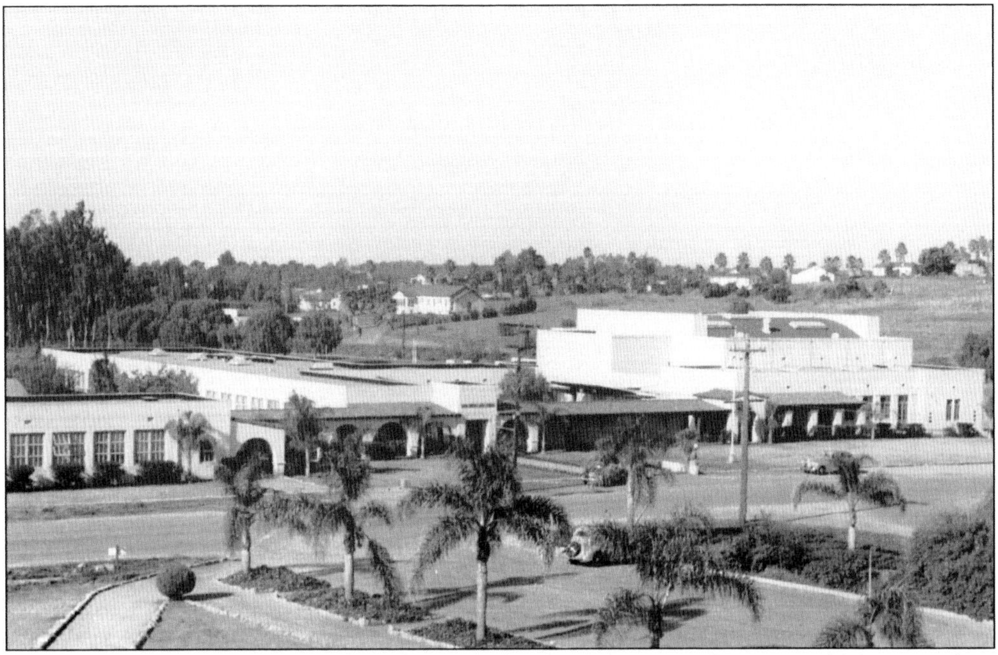

Vistans voted almost unanimously to form a high school district in January 1936. Prior to that, students traveled to Oceanside by bus. This first Vista High School, on Escondido Avenue bordered by Eucalyptus Avenue and East Vista Way, was completed in 1938 at a cost of $200,000. The first senior class graduated in 1938.

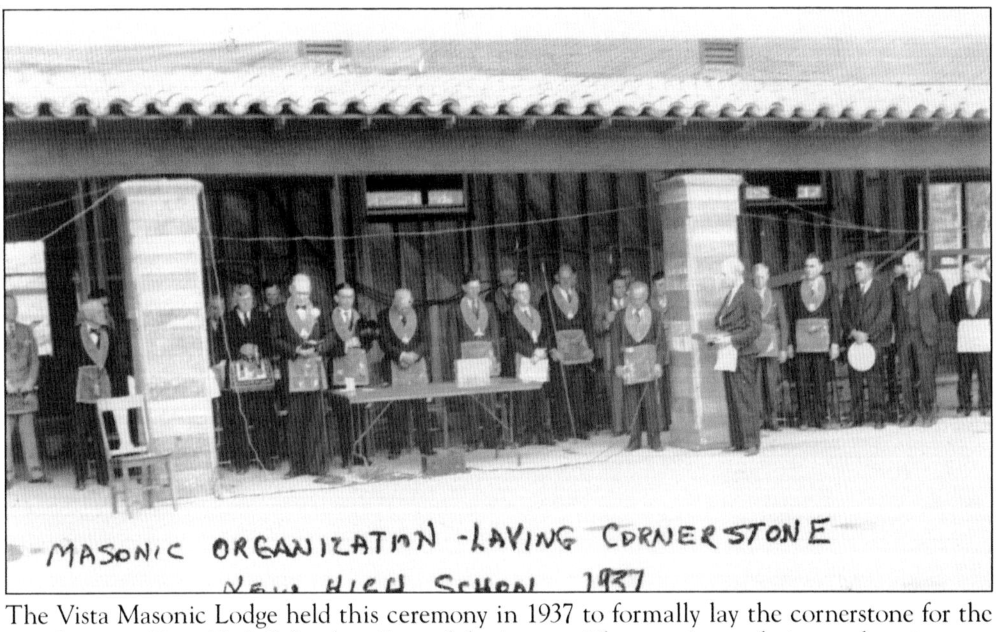

The Vista Masonic Lodge held this ceremony in 1937 to formally lay the cornerstone for the new four-year Vista High School on Escondido Avenue. The town's population at that time was 7,000. When the high school needed more room and moved to a new site on Bobier Drive in 1972, these buildings became Lincoln Middle School. Rancho Buena Vista High School was completed in 1987.

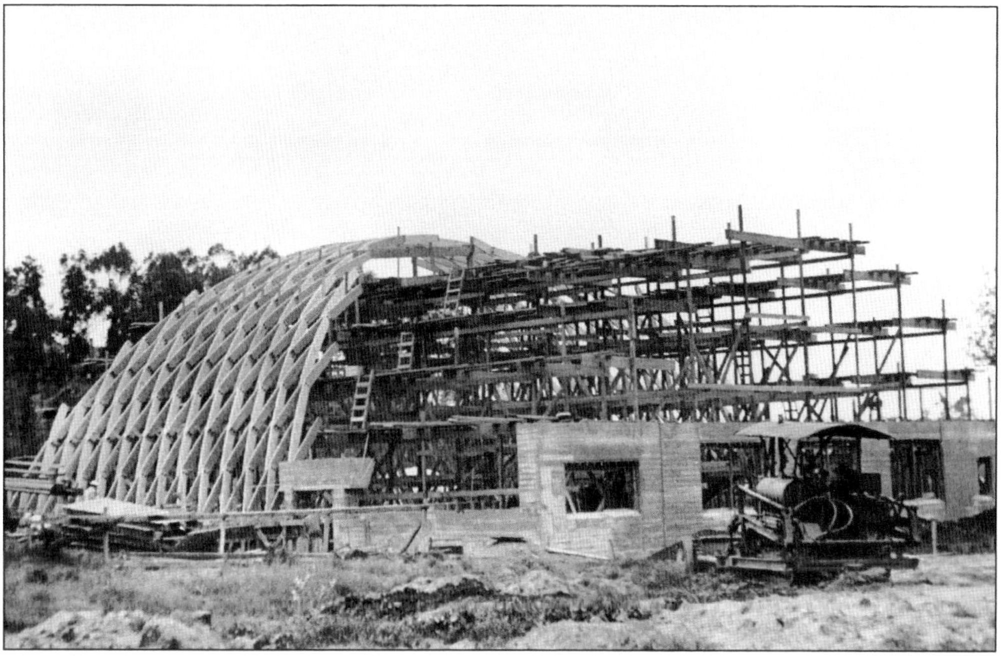

A vital component of Vista's first high school complex was the gymnasium, pictured here under construction in 1937. The school was to have an active sports program under guidance of teacher and coach O. K. "Bub" Williamson, who directed all of the football, baseball, basketball, and track teams in the early years.

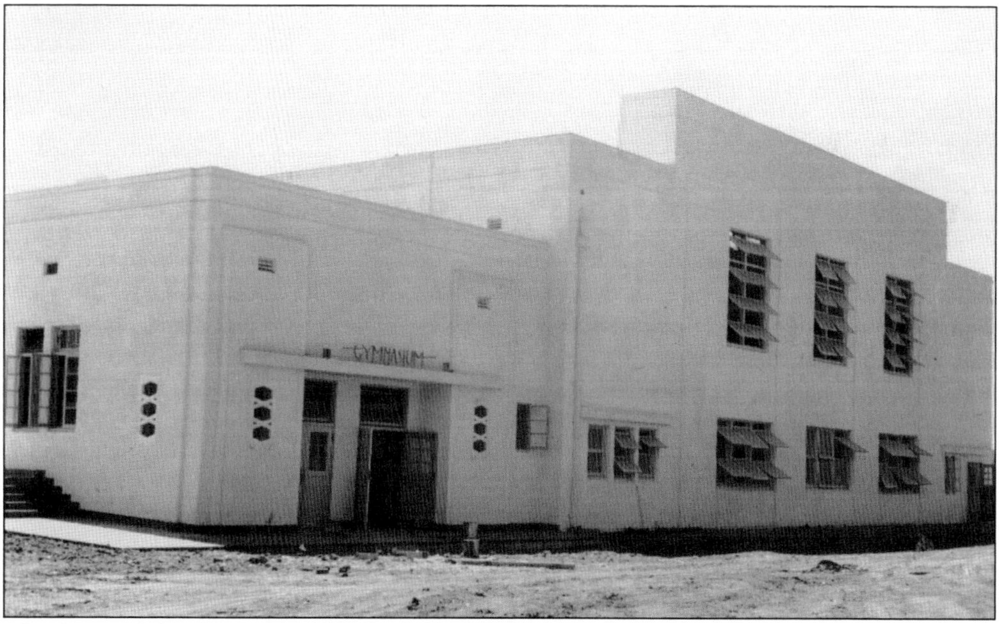

The front of the new Vista High School gymnasium is shown here as construction neared completion for the school's opening. Only the landscaping remained to be added. The gymnasium was used by Vista High School students until 1972, then by Lincoln Middle School students. Rancho Minerva Middle School on Foothill Drive was completed in 2007, and this site became a magnet school.

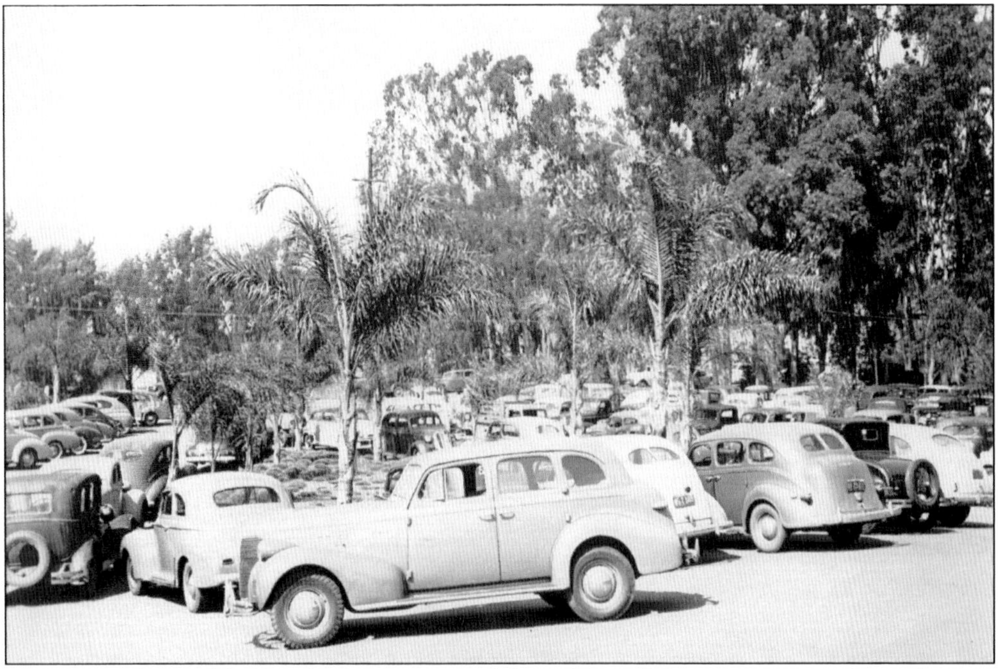

This area in front of the Rancho Buena Vista adobe on Escondido Avenue, across from what was then Vista High School, was used as a parking area in the 1940s. Professional buildings were built on this site in the early 1980s by Rudd and Sally Schoeffel, who purchased the rancho in 1972.

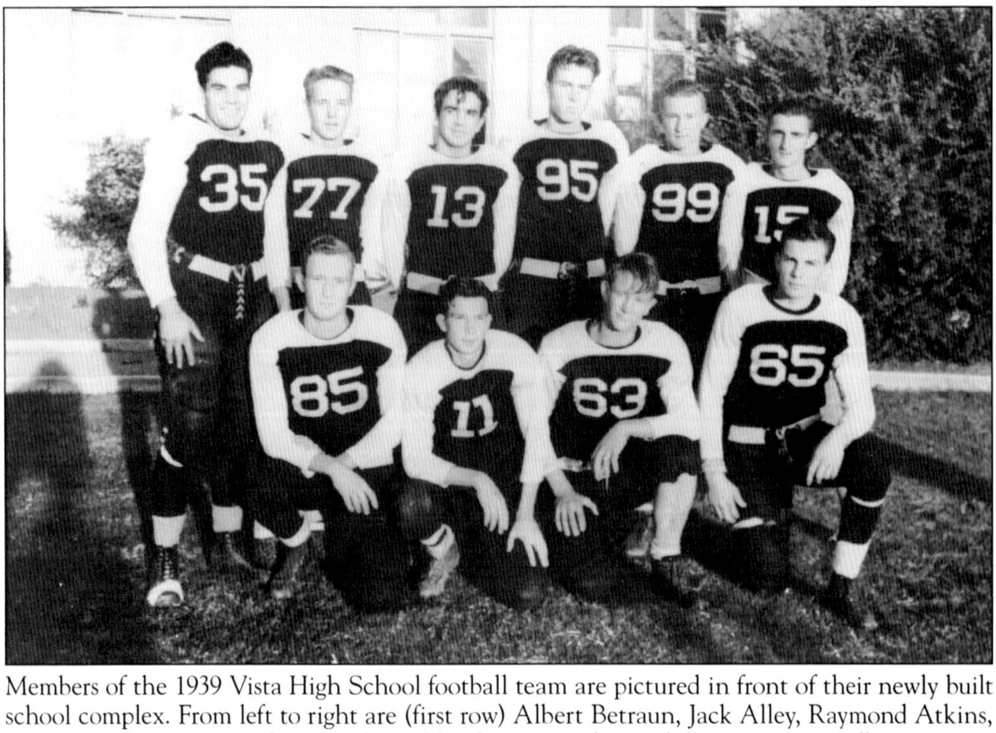

Members of the 1939 Vista High School football team are pictured in front of their newly built school complex. From left to right are (first row) Albert Betraun, Jack Alley, Raymond Atkins, and Glen Greever; (second row) Eddie Hubbard, Don Hayden, Robert King, Don Walker, Norman Tongess, and Roger Galogalli.

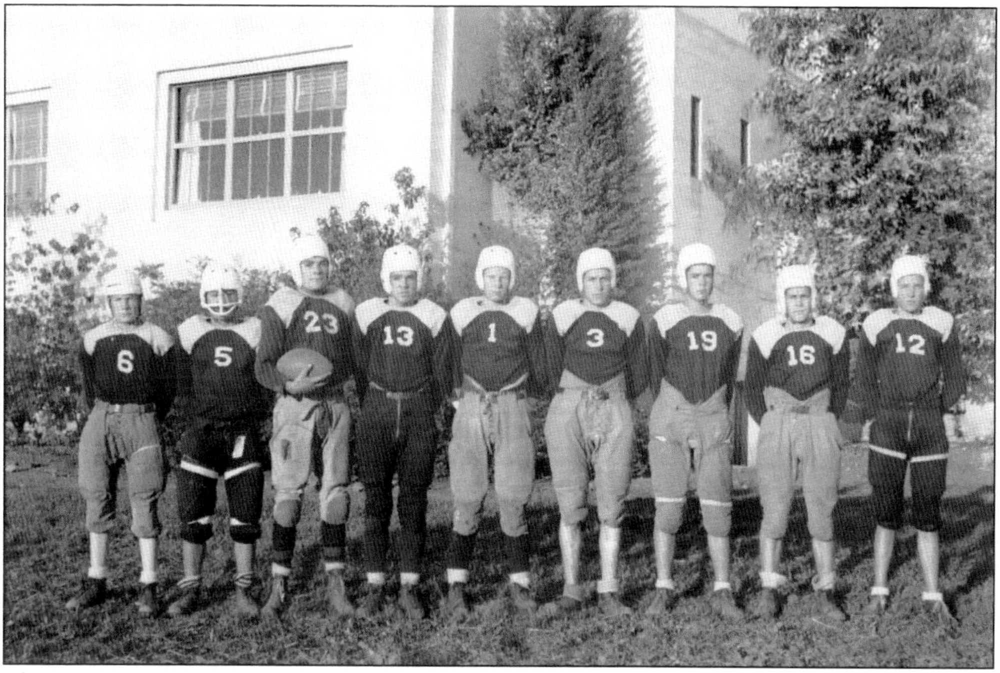

The 1940 Vista High School football team poses in uniforms and helmets for an official photograph. From left to right are Don Palmer, Kenzo Osaki, Eddie Hubbard, Robert King, Pinkey Briley, James Slivkoff, Don Mack, Leonard Armstrong, and Don Hayden. Coach O. K. "Bub" Williamson organized the Southern League, the first high school all-sports league in northern San Diego County.

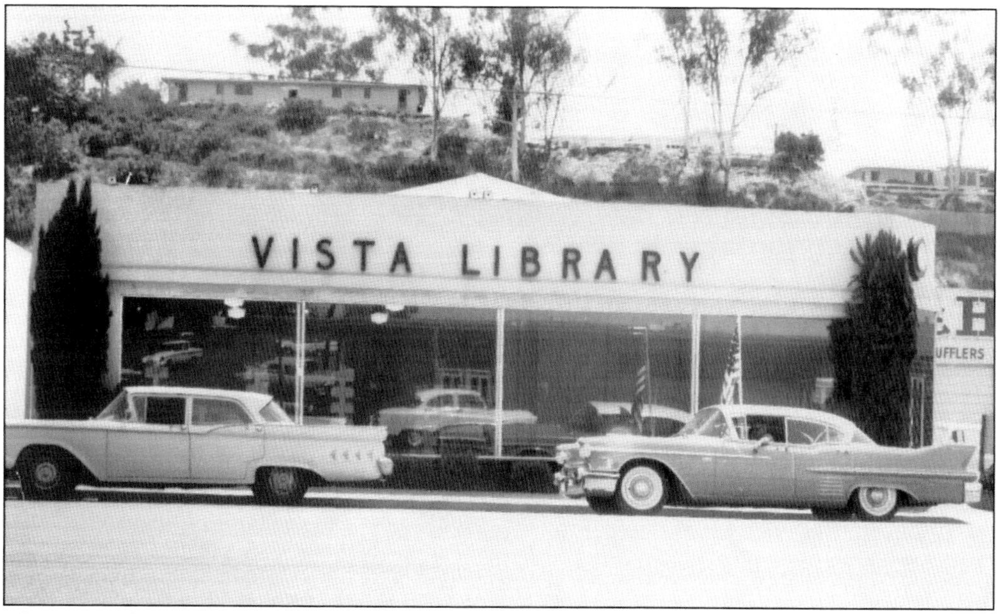

The Vista Library quickly outgrew its first 900-square-foot building near Vista Community Church. In the 1950s and early 1960s, it was located in the 300 block of South Santa Fe Avenue in this former automotive building. The library was moved to the Regional County Center on Melrose Drive in 1964 and remained there until the permanent site was built on Eucalyptus Avenue.

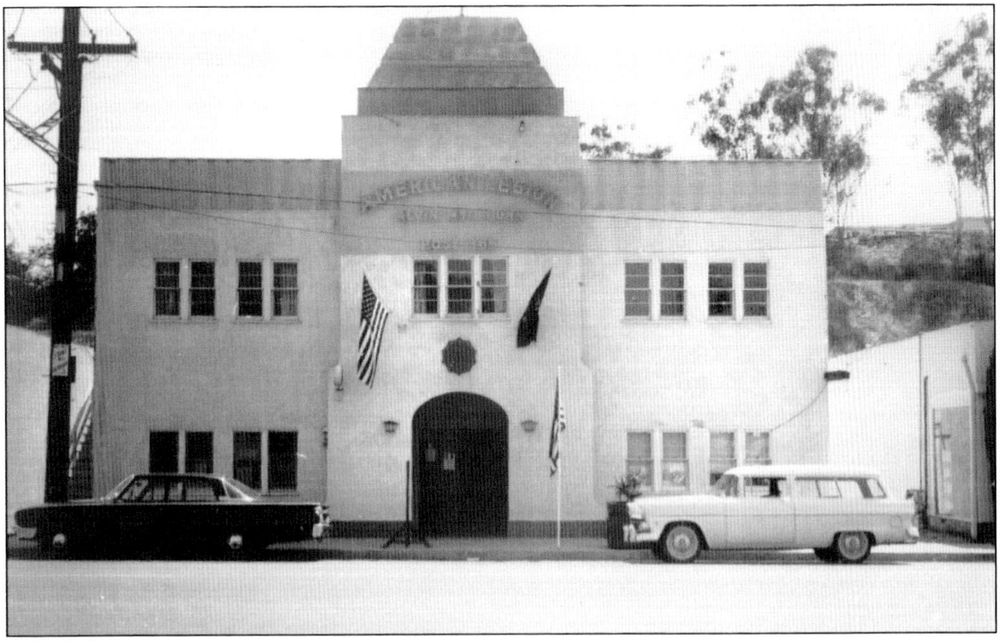

Alvin Myo Dunn Post No. 365 of the American Legion was formed in late 1929. Fund-raisers included the "Days of '49" parade, and the post's first hall was built on East Vista Way across from Wildwood Park. After World War II, expansion was necessary, and Alvin M. Dunn offered the lot on South Santa Fe Avenue on which this building was completed in 1948. The post name honors Dunn's grandson.

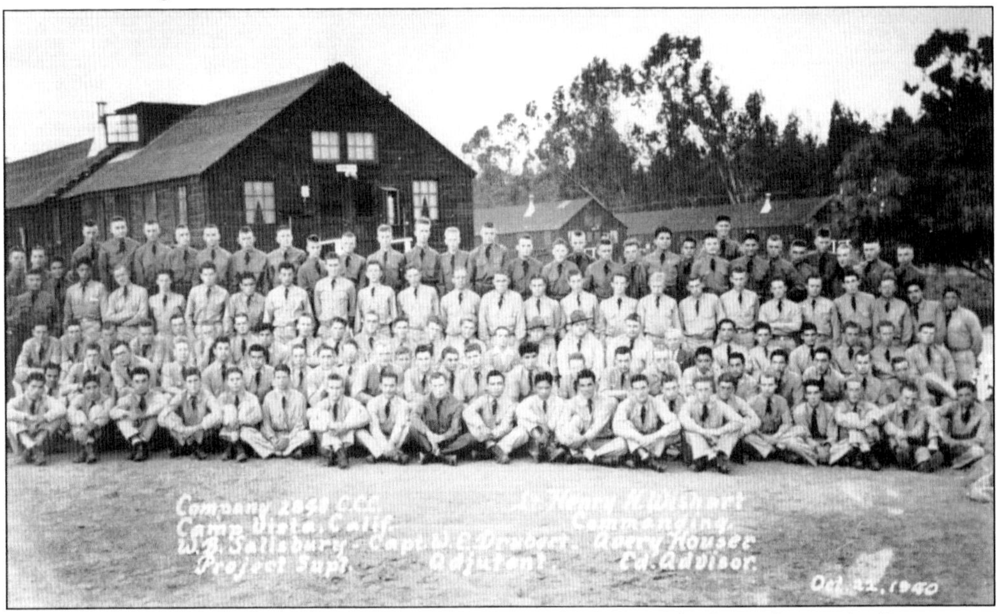

Camp Vista, one of a series of U.S. Civilian Conservation Corps facilities during the Depression era, was located west of Sycamore Avenue and south of Shadowridge Drive on land that is now Green Oak Ranch. From 1935 to the start of World War II, young men lived at the camp and worked on road building and preservation projects. This photograph was taken of Company 2848 on October 22, 1940.

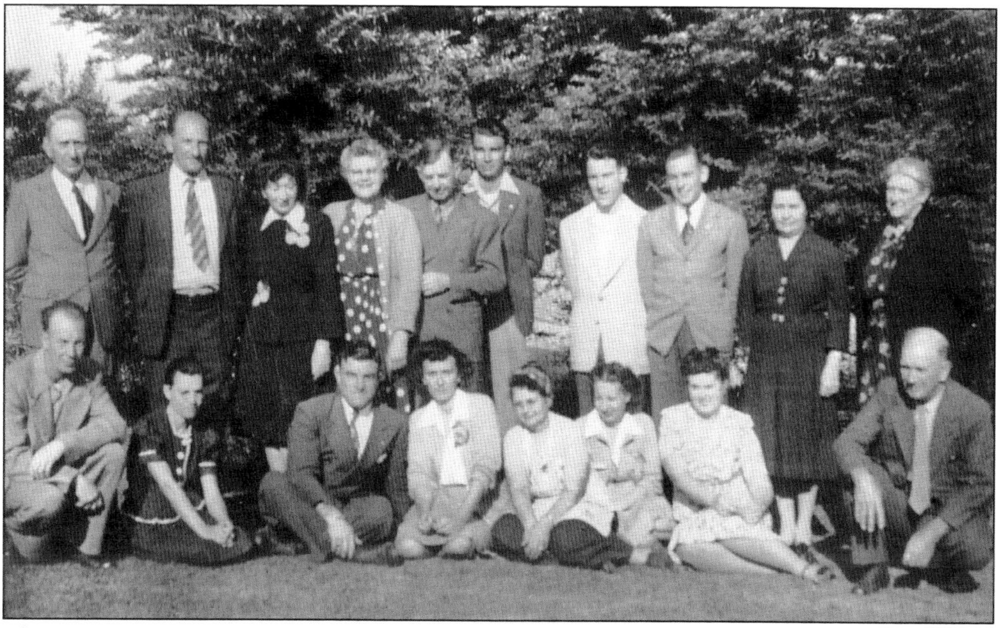

The Vista Post Office staff and their spouses pose during a bridal shower they held for Frances Beck to celebrate her marriage to Ervin Ries in 1946. Shown, not in order, are Edward Beck, Joe Beck, Hazel Bice, Edna Martin, Al Martin, Jim Beck, Roger Bengston, Earl Leak, Mac Floyd, Anna Prosel, Neal Sanat, Ervin Ries, Frances Beck, Anne Skinner, Lillian Bengston, Betty Mack Leach, and Harry Floyd.

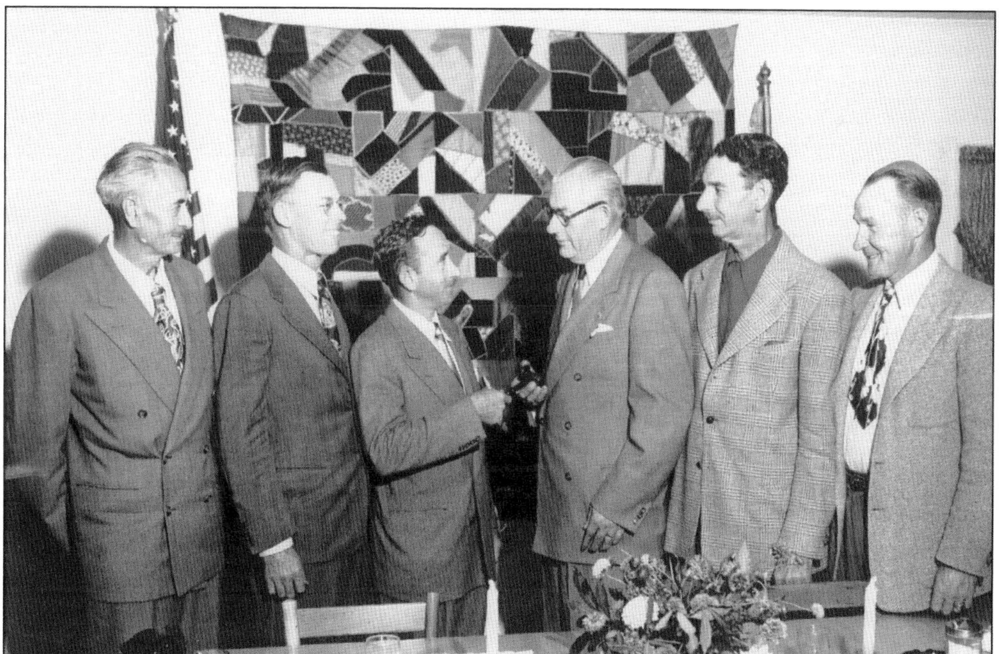

The popular Vista Toastmasters' Club is holding its annual installation ceremony at the Vista Inn in this 1940s photograph. From left to right are Harrison Doyle, William Gordon Wight, James Sutton, an unidentified installing officer from San Diego, Joseph Laib, and Rudy Wellpott.

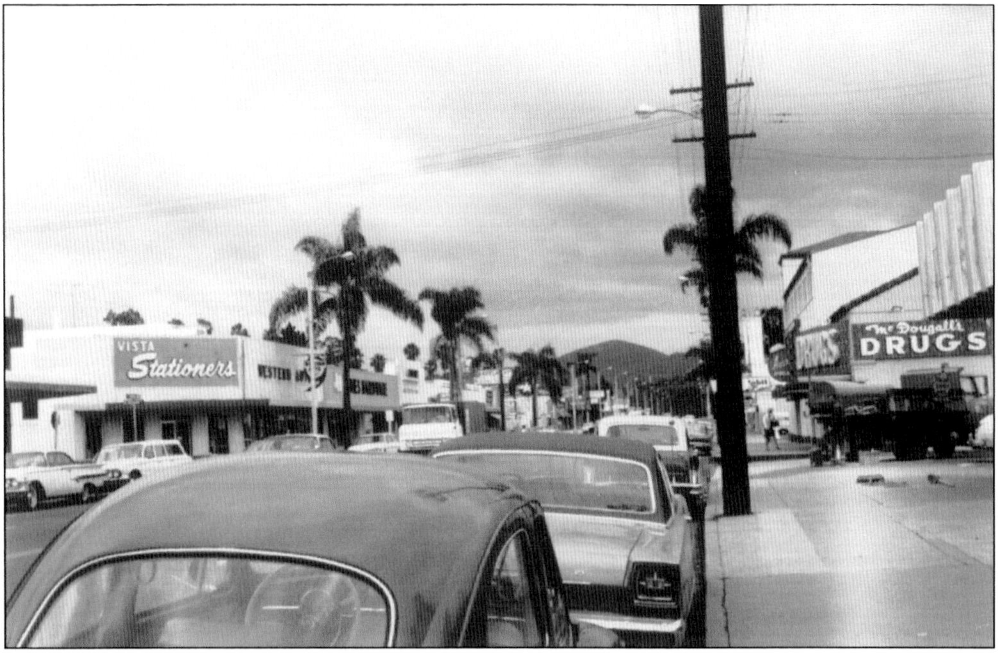

McDougall's Pharmacy was a downtown Vista landmark for almost a half-century, noted almost as much for its hot fudge sundaes as its prescriptions. Alexander McDougall opened a store in the Pechstein Building and later moved across the street into his own building, which is pictured here in 1966. In 1933, he married Julia Pelley, who was the 1929 Miss Vista.

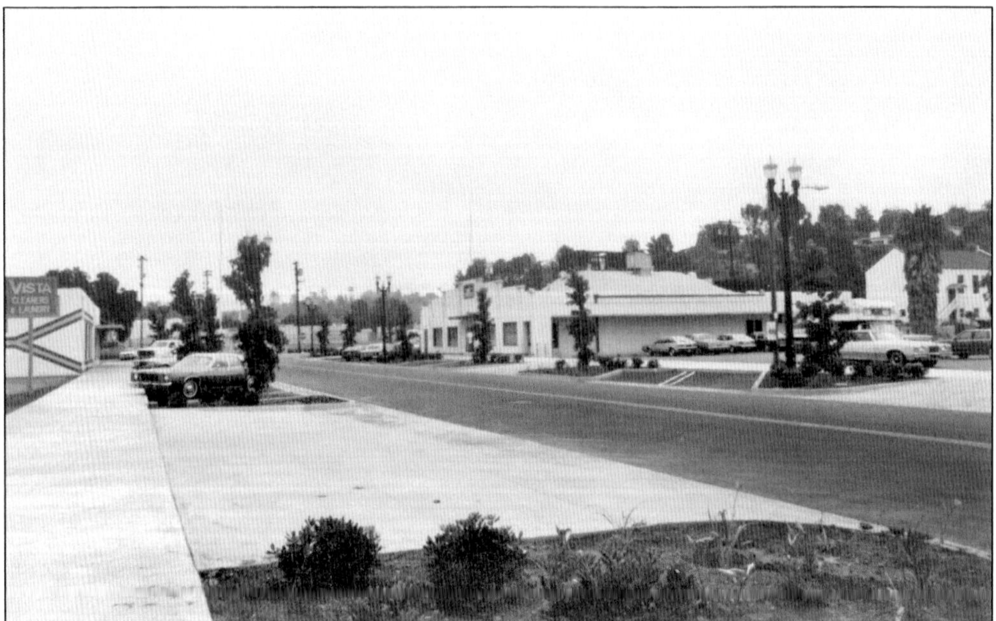

Carpenter's Hall, for many years the headquarters for the local Carpenter's Union, was rented for various events and was the site of many formative meetings for Vista churches and organizations. The hall is at right center in this photograph, which looks east on Broadway.

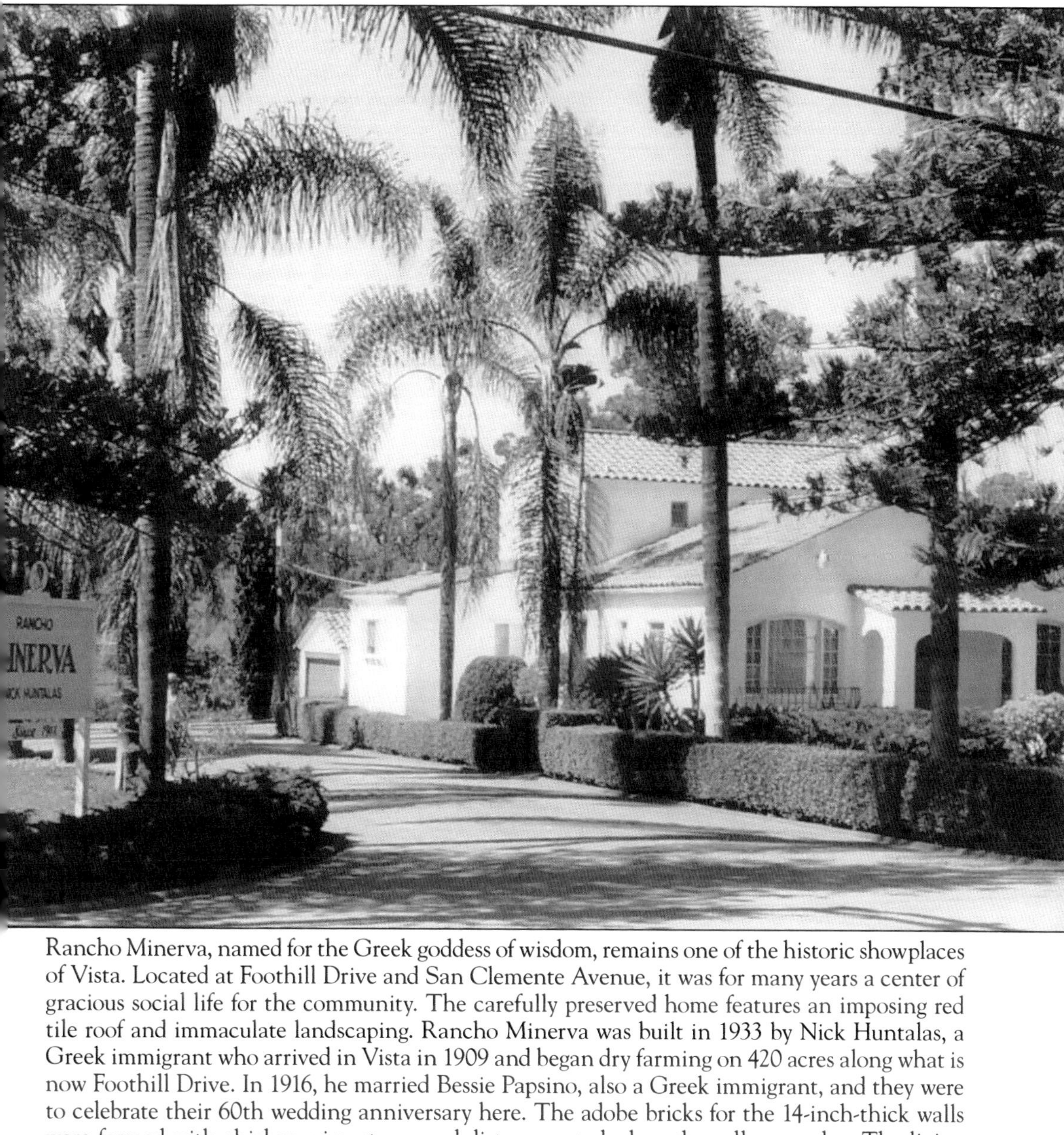

Rancho Minerva, named for the Greek goddess of wisdom, remains one of the historic showplaces of Vista. Located at Foothill Drive and San Clemente Avenue, it was for many years a center of gracious social life for the community. The carefully preserved home features an imposing red tile roof and immaculate landscaping. Rancho Minerva was built in 1933 by Nick Huntalas, a Greek immigrant who arrived in Vista in 1909 and began dry farming on 420 acres along what is now Foothill Drive. In 1916, he married Bessie Papsino, also a Greek immigrant, and they were to celebrate their 60th wedding anniversary here. The adobe bricks for the 14-inch-thick walls were formed with chicken wire, straw, and dirt excavated when the cellar was dug. The living room features an 18-foot-high ceiling.

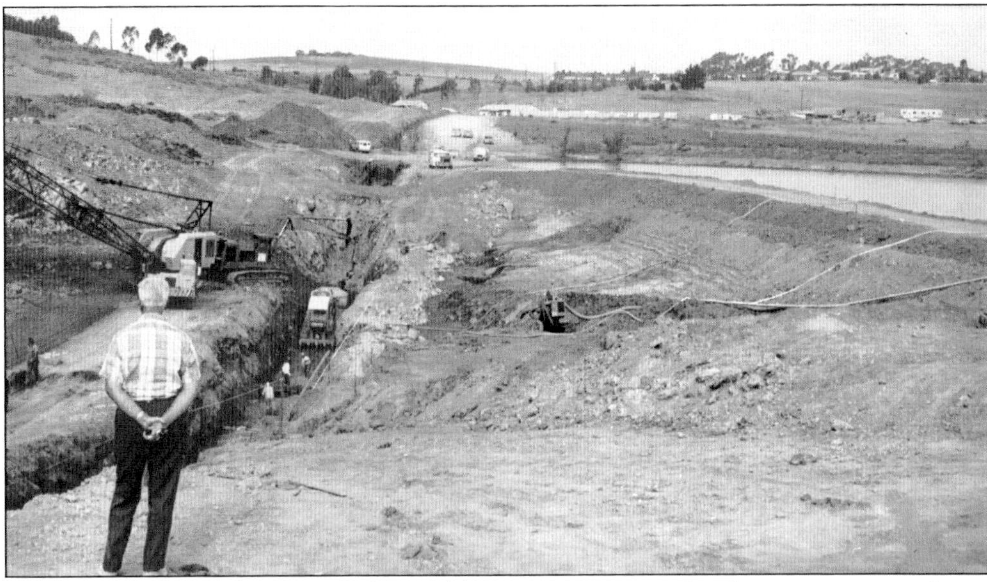

A "sidewalk superintendent" watches with interest as crews utilize heavy equipment during construction of the Vista phase of Highway 78. The opening celebration of the Vista section of the freeway was held February 18, 1963, on the new bridge over Melrose Drive. It was just three weeks after the City of Vista incorporated, and newly elected Mayor Joseph H. Fotheringham headed the list of dignitaries.

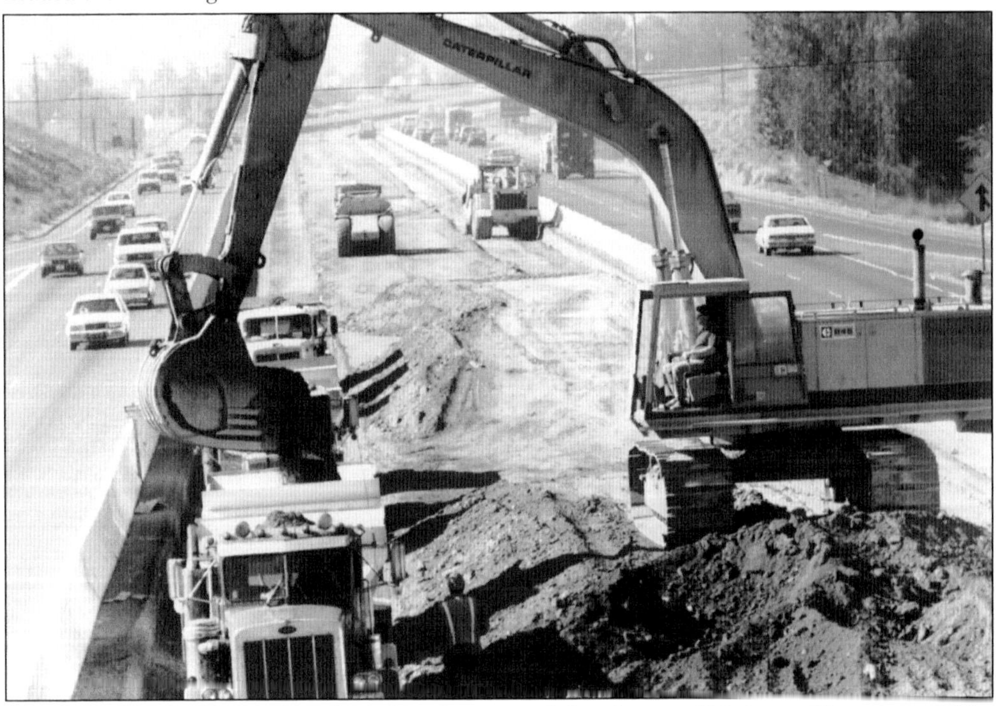

After two decades, it became clear that the original four lanes of Highway 78 soon would be inadequate to handle local traffic and serve efficiently as the only northern San Diego County connector freeway between Interstate 15 to the east and Interstate 5 on the coast. This major widening project in 1989 and 1990 was one of several designed over the years to ease traffic.

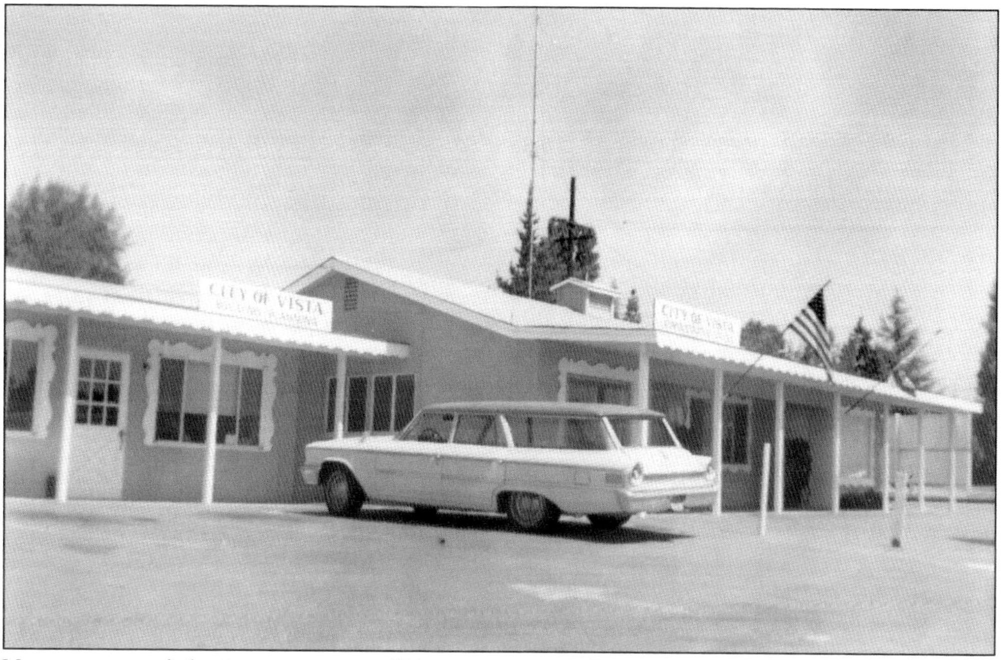

Voters approved the incorporation of Vista as a city on January 15, 1963, and two weeks later, on January 28, the incorporation ceremony was held. From 1963 to 1969, the first city hall was located in these two buildings in the 800 block of East Vista Way. The buildings were constructed in 1950 by Jess and Frances Shiffer and were used as real estate sales offices for many years.

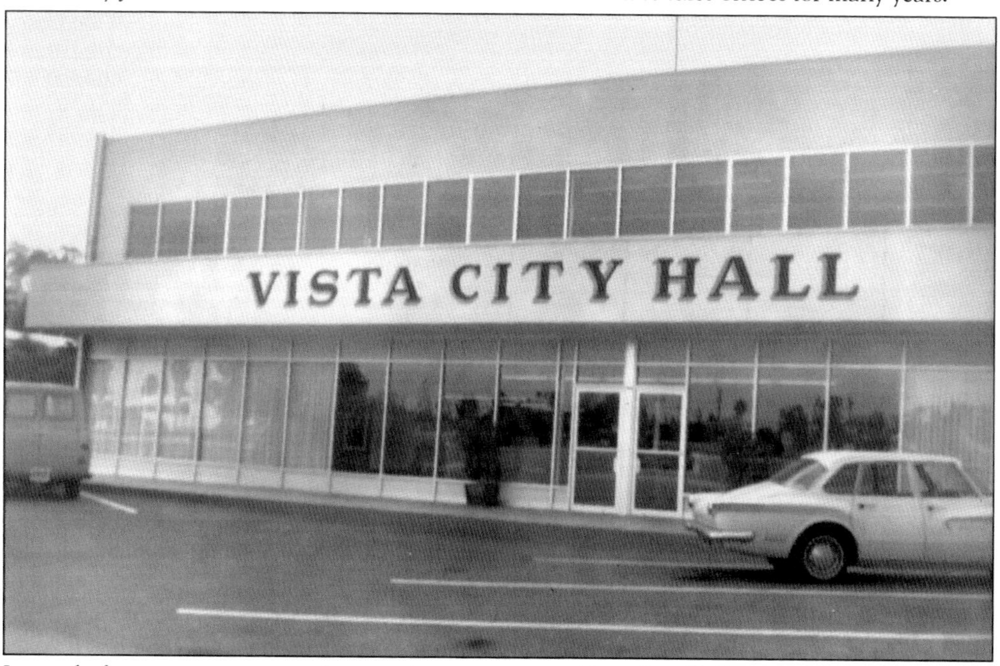

In need of more space to serve the growing community, Vista City Hall was moved into this two-story building in the Broadway shopping center in 1969. A decade later, it was moved once again, this time to its present site at 600 Eucalyptus Avenue. The Broadway center was ultimately razed, and the land became part of the new Main Street complex of shops and restaurants.

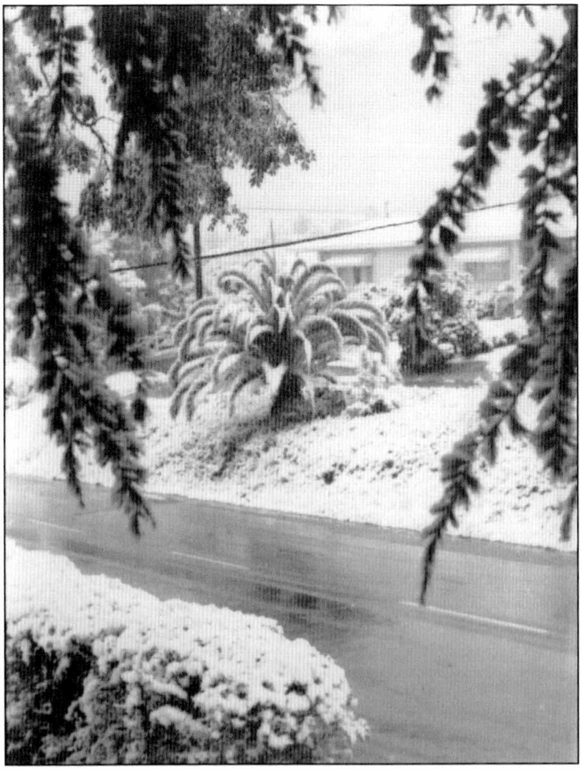

Is this snow in Vista? Some of the early residents recall a few times when there was what they term "kind of a slush that melted fast" but never real snow until December 13, 1967. The temperature dropped to 28 degrees, and 3 solid inches of the white stuff blanketed the surprised community. George Sexsmith, a Vistan since 1929 and dedicated amateur photographer, took these photographs. Pictured below is the street marker at Escondido Avenue and Morningside Drive, with a crystal-coated tree on the left. Pictured at left is a snow-covered sago palm tree in the front yard of a home on Escondido Avenue.

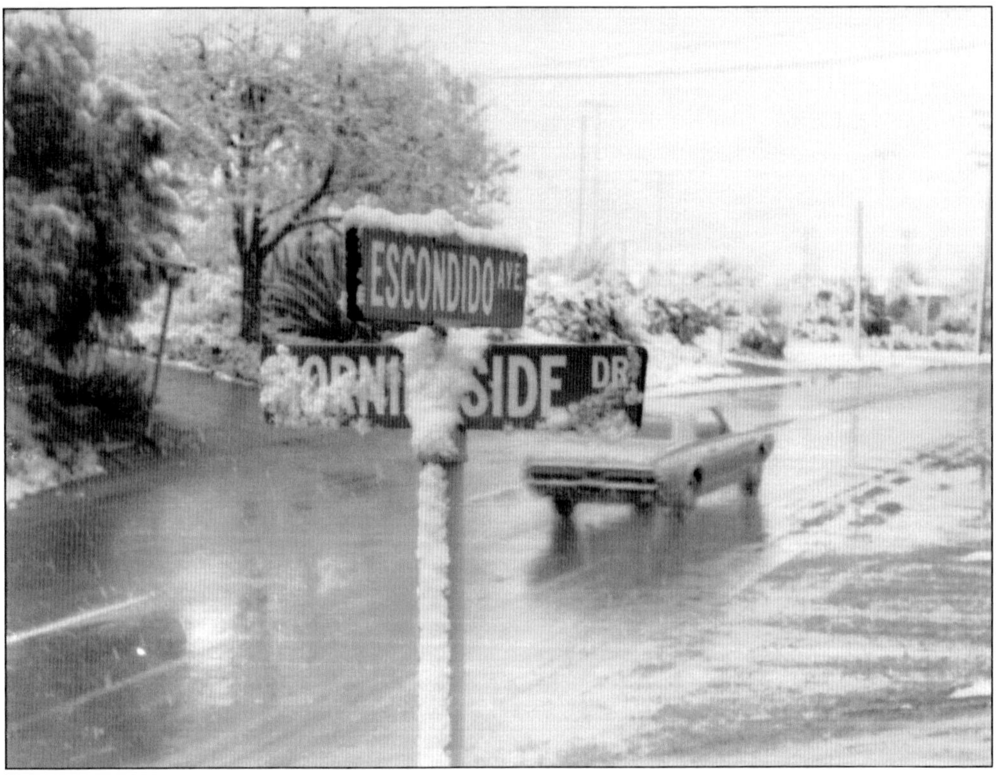

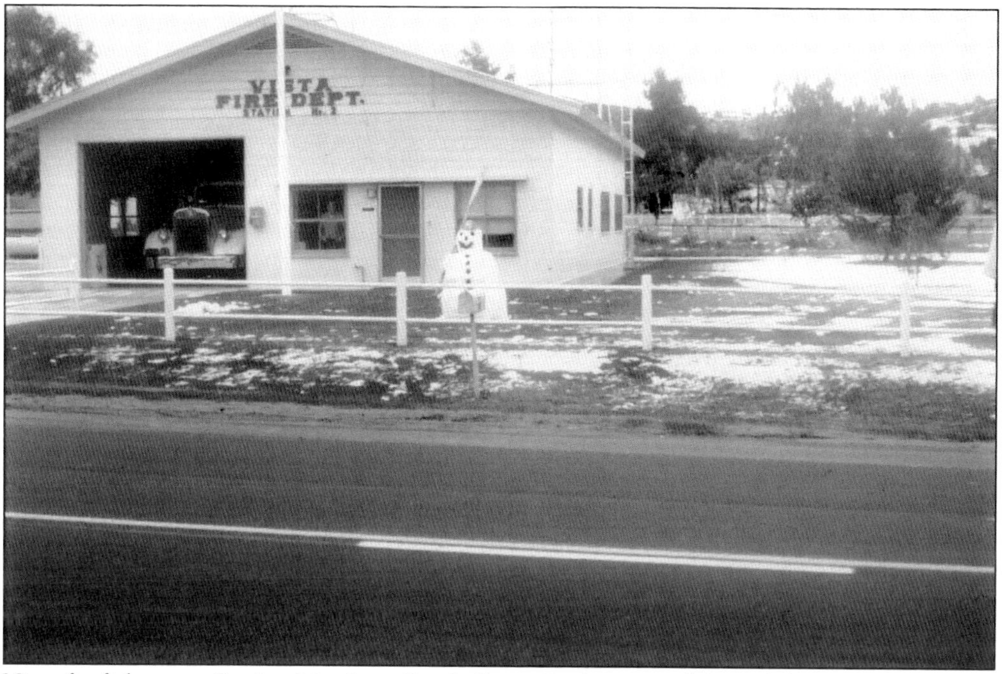

Vista firefighters at Station No. 2 on South Santa Fe Avenue celebrated the unprecedented 3 inches of snowfall on December 13, 1967, by building a snowman in their front yard.

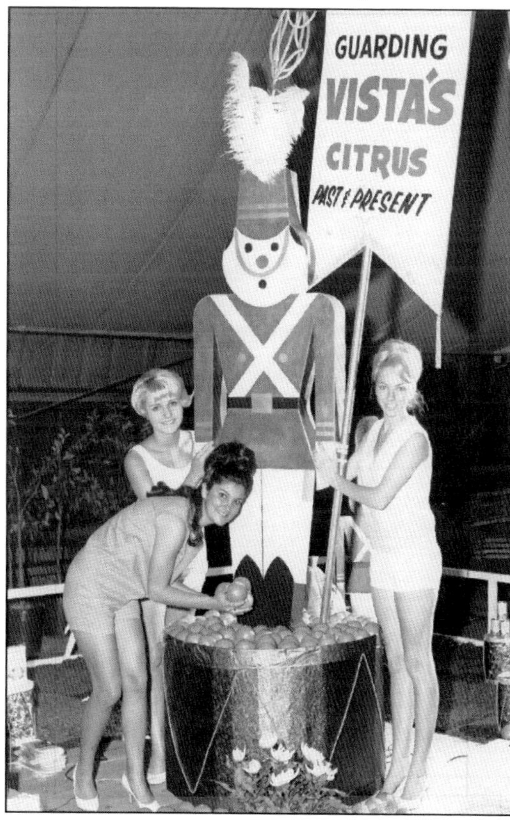

Vista teenagers assisted in informing the public about their city's agricultural industry during this 1966 chamber of commerce exhibit at the Del Mar Fair. The housing boom after World War II acquired land formerly used for groves, but citrus growing was still a major entity in the newly incorporated city. The fair is held each year from mid-June to early July, and Vista families have historically been major participators.

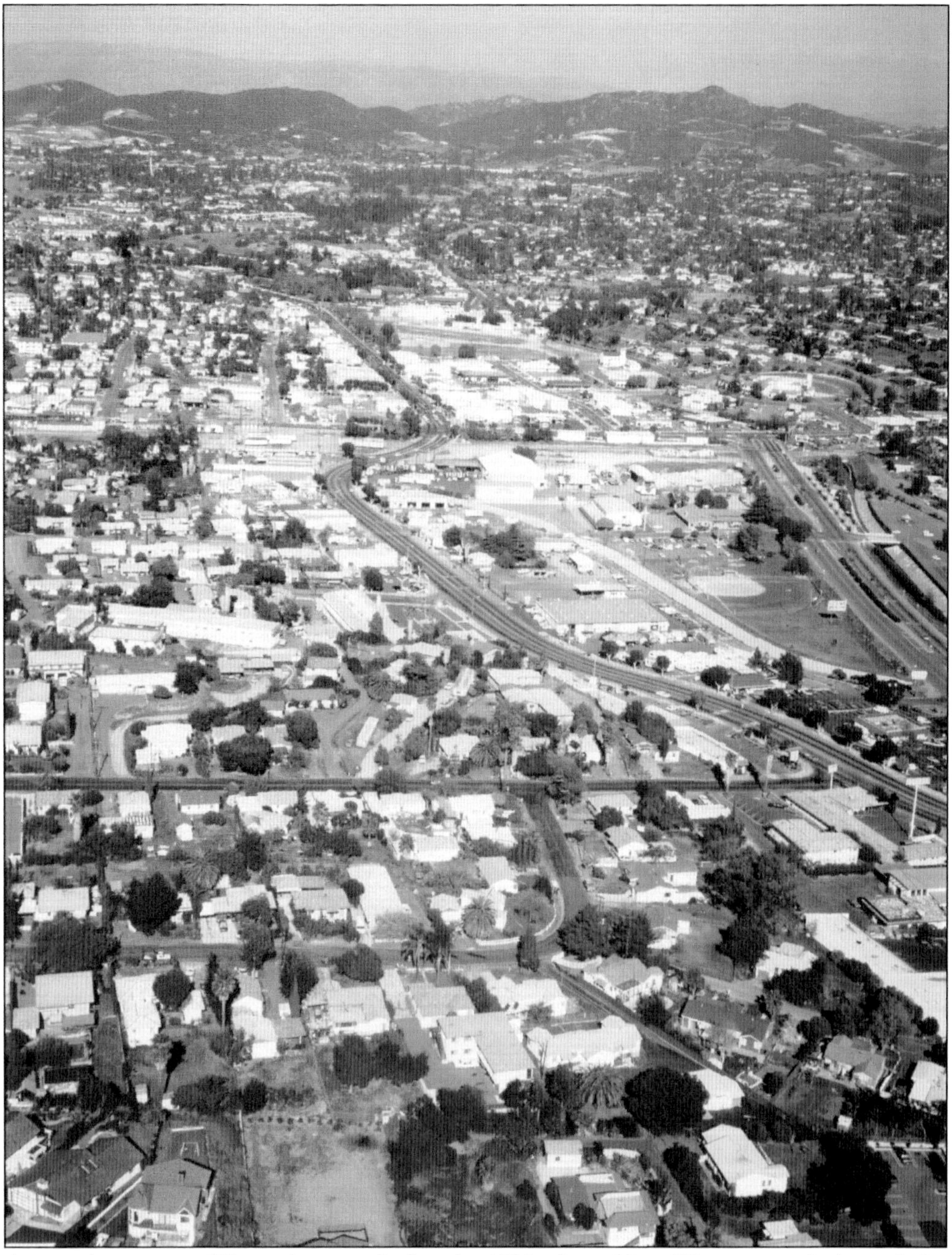

An aerial overview of Vista, photographed in the 1980s, shows Vista Way as it winds through the center of the city. This major artery through Vista has since been reconfigured and named Vista Village Drive west of Escondido Avenue. The historic downtown area was bypassed during this construction, renamed Main Street, and updated to become part of a shopping and dining area that now extends for several additional blocks. At center right is Vista's first recreation center, built in 1939, and adjacent park, with the National Guard Armory to the left. The park was later replaced by the popular Wave family waterpark, and the recreation center, armory, and adjacent properties were demolished in 2000 to make way for the Main Street extension.

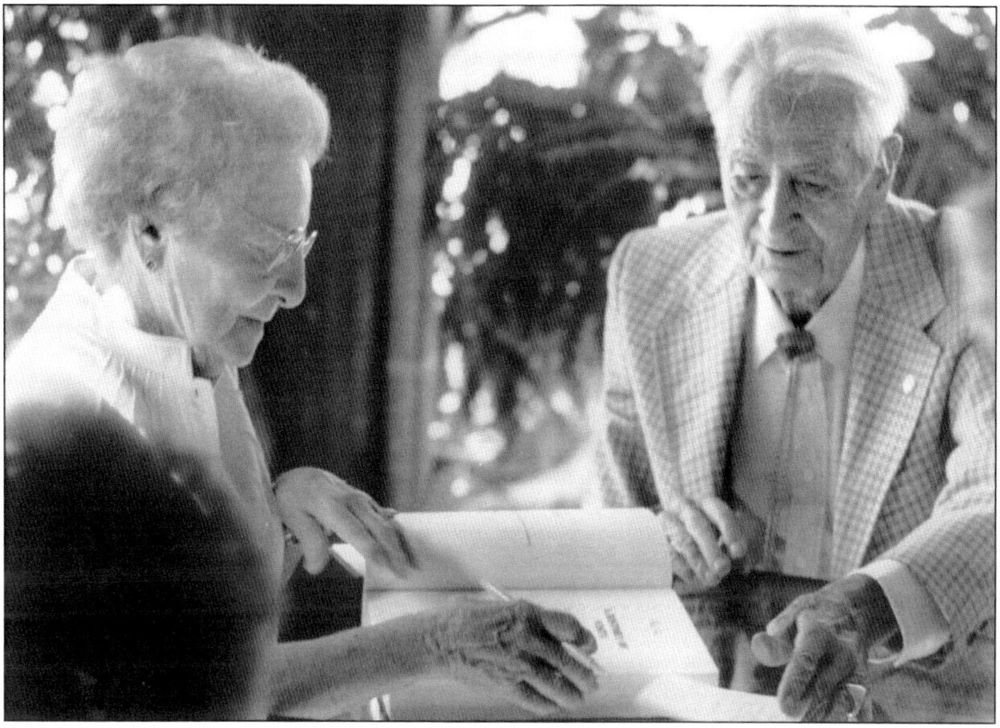

At a book-signing at historic Rancho Buena Vista in 1983, Harrison and Ruth Doyle autograph copies of their newly coauthored, 407-page *A History of Vista*. The Doyles were active in philanthropic and civic affairs from their arrival in the community in 1941. Harrison Doyle was elected in 1964 to the first full-term Vista City Council following the city's incorporation and served as mayor from 1966 to 1968.

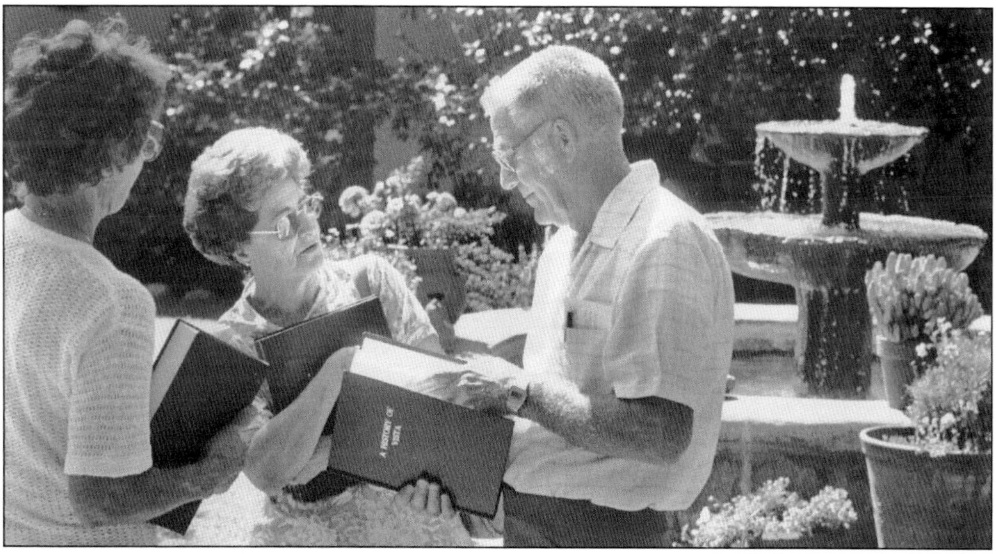

Robert and Aimee Bobbett peruse their newly autographed copies of *A History of Vista* at Rancho Buena Vista. Robert Bobbett worked for the Santa Fe Railroad from 1939 to 1971 and for 27 years was the railroad agent at the Santa Fe depot in Vista. His family purchased land in Vista in 1929. (Courtesy of *Escondido Times-Advocate*.)

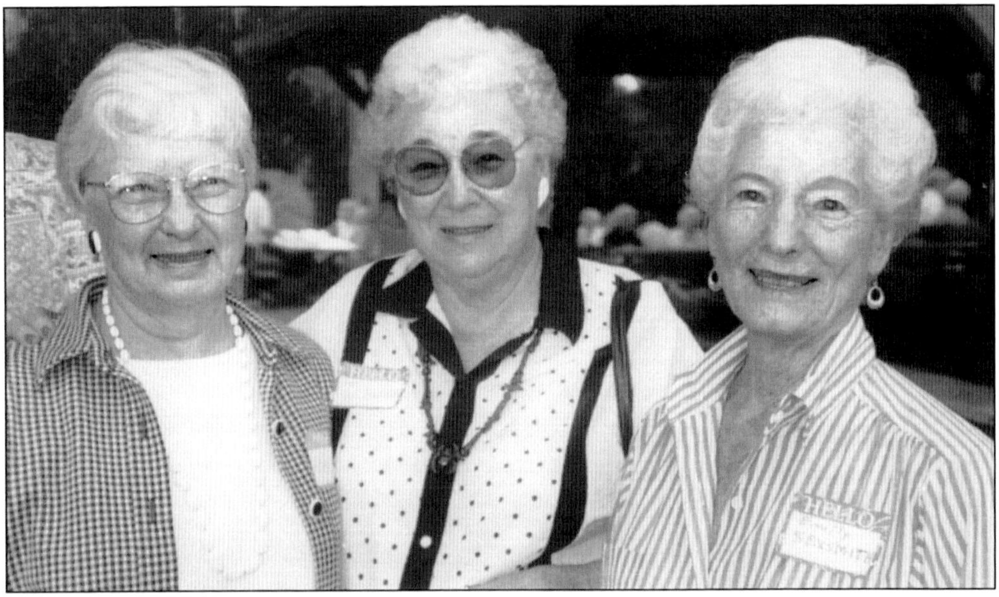

A trio of Vista's most prominent longtime residents enjoys time together at the 1993 Vista Historical Society Barbecue. From left to right are Betty Minor, elected to the Vista Unified School District board of trustees in 1971; Orbee Mihalek, three-term Vista City Council member and mayor from 1970 to 1972; and Emily Sexsmith, active in civic and philanthropic endeavors from her arrival in Vista in 1932.

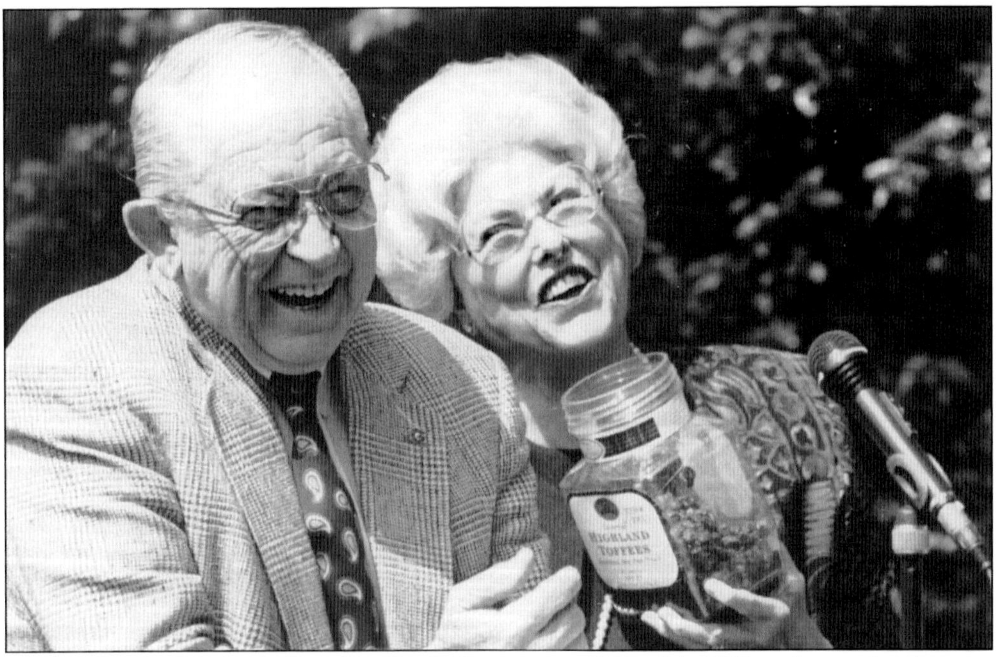

California state senator Bill Craven and Vista mayor Gloria McClellan share a laugh at an "Appreciation Day" luncheon for Craven. Mayor McClellan was elected to the city council in 1972 and served as councilwoman and then mayor consecutively until her death in 2002. Senator Craven was elected to the San Diego County Board of Supervisors in 1970, then to the California State Assembly, and later to the state senate.

Five

Parks and the Arts

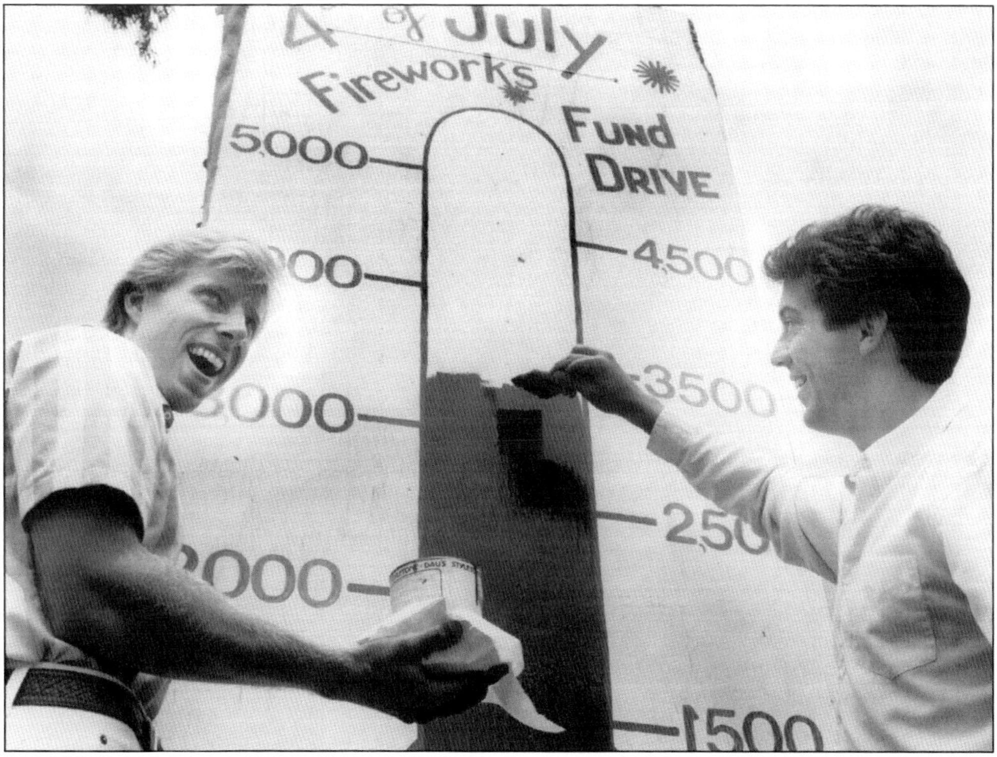

A highlight of the year for Vistans is the fireworks display held every Fourth of July at Brengle Terrace Park. Games and entertainment are provided throughout the afternoon and evening as families picnic on the lawns and await one of the most elaborate fireworks shows in the county. Citizens pitch in with donations, and Frank Sheckler (left) and Ed Estes Jr. are painting new figures on a fund-raiser thermometer in this 1989 photograph.

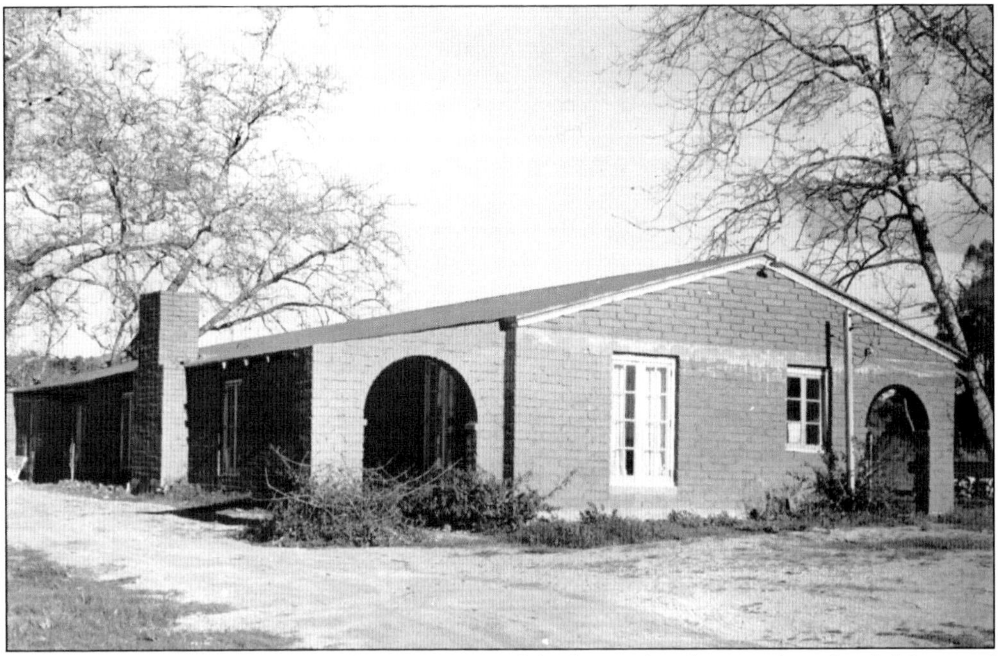

In response to the growing need for a recreational facility and gathering place for children and adults, the Committee for the Recreation Center was formed in the late 1930s. The citizenry came together with fund-raisers and offers of volunteer labor. In May 1939, cement for the foundation was mixed on-site and poured by wheelbarrow. Local contractors Luz and Tony Duran and L. G. and Dan Lara directed construction, using hand-hewn timbers and thousands of adobe bricks made by Hispano Club members. The high school superintendent declared a holiday so the boys could dig the block-long sewer line along Recreation Drive to East Vista Way while the girls cooked for them. After incorporation in 1963, the Parks and Community Services Department took over the recreation center. It was demolished to make way for Main Street commercial development in 2000.

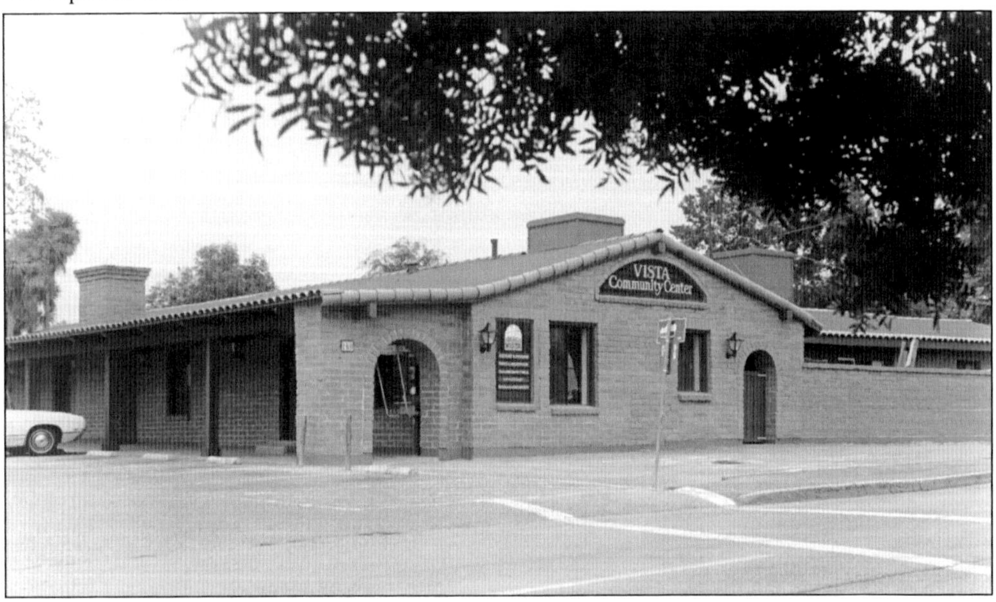

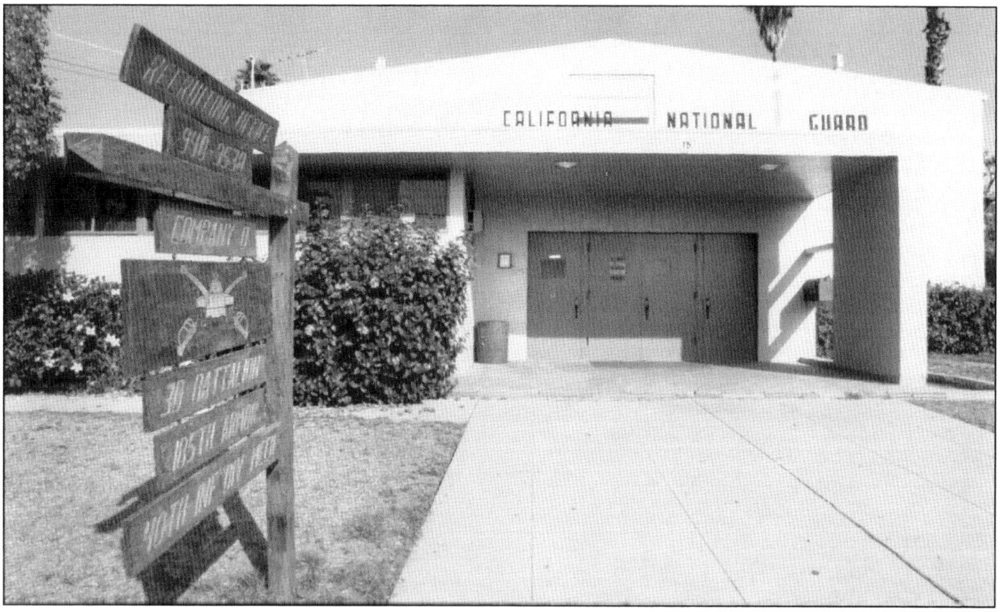

A dedication ceremony for the California National Guard Armory on Recreation Drive was held on January 13, 1950. The building stood next to the community's first recreation center for a half-century, until both buildings were razed in 2000 for construction of Main Street commercial enterprises. The sign at left reads, "Recruiting Office, Company II, 30 Battalion, 185th Armor, 40th Inf Div Mech."

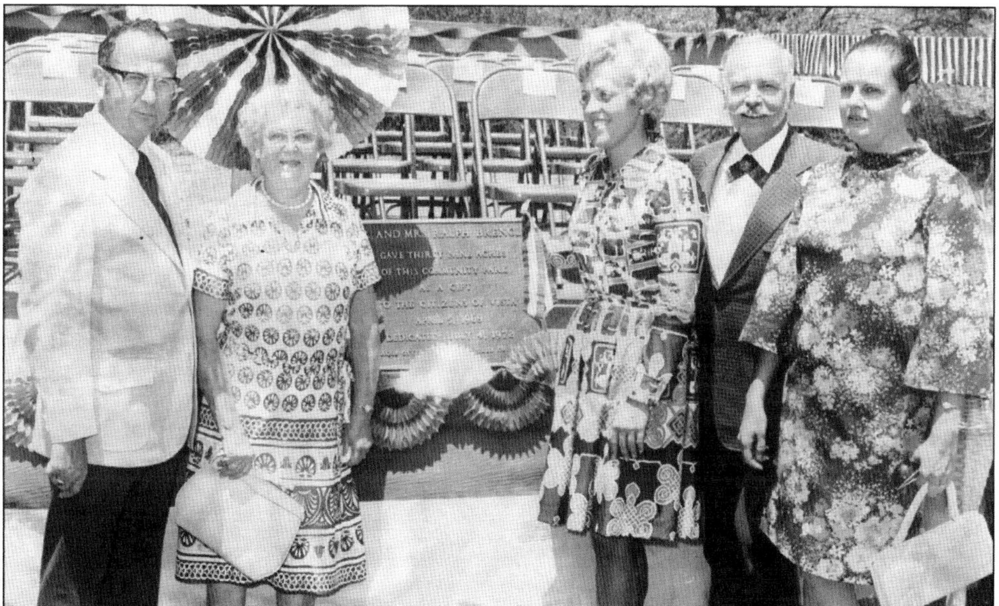

Ralph and Emma Brengle donated 39 of the original 56 acres that comprised Brengle Terrace Park in April 1968. Pictured here with the official plaque at the July 4, 1972, dedication ceremony are, from left to right, Mayor Kenneth Annin; Emma Brengle; Janis Perry Loftus, director of Parks and Community Services; and two unidentified relatives of Emma Brengle. (Courtesy of Vista Parks and Community Services Department.)

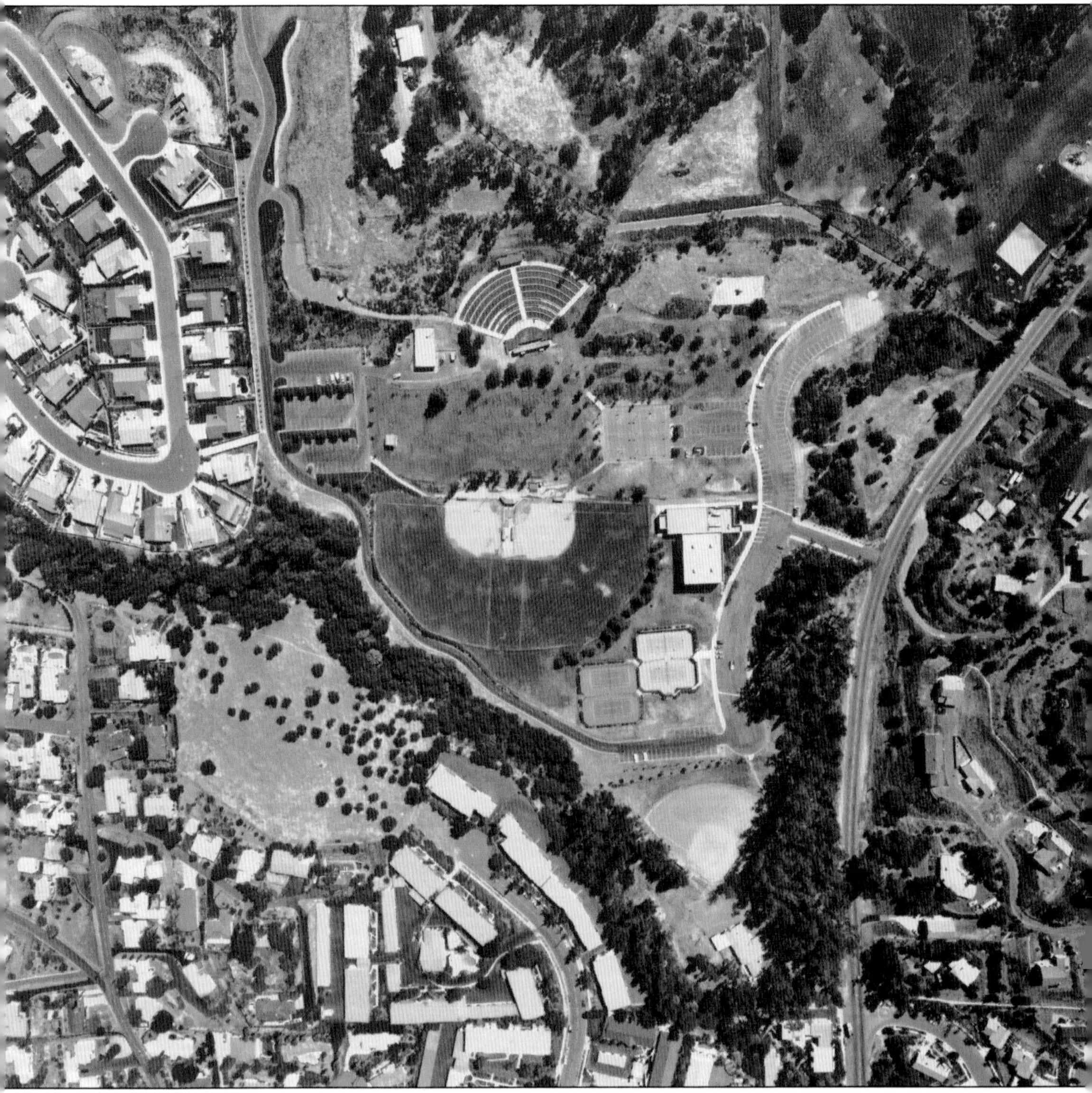

This 1988 aerial overview of city-owned Brengle Terrace Park shows the multiple recreational uses created at the site. At upper center is the amphitheater, used for a variety of outdoor performances and most particularly for the popular Moonlight Amphitheatre summer musicals, which attract audiences from a wide area. In the lower section are tennis courts and ball fields, with the Brengle Terrace Recreation Center and indoor gymnasium just above the tennis courts. Picnic areas and children's playgrounds are to the right of the amphitheater and among the trees adjacent to Vale Terrace, the road that leads past the park to residential areas beyond. At upper right of the amphitheater is the newly graded site for the initial phase of the Vista Senior Center. (Courtesy of Vista Parks and Community Services Department.)

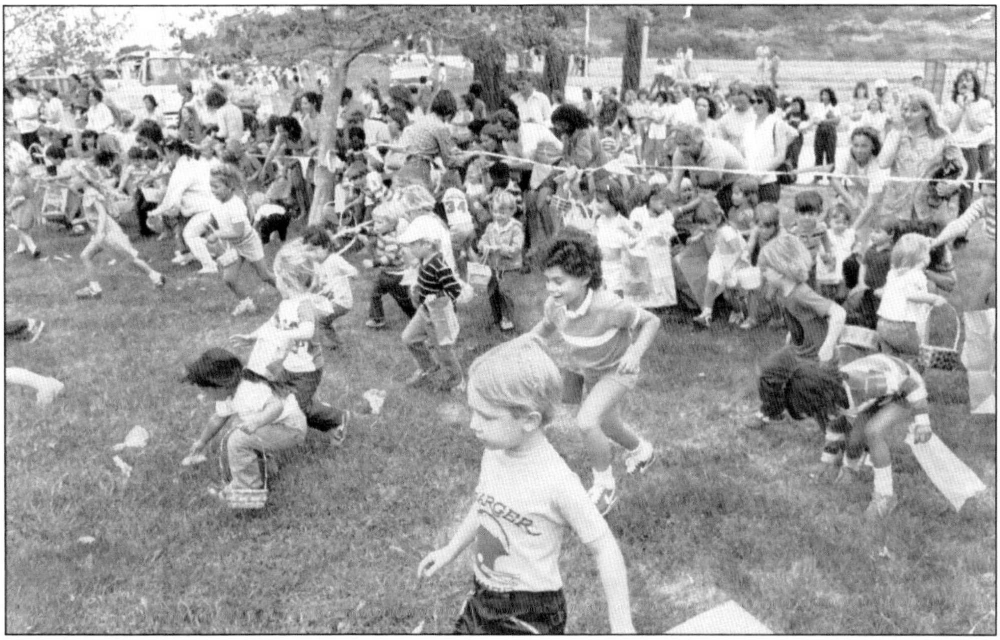

Vista children are off and running at the annual Easter Egg Hunt, sponsored by the city since incorporation in 1963. Families gather early on the vast Brengle Terrace Park lawn, where Parks and Community Services Department staff members have worked since dawn to hide ample treats for each child. A bonnet contest and visit with the Easter Bunny are traditional. (Courtesy of Vista Parks and Community Services Department.)

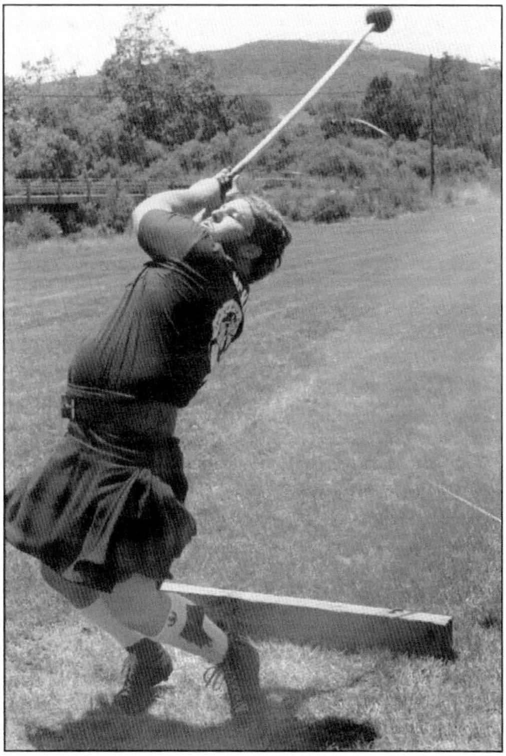

The Scottish Highland Games, held each June at Brengle Terrace Park, draws competitors and visitors from throughout Southern California. Pictured here is David McNabb of Los Angeles, clad in the kilt of his clan as he throws the 16-pound hammer. A large area of the park is fenced off for several days to accommodate sports competitions, the drum and bagpipe corps, and various booths.

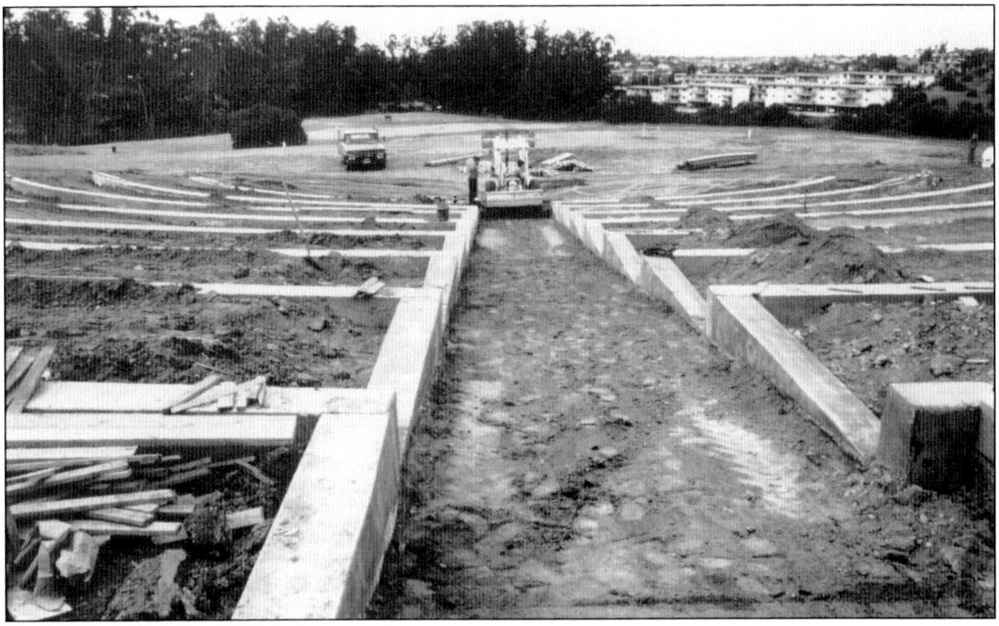

This April 1976 photograph shows newly poured concrete tiers as Vista's amphitheater takes shape in Brengle Terrace Park. Under the chairmanship of attorney Frank Tiesen, along with the efforts of the Vista Foundation and Vista Bicentennial Committee, plus generous donations of funds, materials, and labor, the amphitheater was presented to the citizens of Vista debt-free on July 4, 1976. (Courtesy of Vista Parks and Community Services Department.)

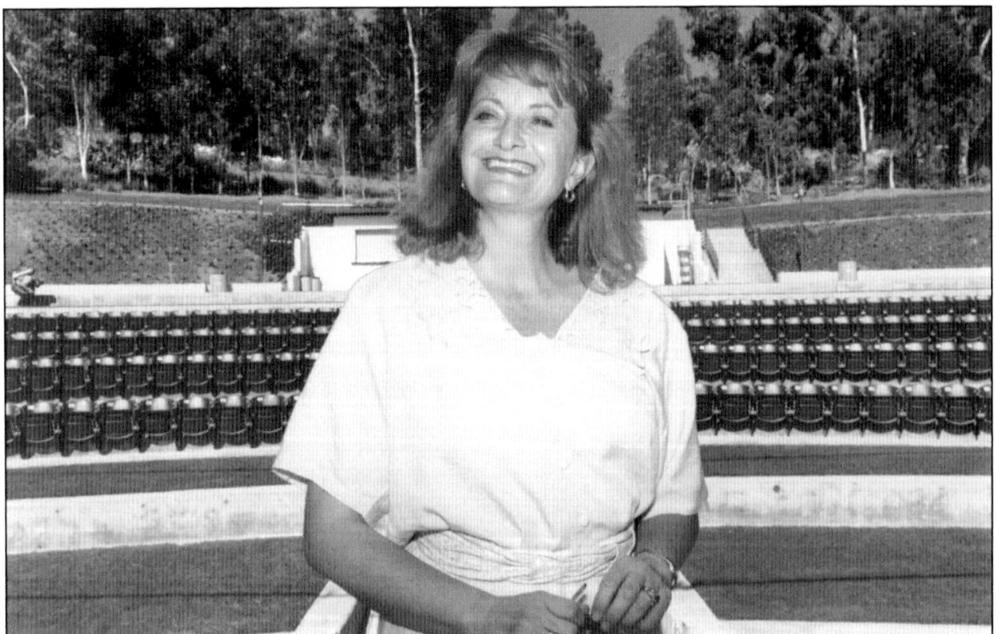

Kathy Brombacher, producing artistic director for Moonlight Stage Productions, shared her vision for the new amphitheater with James Porter, then director of the Parks and Community Services Department. In 1981, she produced *Oliver* and *The Boyfriend* to rave reviews. (Courtesy of *Escondido Times-Advocate*.)

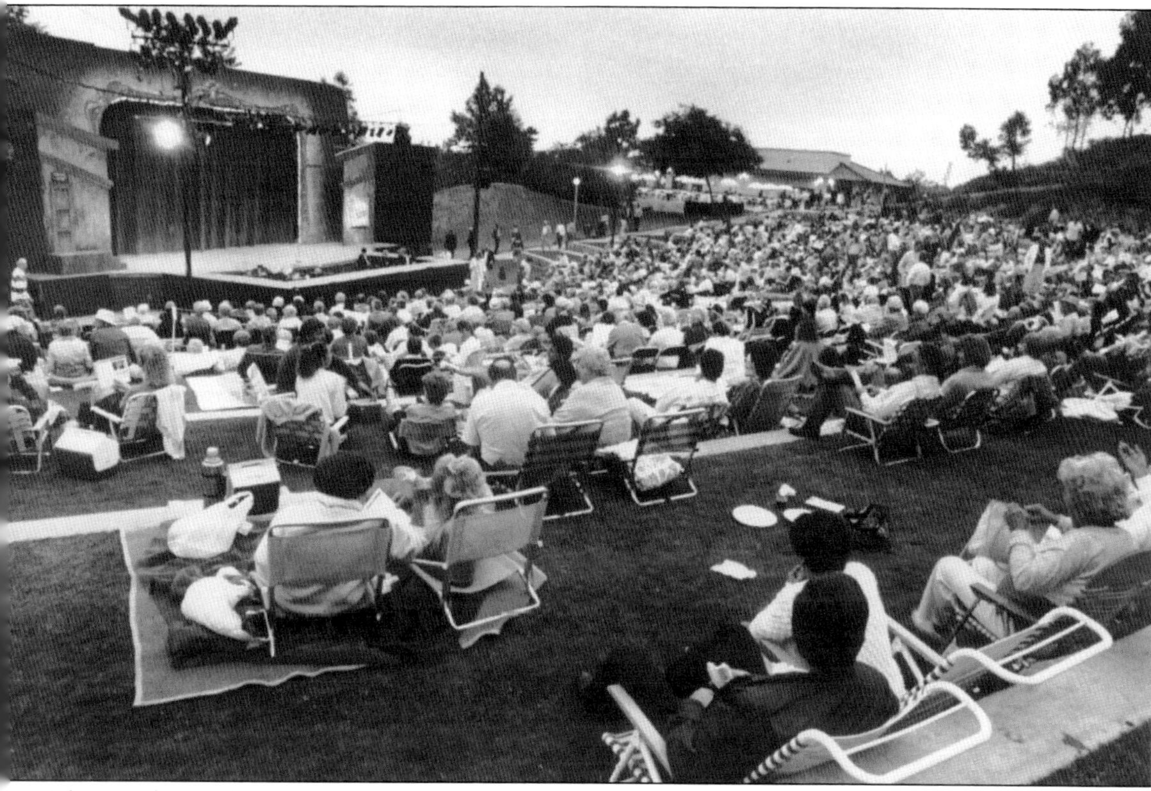

The popularity of Moonlight Amphitheatre musicals has grown steadily over the years, and with new revenues have come improvements to the stage and dressing rooms, the addition of rows of permanent seating, and a building with a patio where food is available. Picnics, many of them epicurean, are always popular. Pictured is the 1988 opening-night crowd for *Gypsy*. (Courtesy of *Escondido Times-Advocate*.)

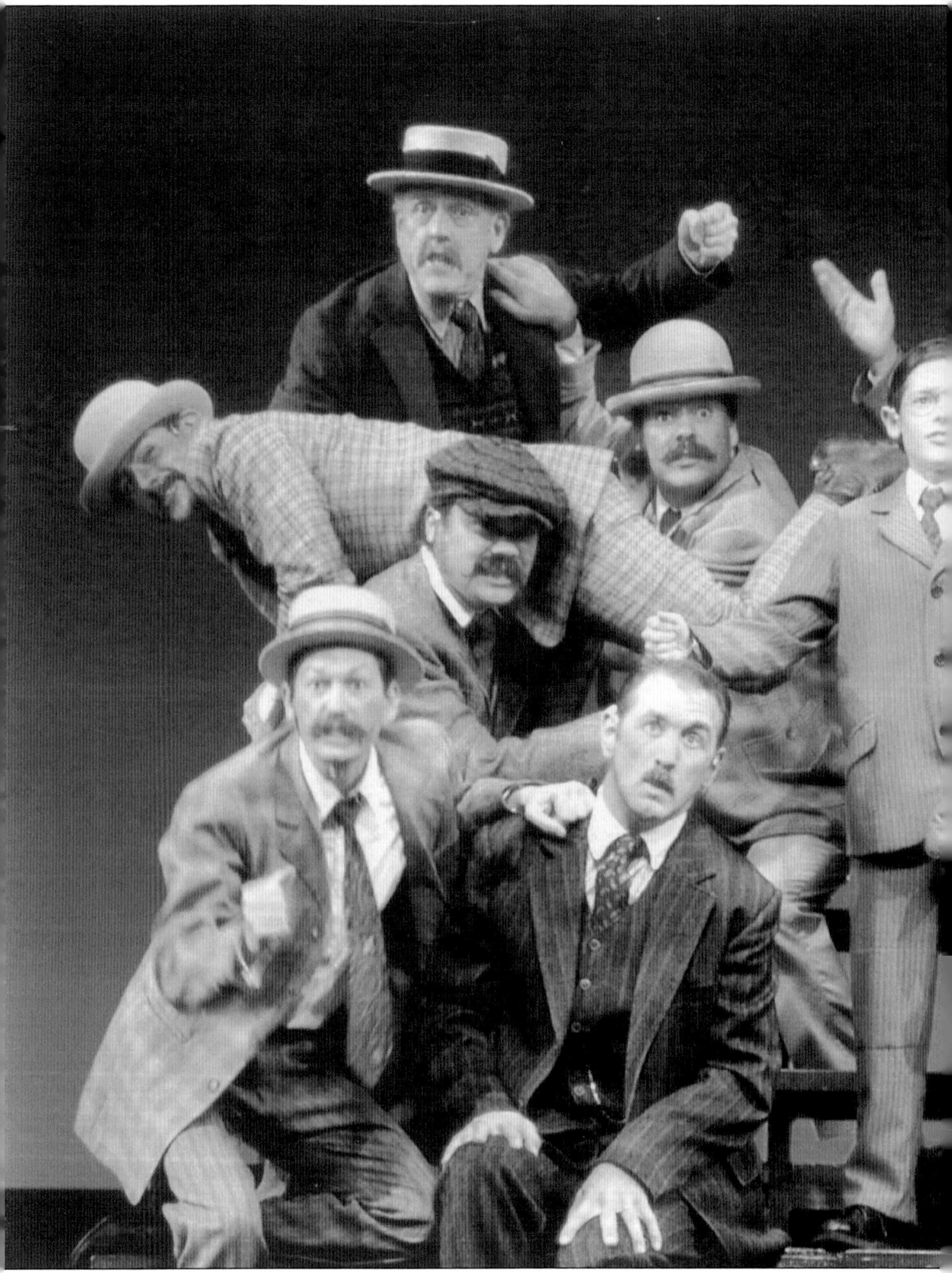

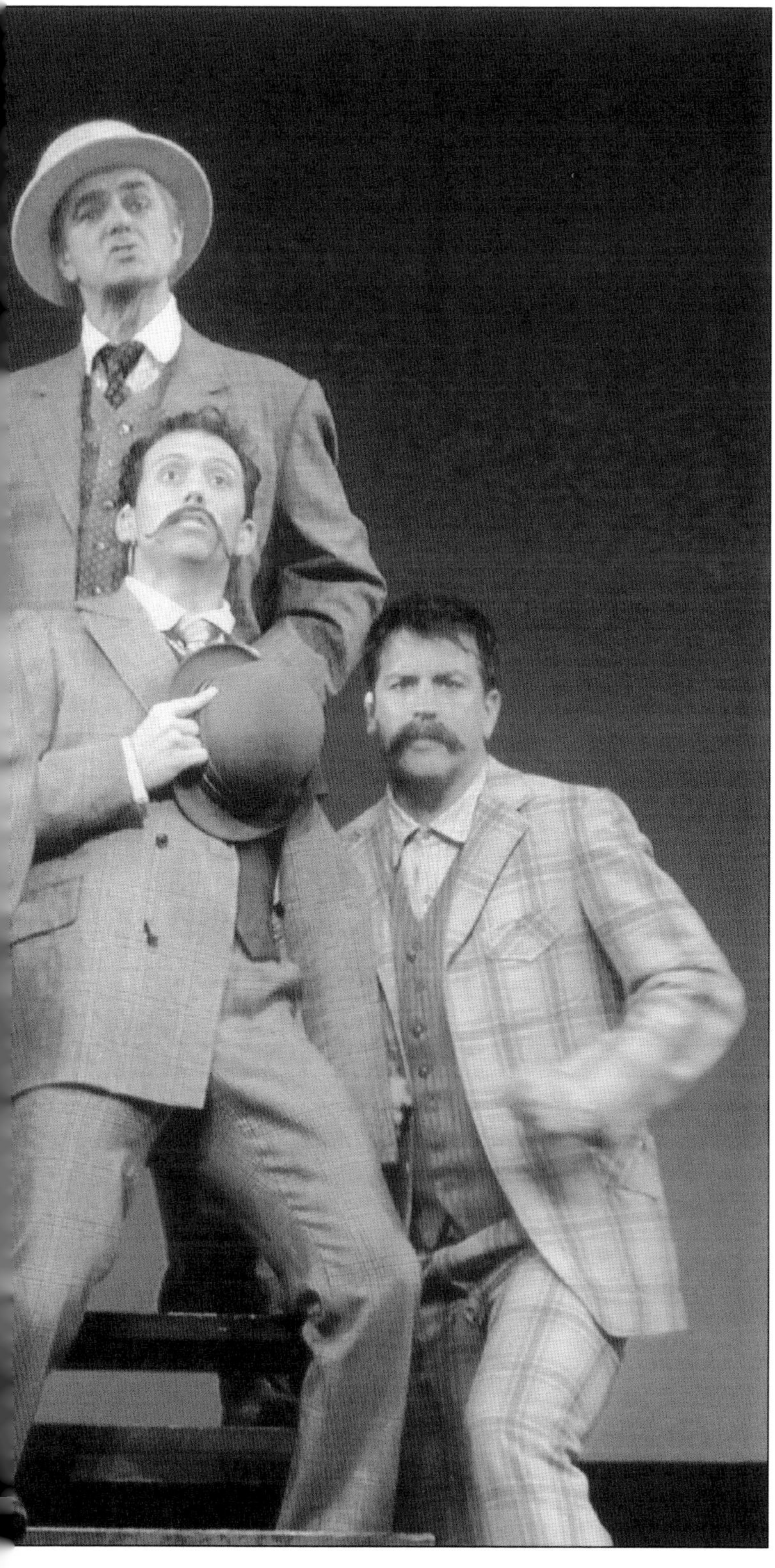

As with so many Moonlight Amphitheatre productions, the 2002 production of *Ragtime, The Musical* won multiple awards. Included were the San Diego Theatre Critic Circle awards for Outstanding Performance in a Musical and Outstanding Resident Musical. Kathy Brombacher, producing artistic director for Moonlight, directed the show. The choreographer was Paul David Bryant, with musical direction by Elan McMahan and Kenneth Gammie as orchestra conductor. (Courtesy of Vista Parks and Community Services Department.)

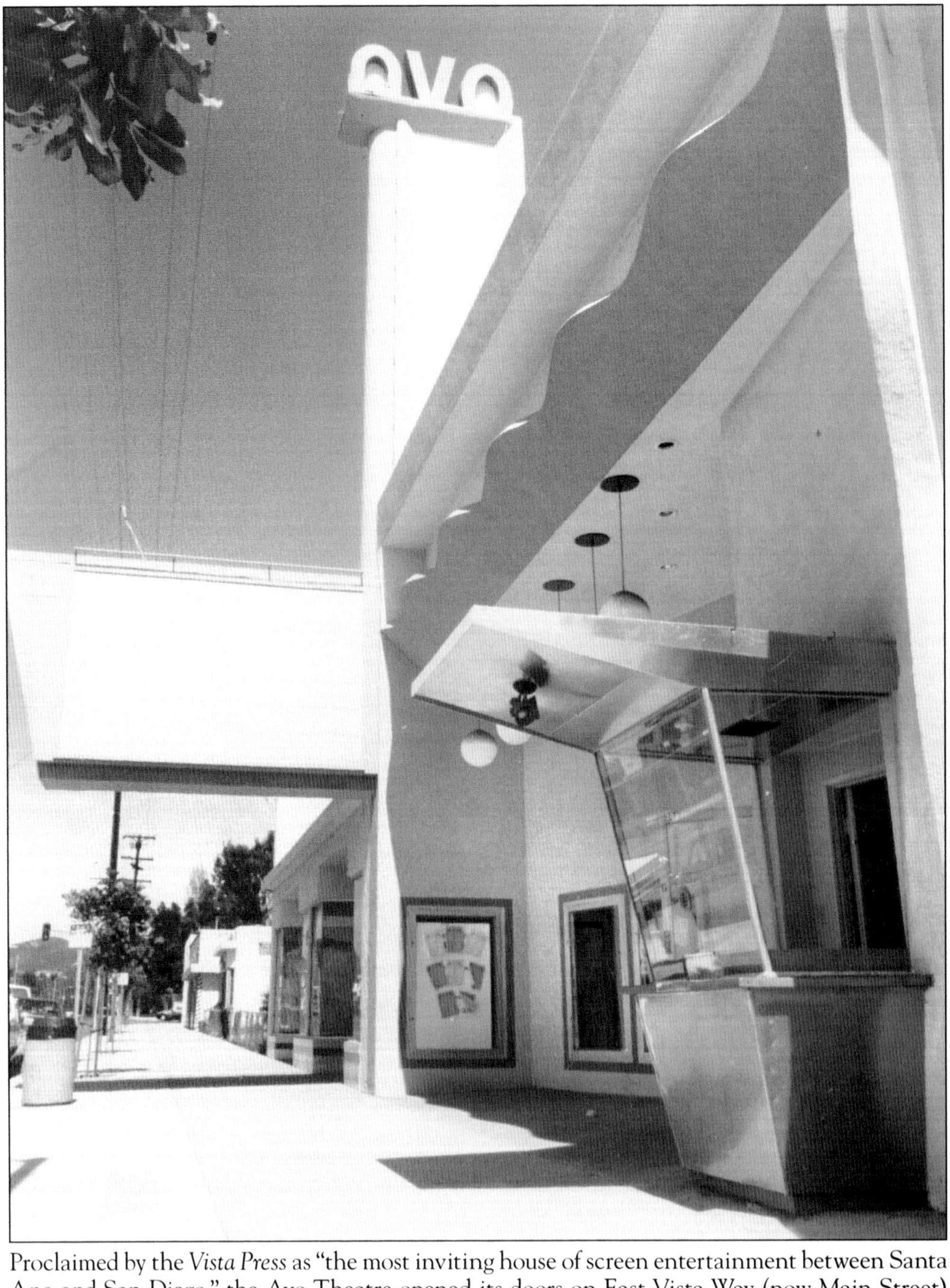

Proclaimed by the *Vista Press* as "the most inviting house of screen entertainment between Santa Ana and San Diego," the Avo Theatre opened its doors on East Vista Way (now Main Street) for the first time on Saturday, December 11, 1948. The $100,000 theater had 800 seats, with loge seats going for 90¢. Local businessman Abe Shelhoup built and owned the theater. His associate partner was Joseph Fotheringham, later the first mayor of Vista; the first manager was Clell E. McElroy. The theater hosted the Miss Vista contest and various theatrical and musical performances as well as movies. It was named the Avo to honor Vista's status as the avocado capital of the world.

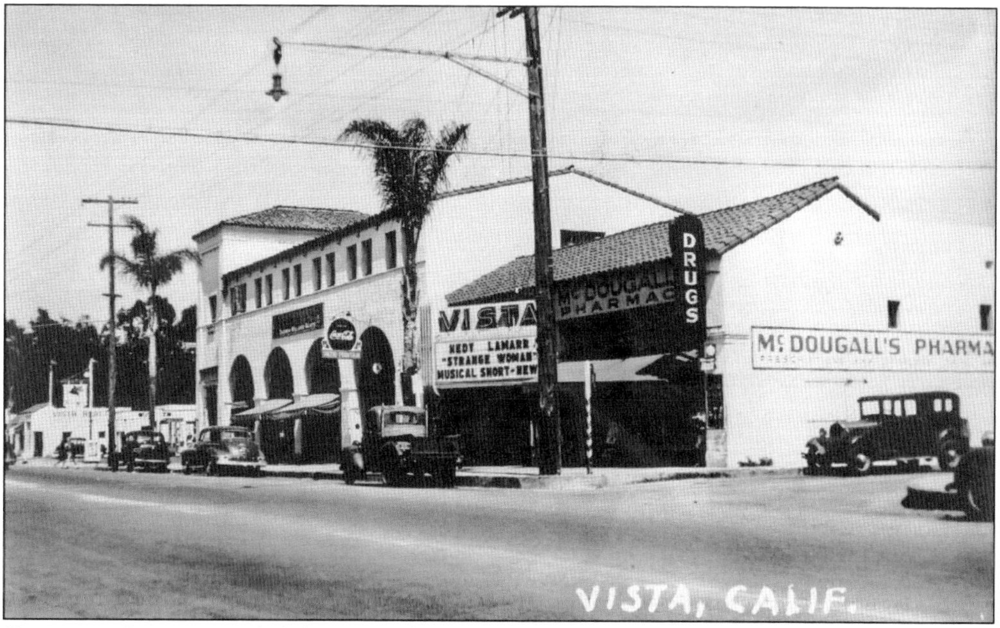

One movie house preceded the Avo. The Vista Theatre opened in the McDougall Building on May 2, 1941, praised in the *Vista Press* as "a remarkable demonstration of luxury and compactness." It operated for a while after the Avo opened in 1948. It then became a Spanish-language theater and ultimately was closed and the space taken over by an expansion of the adjacent McDougall's Pharmacy.

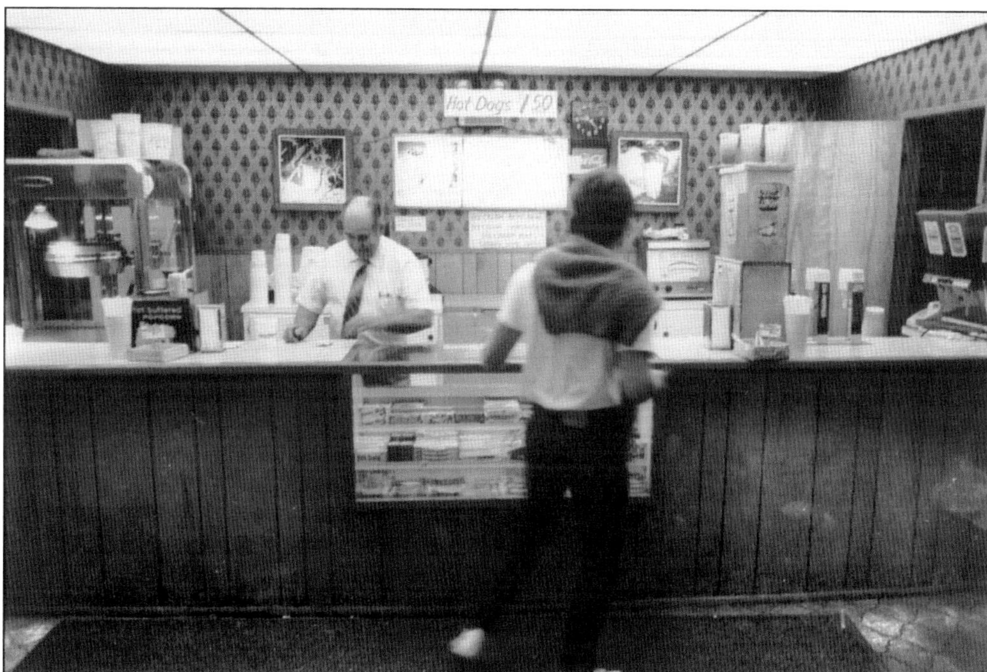

Earl Willis, longtime manager of the Avo Theatre, helps a young customer at the snack bar. The popular theater was unable to keep up with the multiplex movie houses that cropped up in northern San Diego County and closed its doors in 1989.

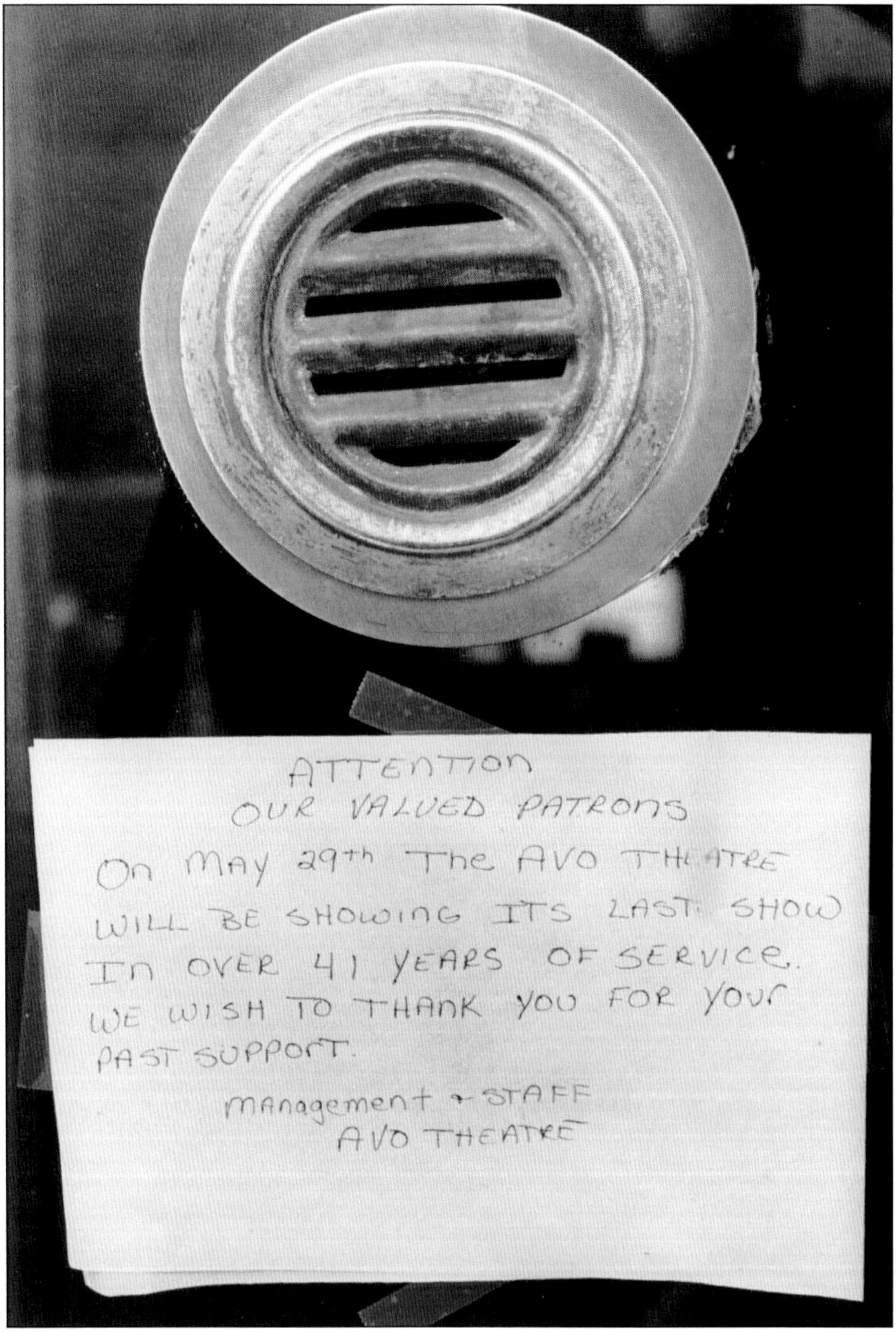

This photograph tells it all. After 41 years, the staff and management of the Avo Theatre sadly closed their doors on May 29, 1989, and the building sat empty for several years. The Friends of the Avo formed and held a "Memories of the Avo" essay contest and "Nostalgia Night" in an effort to save the theater and honor its past. The City of Vista purchased the building and adjacent café in 1994, renovated it, and reopened in 1995 as the Avo Playhouse, home of the Winter Moonlight series of plays. It is also available for youth theater, concerts, and major business meetings.

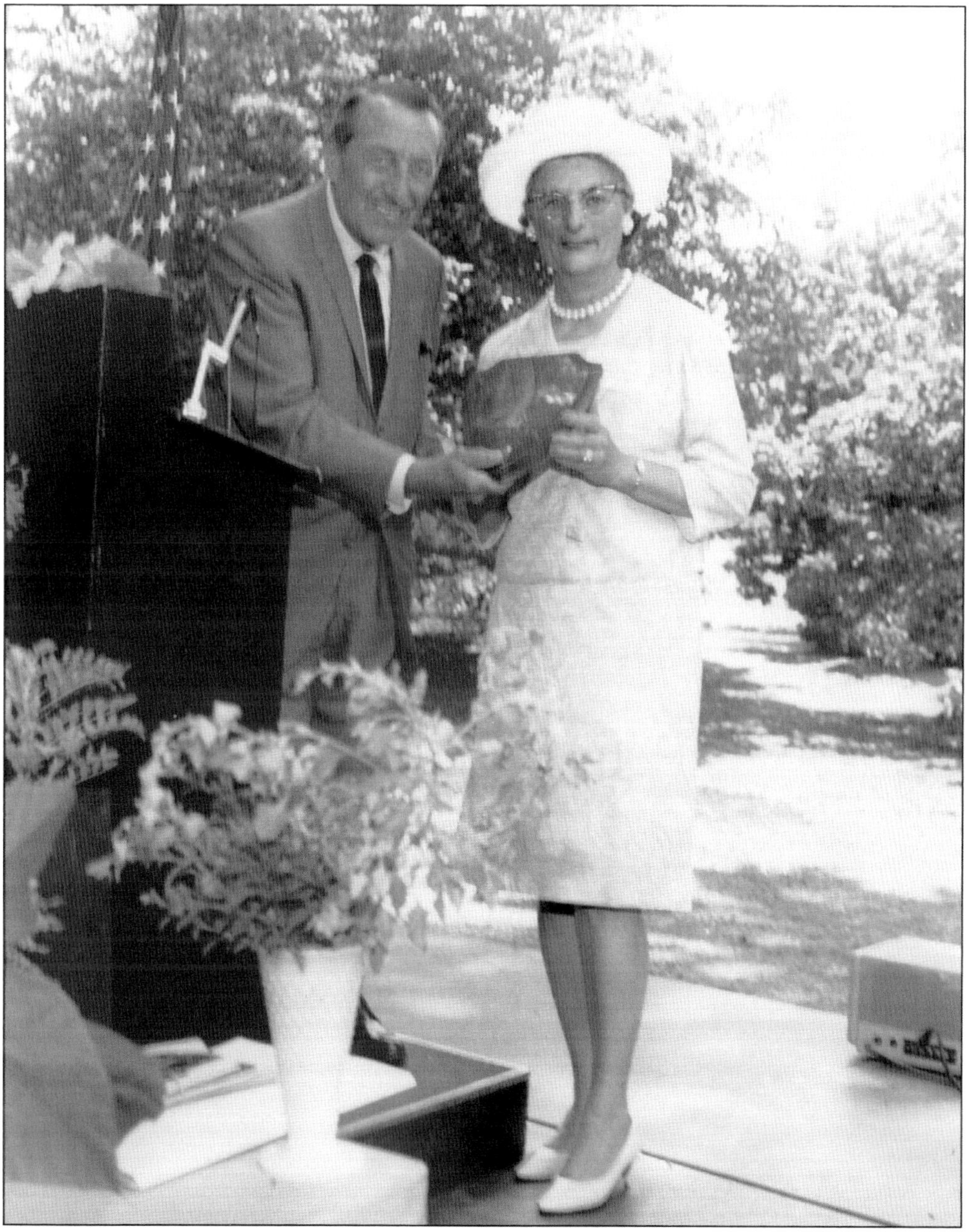

Elva Dawson, chairman of Vista Beautiful, receives the 1967 Grand Award for outstanding community beautification achievements from Frank G. Bonelli, chairman of the Los Angeles Board of Supervisors. Vista is noted for having six times the national average of park space and for its many recreation facilities and beautification efforts. Vista Beautiful, created by the city council in 1965 to promote commercial and residential pride, was judged "Most Outstanding Community Group" from among 300 Southern California organizations in 1967. The Los Angeles Beautiful "Celebrate With Color" awards luncheon was held at the Arcadia arboretum.

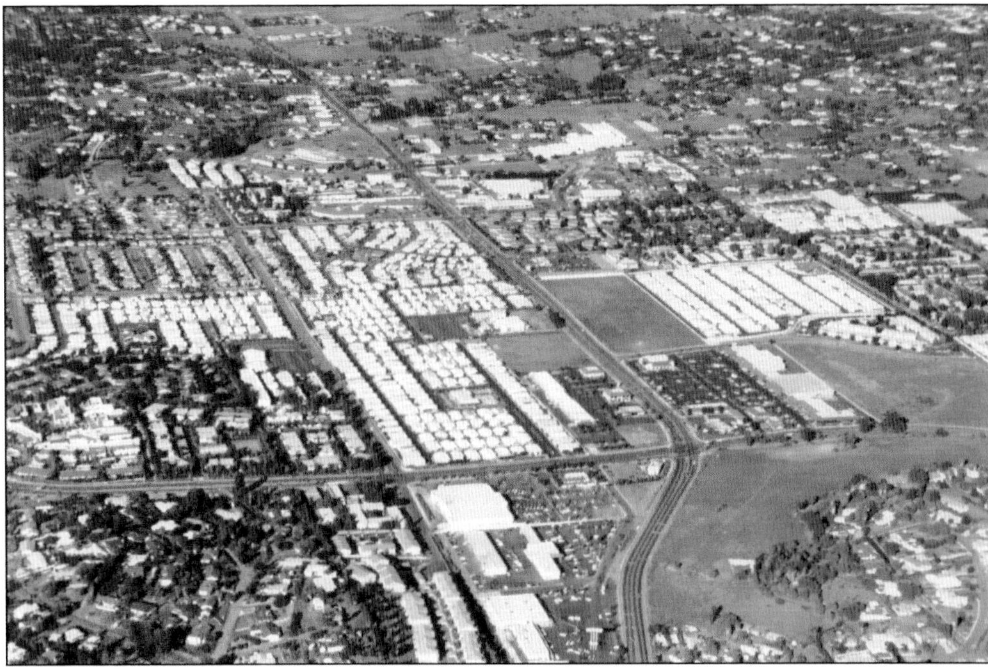

In the early 1970s, a new kind of structure and an influx of senior citizens arrived in Vista simultaneously. This aerial view shows four mobile home parks within a square-mile radius: Vista Royalodge Mobile Estates on Bobier Drive, at lower center; Vista Cascade Mobile Home Park on East Vista Way, at upper center; Corona del Vista on Anza Avenue, at left; and Royal Oaks on Oak Drive, on the right.

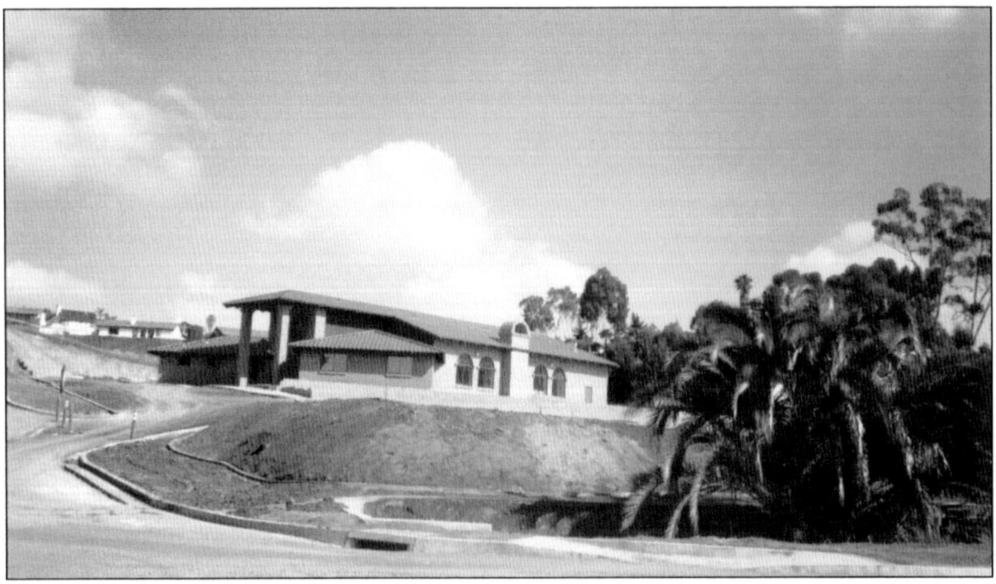

By 1984, it became essential that a facility be provided for the growing senior citizen population that would house the nutrition center as well as additional social, educational, and recreational activities. After various funding sources were in place, the 8,100-square-foot building pictured above was constructed on Vale Terrace Drive at the east end of Brengle Terrace Park at a cost of $1,319,000. (Courtesy of Vista Parks and Community Services Department.)

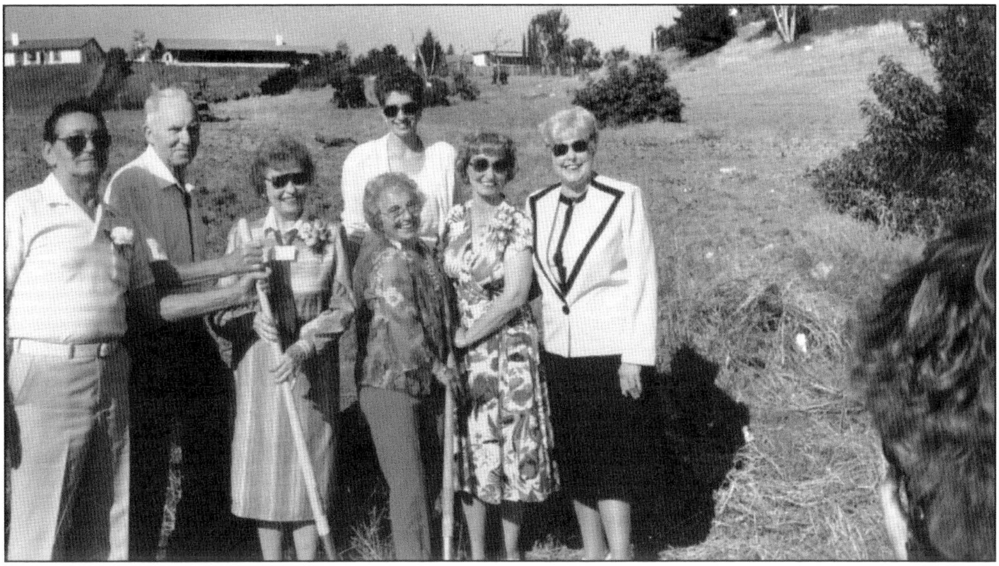

Senior citizens and local dignitaries presided at the 1987 ground-breaking ceremony. At the far right is Mayor Gloria McClellan, in whose honor the center was later named. A dedication celebration attended by more than 800 citizens and dignitaries was held on April 24, 1989. The nutrition center moved into a modern 252-seat dining room from a meeting space at city hall that it had actually shared with the Vista City Council. (Courtesy of Vista Parks and Community Services Department.)

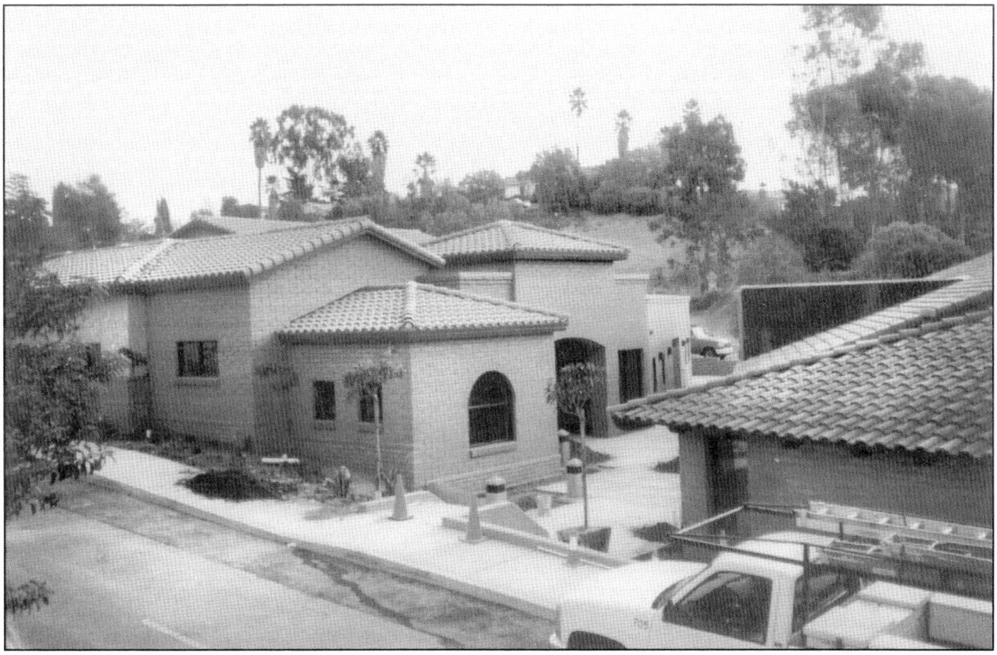

In 2001, this 8,000-square-foot addition to the Brengle Senior Center was dedicated and the entire center was named in honor of the late longtime mayor and senior advocate Gloria E. McClellan. Services that had been provided at the Jefferson Senior Center, on what is now Vista Village Drive, were expanded and combined with operations at the new facility. (Courtesy of Vista Parks and Community Services Department.)

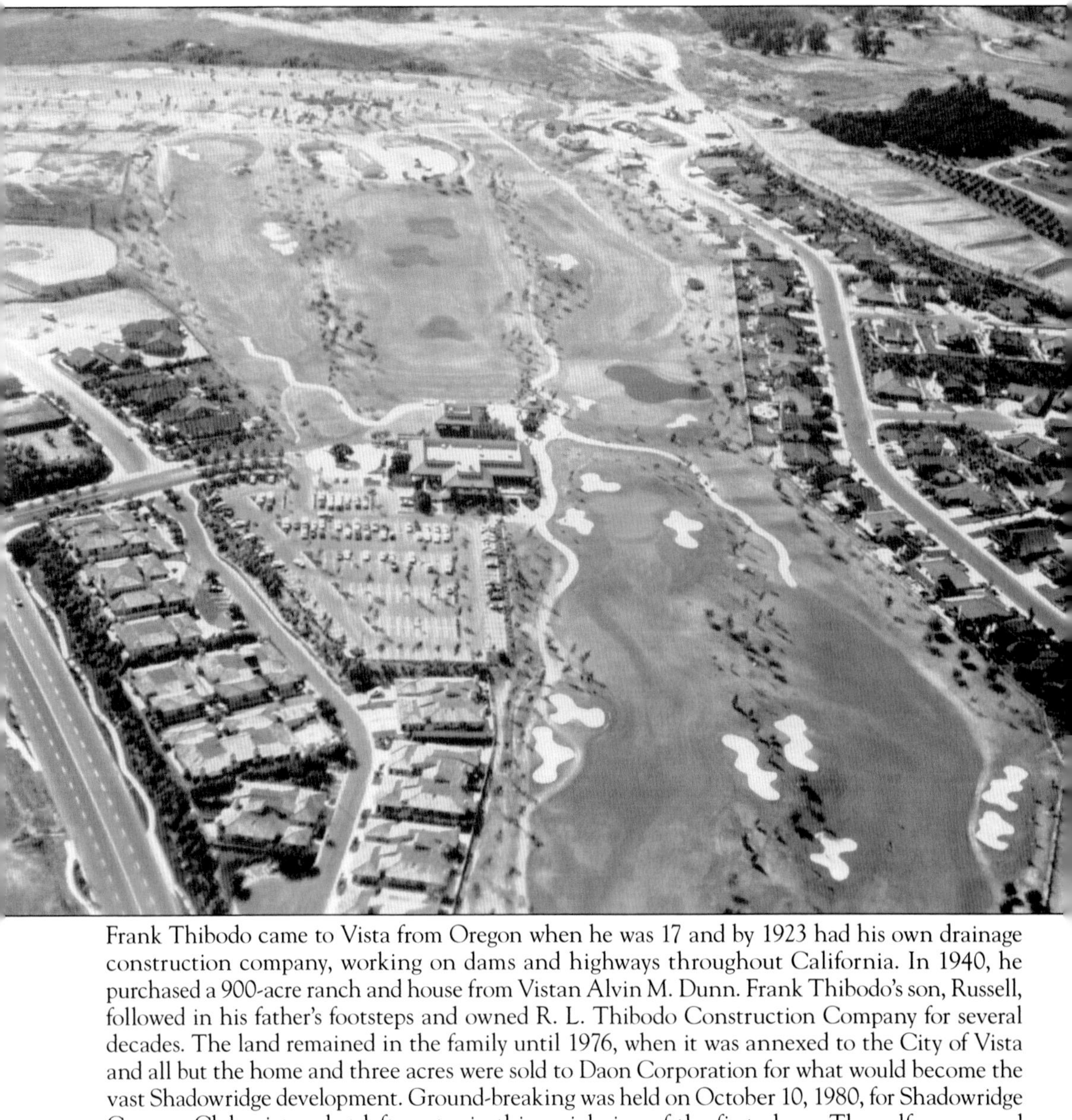

Frank Thibodo came to Vista from Oregon when he was 17 and by 1923 had his own drainage construction company, working on dams and highways throughout California. In 1940, he purchased a 900-acre ranch and house from Vistan Alvin M. Dunn. Frank Thibodo's son, Russell, followed in his father's footsteps and owned R. L. Thibodo Construction Company for several decades. The land remained in the family until 1976, when it was annexed to the City of Vista and all but the home and three acres were sold to Daon Corporation for what would become the vast Shadowridge development. Ground-breaking was held on October 10, 1980, for Shadowridge Country Club, pictured at left center in this aerial view of the first phase. The golf course and country club served as the centerpiece for the initial $270-million, 3,590-unit housing development. Additional neighborhoods of homes, condominiums, and apartments, and a number of shopping and service areas, have been added over the years.

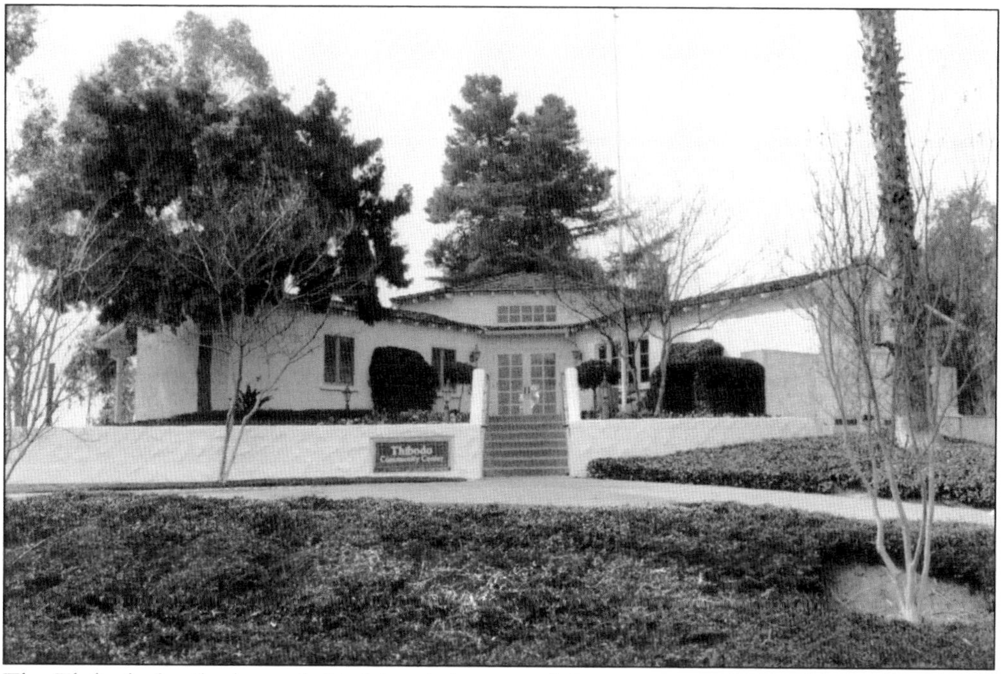

The Thibodo family donated this historic home and the remaining three of their 900 acres to the City of Vista toward a park site. Thibodo Park was dedicated on June 4, 1982. The house, typical of the modified California ranch dwellings built in the 1930s and early 1940s, was then fully restored by the City of Vista and dedicated as a community center on September 30, 1987.

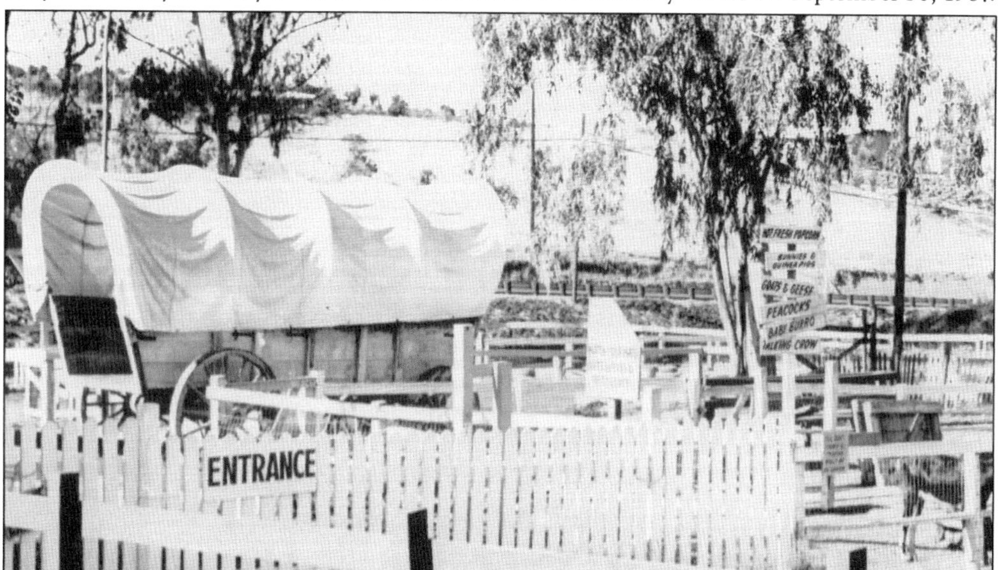

Robert Tupa opened Bob's Burro Farm on East Vista Way on January 1, 1957. Also known as Hee Haw Valley, the farm became so popular that it was featured in a *Sunset Magazine* article in September 1971: "The farm is a place where children can cuddle a duck, feed a goat from a nursing bottle . . . and frolic with a squealing pig." Rising feed prices forced Tupa to close in February 1974.

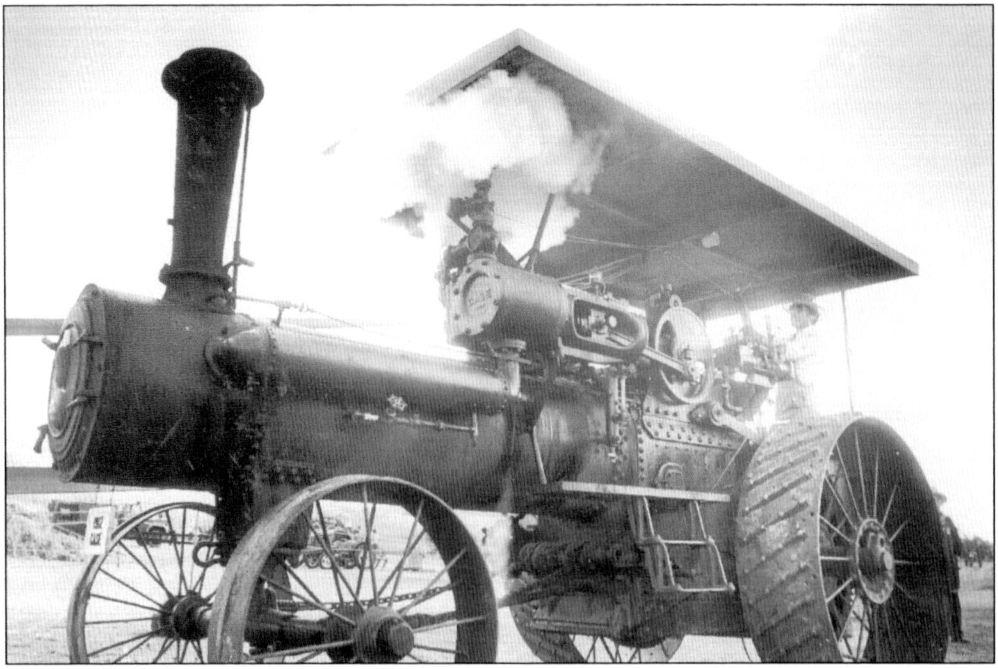

Antique Gas and Steam Engine Museum member Chuck Wischstadt fires up the pride of the fleet, a 1912 Case steam-driven tractor. Museum members and visitors from all over Southern California turn out for the Spring Show in June and the Harvest Festival in October, which feature narrated parades of antique gas and steam equipment, farming and blacksmithing demonstrations, an authentic farmhouse, a multitude of exhibits, entertainment, and down-home cooking. (Courtesy of *Escondido Times-Advocate.*)

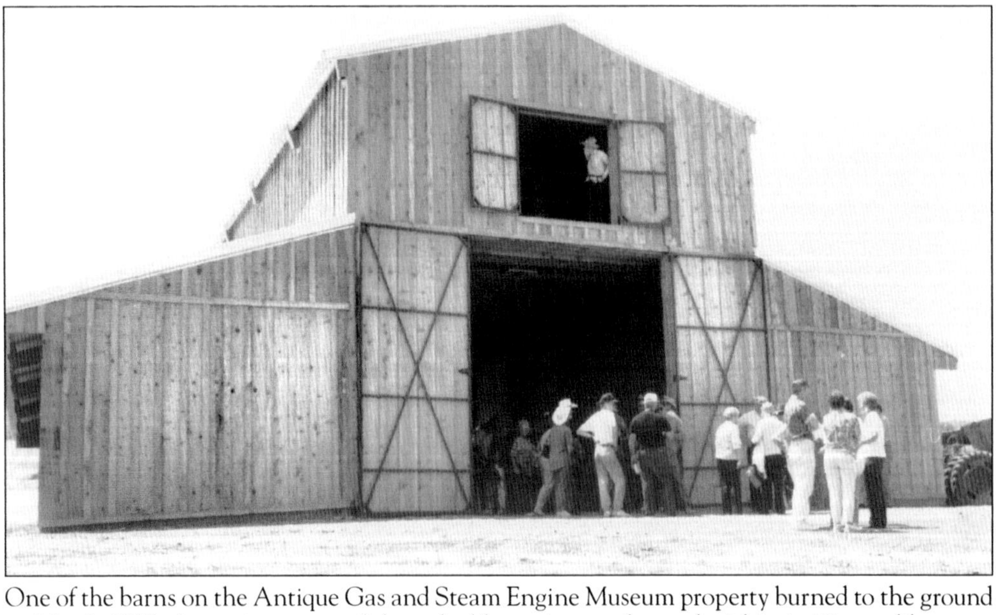

One of the barns on the Antique Gas and Steam Engine Museum property burned to the ground in March 1986, destroying some of the valuable equipment housed within it. Pictured here are guests at 1993 dedication ceremonies for the new California-style barn that replaced it. The museum is open to visitors daily. (Courtesy of Thomas W. Fehr.)

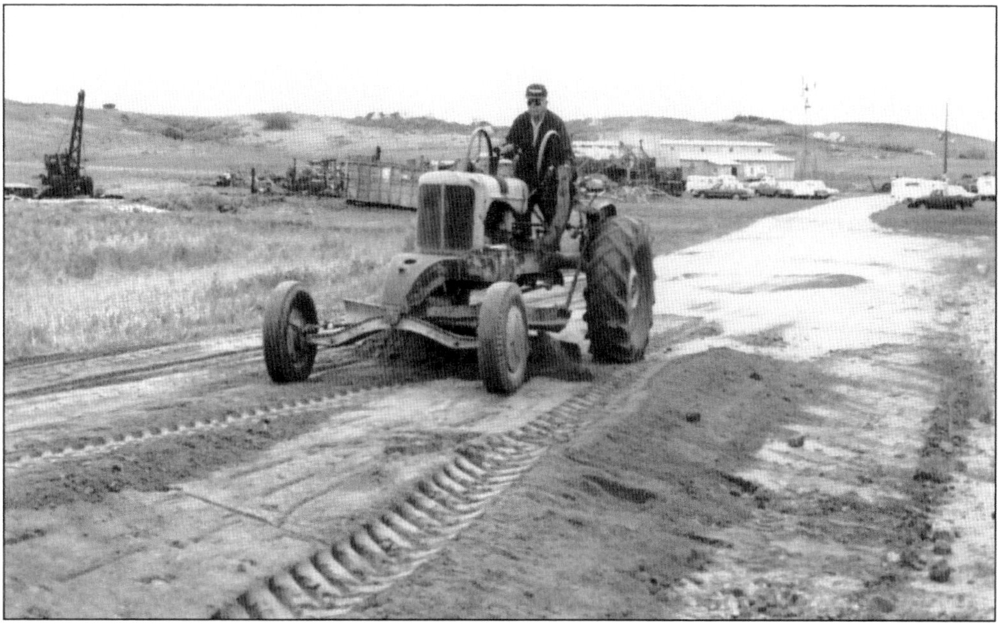

This photograph provides a view of the picturesque 55-acre Antique Gas and Steam Engine Museum site, situated on the outskirts of Vista near historic Rancho Guajome. Ernie Walker, who lives on the museum grounds with other caretakers, is shown driving one of the dozens of old-time tractors and other venerable pieces of equipment displayed on the property. (Courtesy of Antique Gas and Steam Engine Museum.)

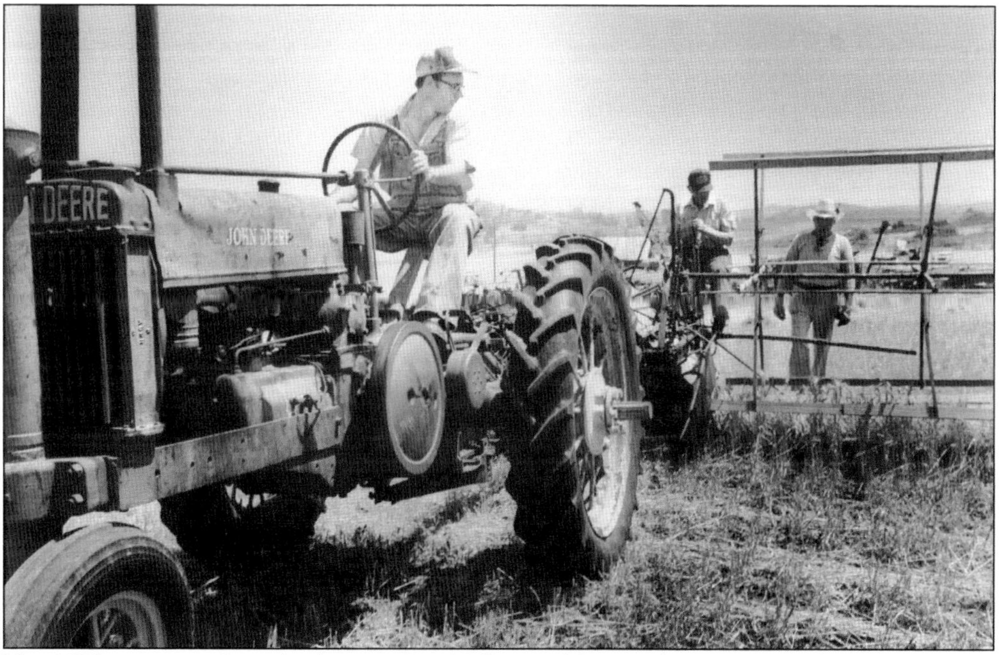

Virgil White, a member who lives in Sun Valley, California, drives a 1936 John Deere tractor pulling equipment that harvests and bundles wheat. The museum dry farmed oats and hay, but there is no longer enough rain. Current crops are sorghum and corn. (Courtesy of Antique Gas and Steam Engine Museum.)

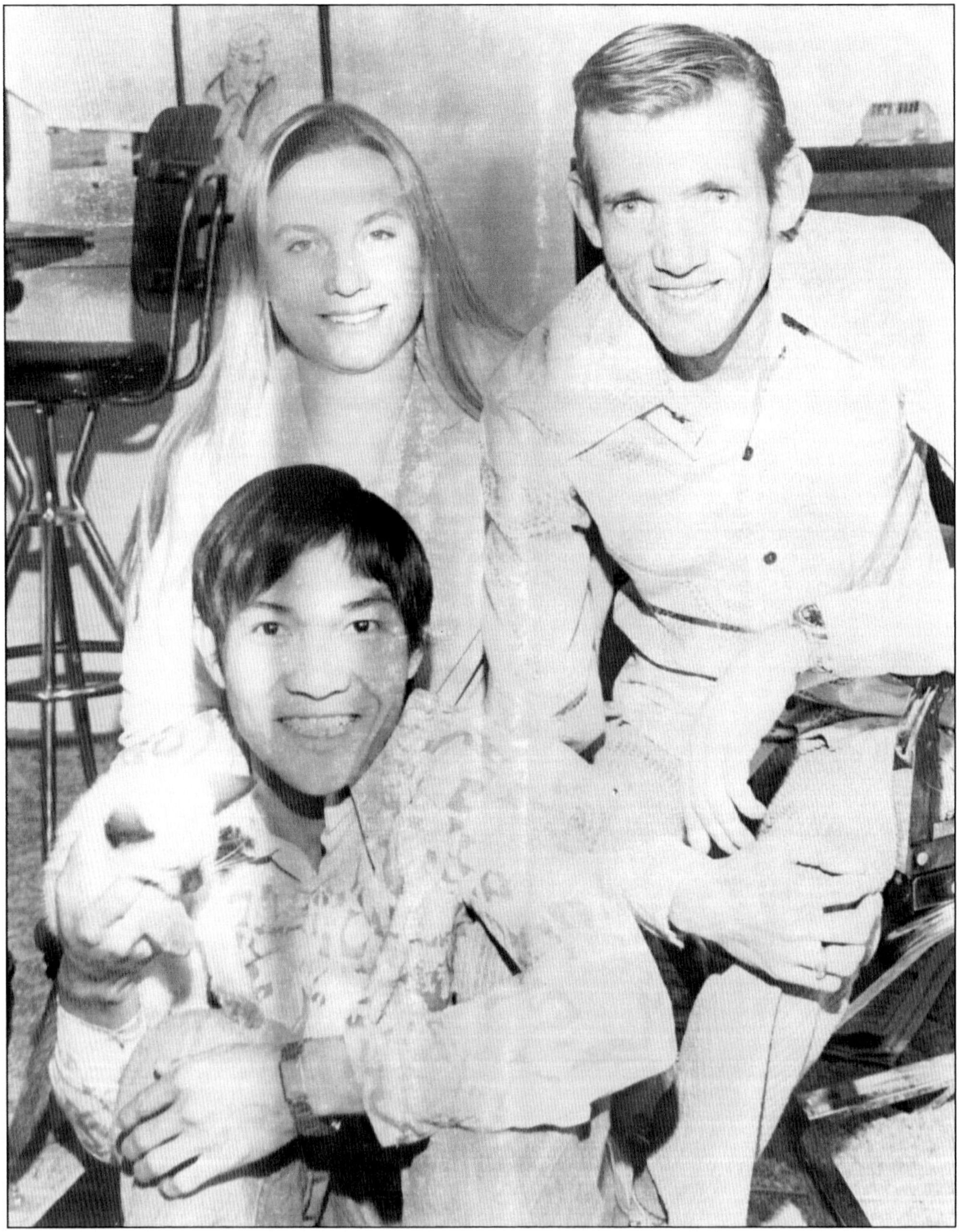

Vista artist-photographer Thomas G. Ebersold (right) was celebrated throughout the Southwest for contemporary cloisonné, his original art form. He began his career in the late 1960s, using traditional Oriental cloisonné and modern materials to produce works of intricate detail and vivid color. His subjects range from Egyptian and Mayan to Southwestern themes. He also served as a photographer for the *Vista Press*. In 1975, Ebersold sponsored Trinh Tran, one of the first Vietnamese to be displaced to Camp Pendleton after the war. Behind Trinh Tran is Margaret Soyland, who grew up with Ebersold and assisted him in his Vista art studio. He was the son of Raymond and Harriet Ebersold, who came to Vista in 1946 and have been active in business, civic, and social activities. Thomas Ebersold passed away in March 1976 at the age of 32.

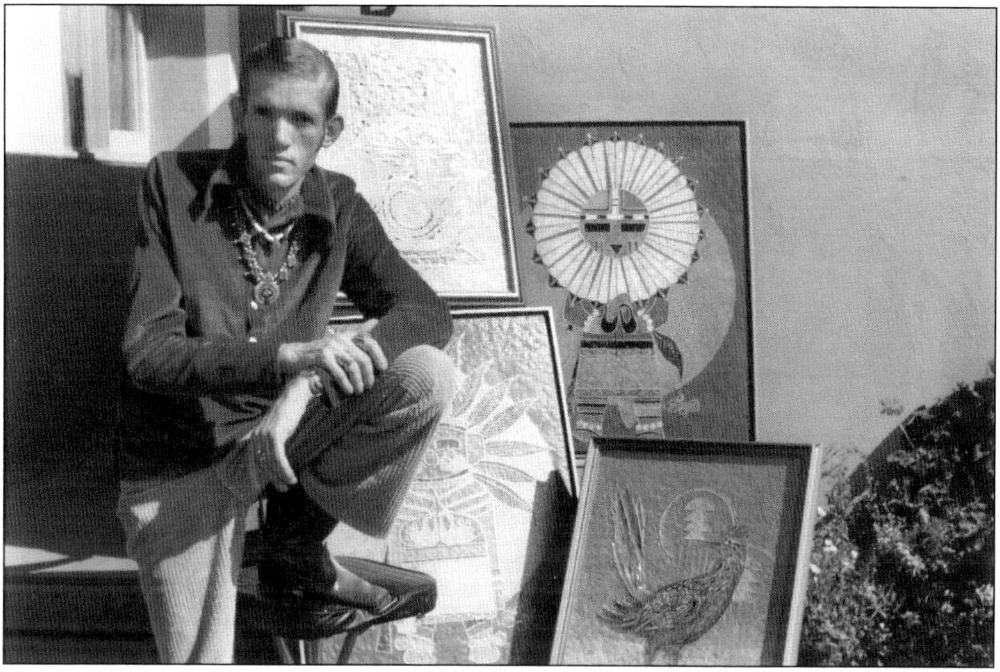

Thomas Ebersold is shown in the early 1970s with some of his works in contemporary cloisonné, the unique art form he created after 10 years of experimentation. He graduated from the University of California at Los Angeles with a bachelor's degree in design and traveled widely to discover new themes for his artwork.

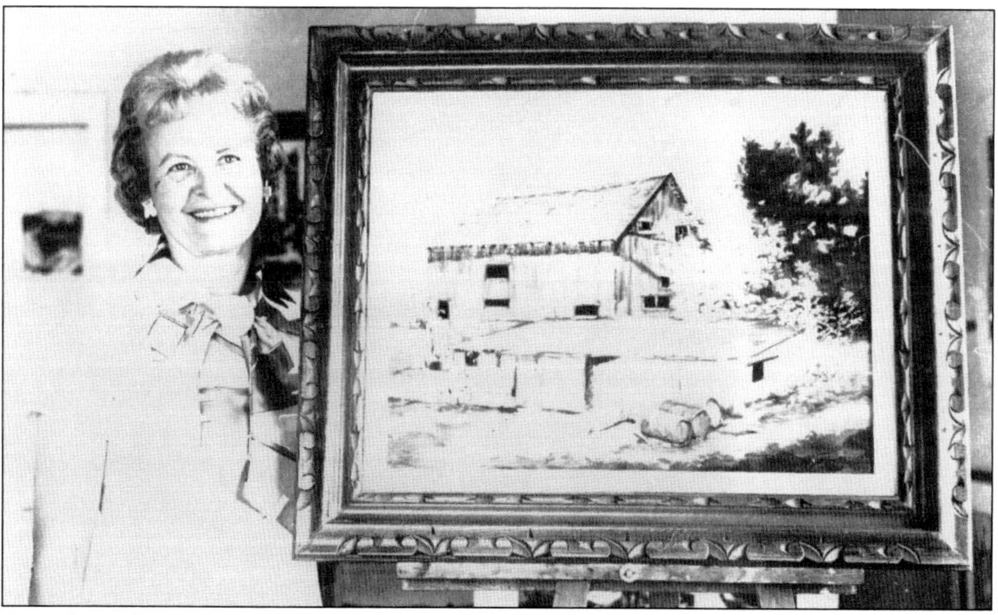

A resident of Vista for more than a half-century, Thelma Speed Houston was an internationally known artist and fabric designer. She was a world traveler and lectured extensively on art. Her works were shown throughout Southern California over many years. A member of the San Diego Water Color Society and the San Diego Art Institute, she also served as president of the Vista Art Guild.

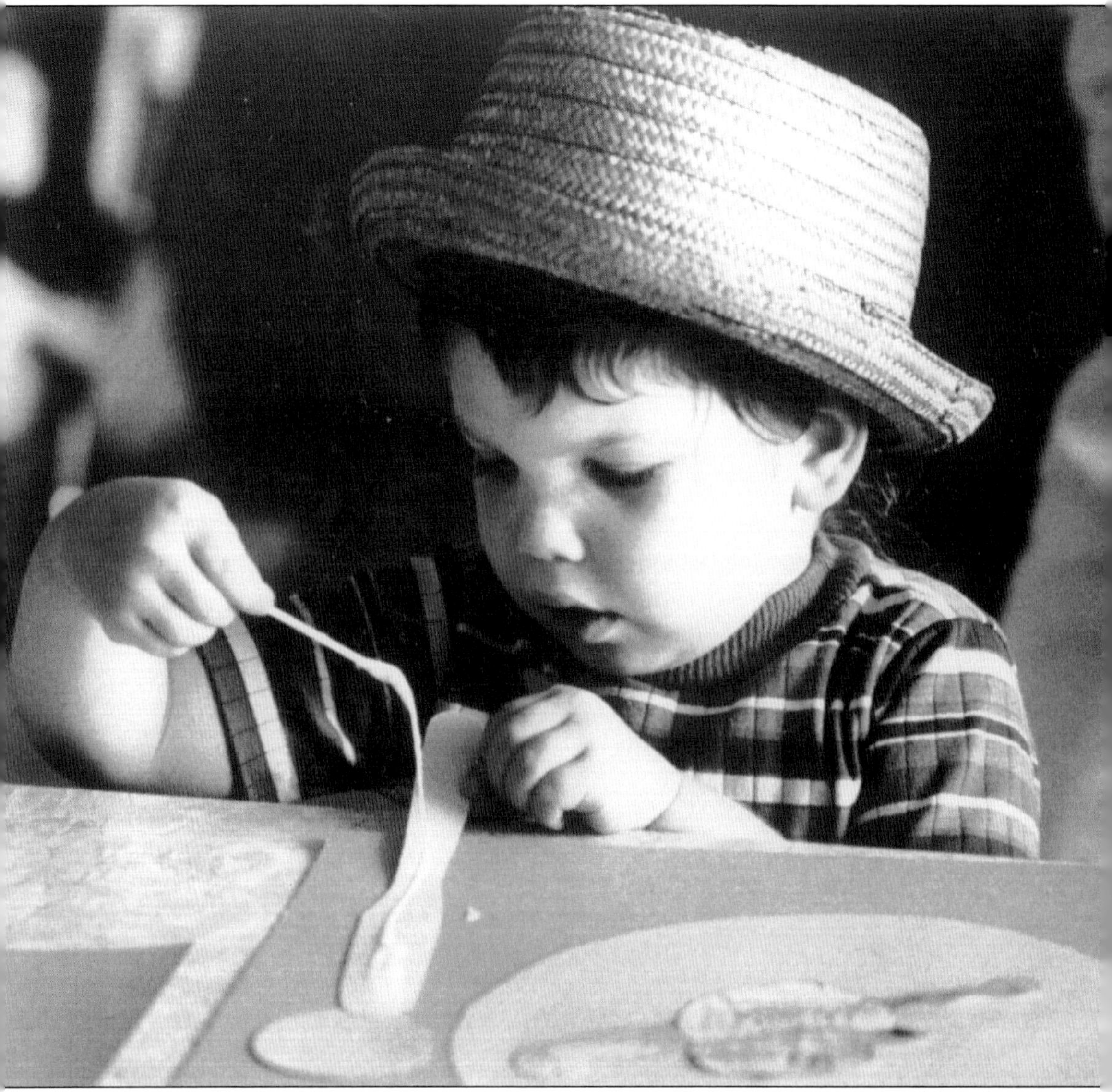

Three-year-old Eric Fletcher carefully glues a crafts project at the Vista Branch of the San Diego County Library in this August 1986 photograph. Educational programs for all ages are ongoing at the library. The 30,000-square-foot building was built on Eucalyptus Avenue, adjacent to Vista City Hall property. Vista's first library was opened with 50 books in the home of Nellie Acker in 1915. In 1921, the Women's Current Events Club welcomed the library to their own new building near North Santa Fe Avenue and Jefferson Street. It was later housed in a building on the property known as the circle, near the Woman's Club of Vista and Vista Community Church, and then in a former automotive store on South Santa Fe Avenue and the courthouse complex before being moved to its present, permanent site. (Courtesy of *Escondido Times-Advocate.*)

Six

NURTURING THE DREAM

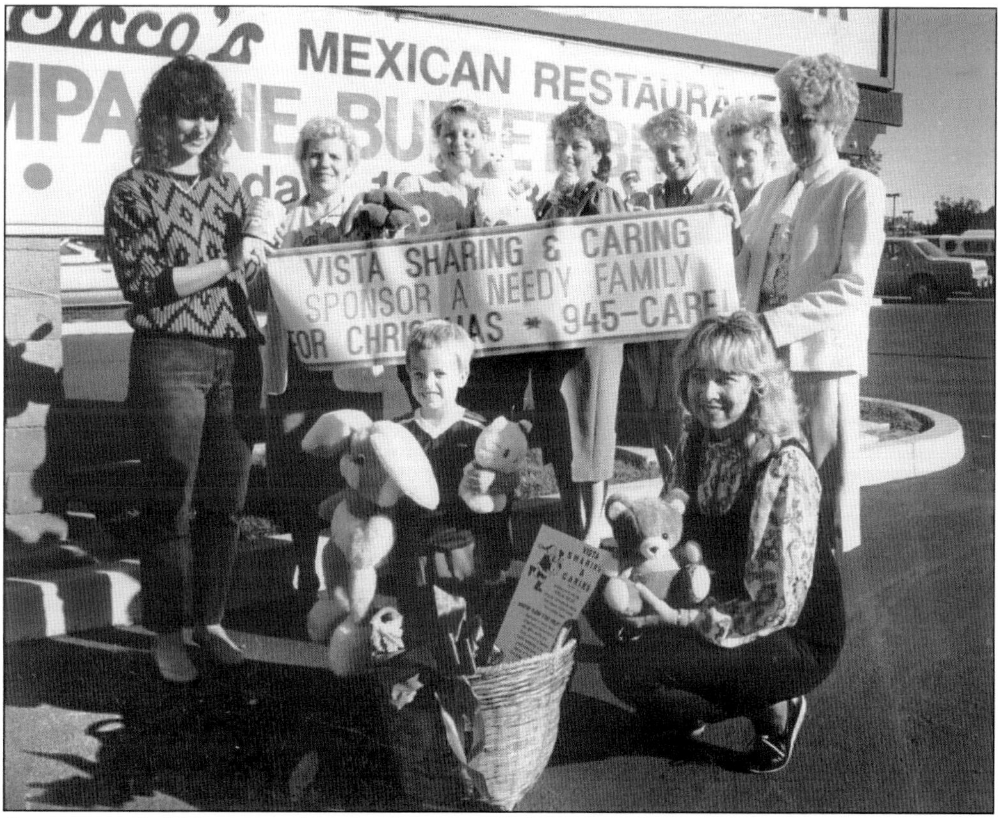

Service-minded Vistans gather for the annual Sharing and Caring Program kick-off in this November 1986 photograph. Residents are invited to sponsor a needy family, providing gifts and food for the holiday season. From left to right are (first row) Christopher Weston and Nadine Rutman; (second row) Candi Carlon, Theresa Plamondon, Sally Weston, Amy Fogle, Stacy Sieger, Donna Schrell, and Carole Burton. (Courtesy of *Escondido Times-Advocate*.)

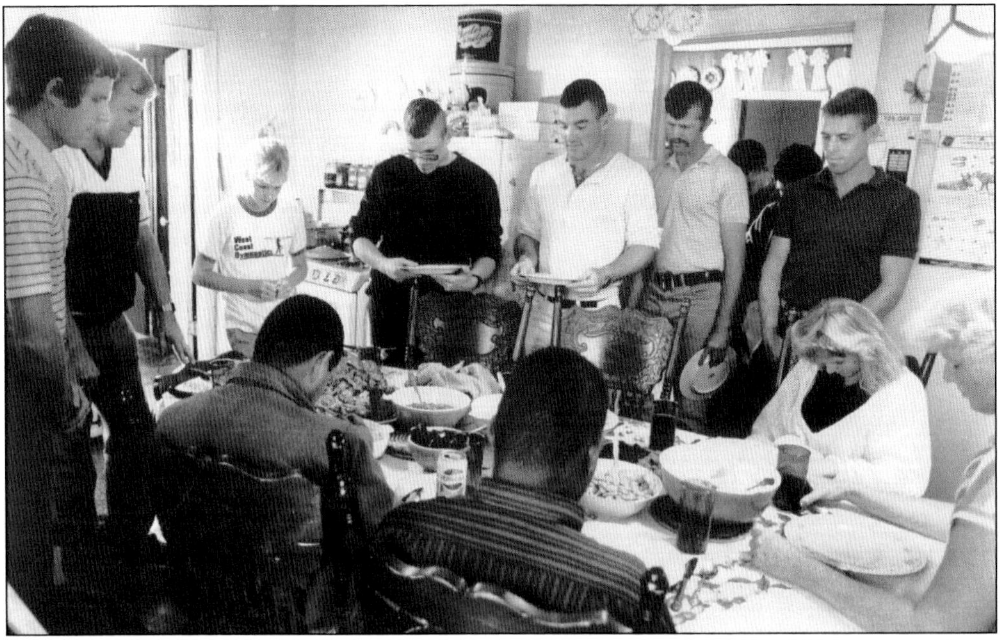

Camp Pendleton borders Vista to the north, and the Marine Corps base and Vista citizens have always been good neighbors. During the holidays, servicemen are invited to share the homes and traditions of local families. In this 1986 photograph, members of the Don Kirk family and the seven marines they have invited give thanks before sharing Thanksgiving dinner. (Courtesy of *Escondido Times-Advocate*.)

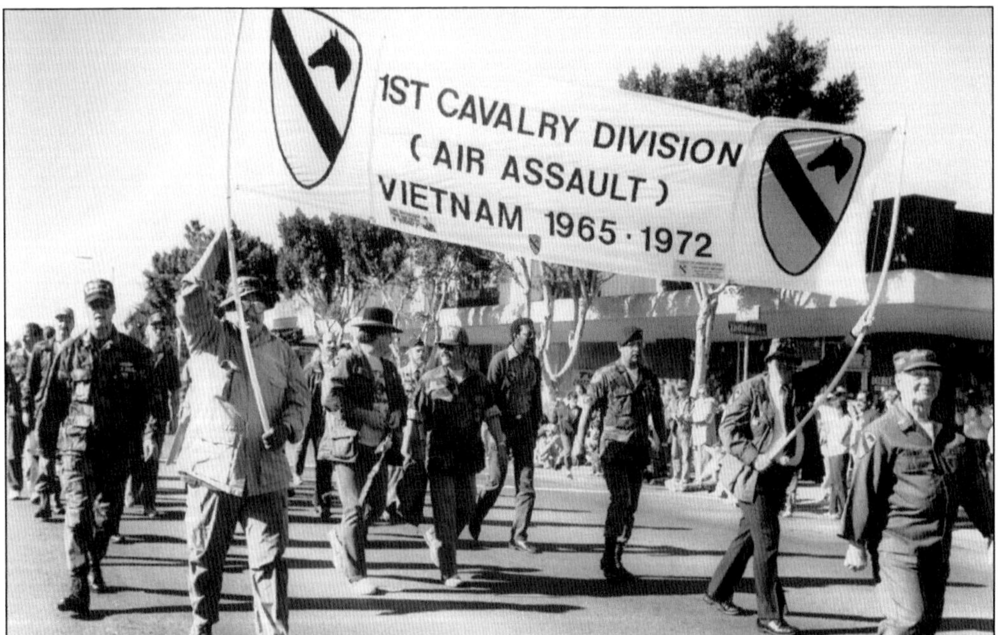

A group of Vietnam veterans from the 1st Cavalry Division marches down Main Street on December 14, 1985, in Vista's annual Christmas parade. Area residents line the streets to watch as bands, floats, and civic and service organizations participate in the parade.

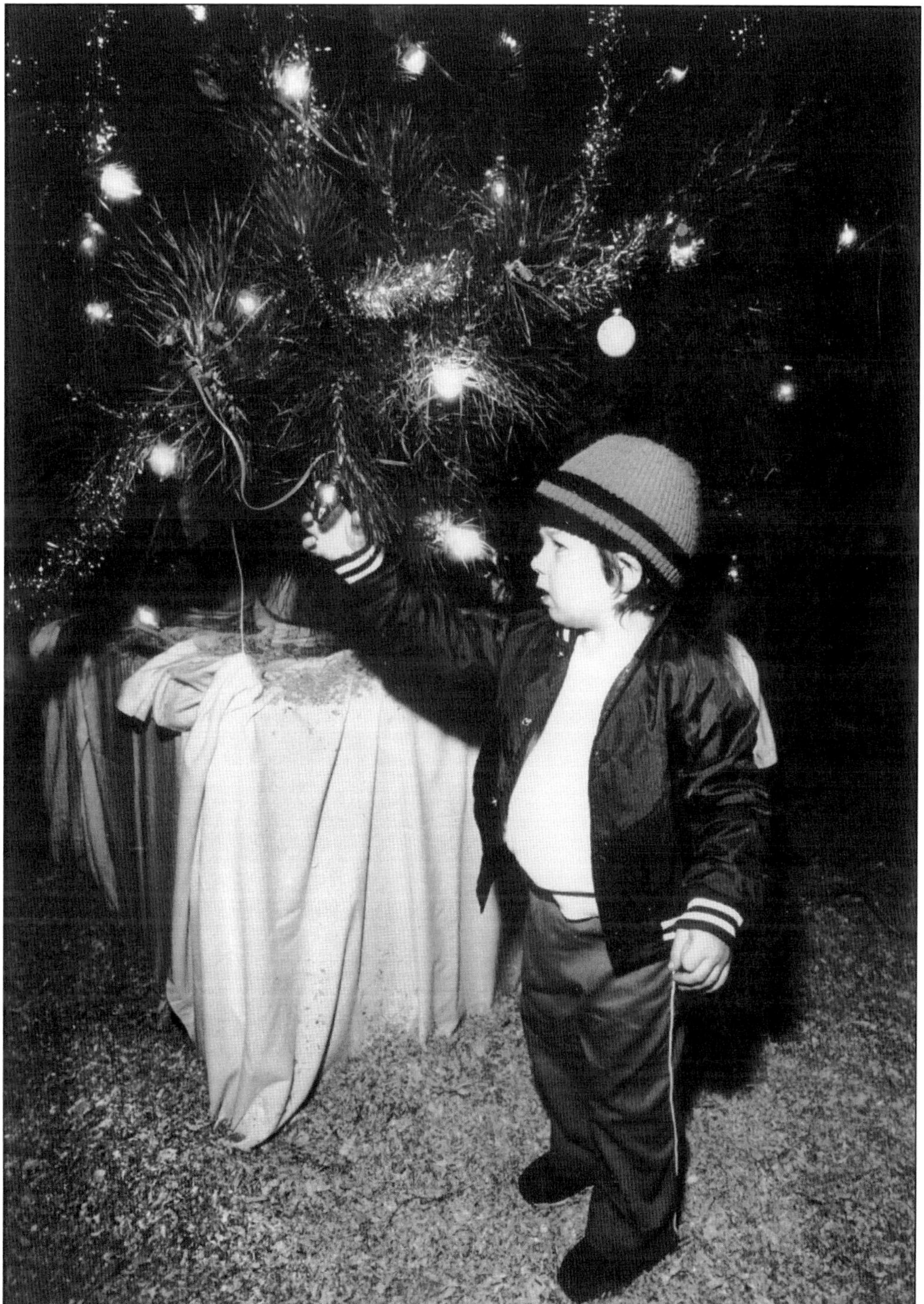

For many years, a feature of every holiday season has been the ceremonial lighting of Vista's own community Christmas tree. Mike James of Vista was just two years old when this December 4, 1986, photograph was taken. He couldn't resist checking out one of the shiny ornaments. (Courtesy of *Escondido Times-Advocate*.)

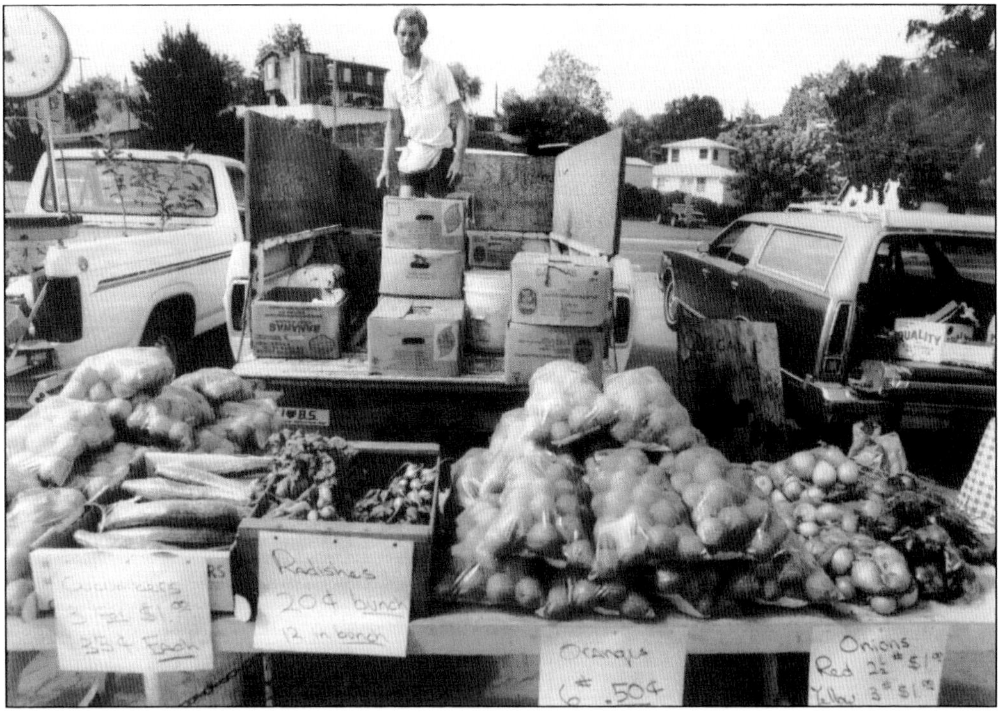

Vista's popular Farmer's Market has attracted crowds on Saturday mornings since 1981. In this July 1984 photograph, Roger Steeve arrives early to stock his stand with fresh produce. The first year, the market was held only during four good-weather months, but demand quickly made it year-round. It was run by the Baughman family until January 2008, when Mark Wall of Just Balance took over operations.

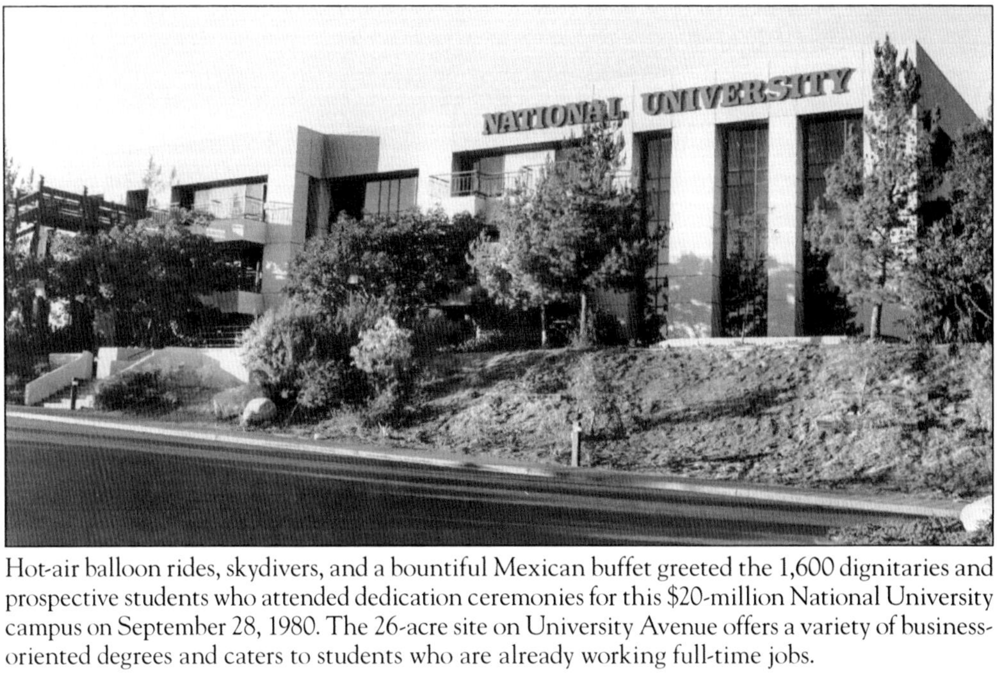

Hot-air balloon rides, skydivers, and a bountiful Mexican buffet greeted the 1,600 dignitaries and prospective students who attended dedication ceremonies for this $20-million National University campus on September 28, 1980. The 26-acre site on University Avenue offers a variety of business-oriented degrees and caters to students who are already working full-time jobs.

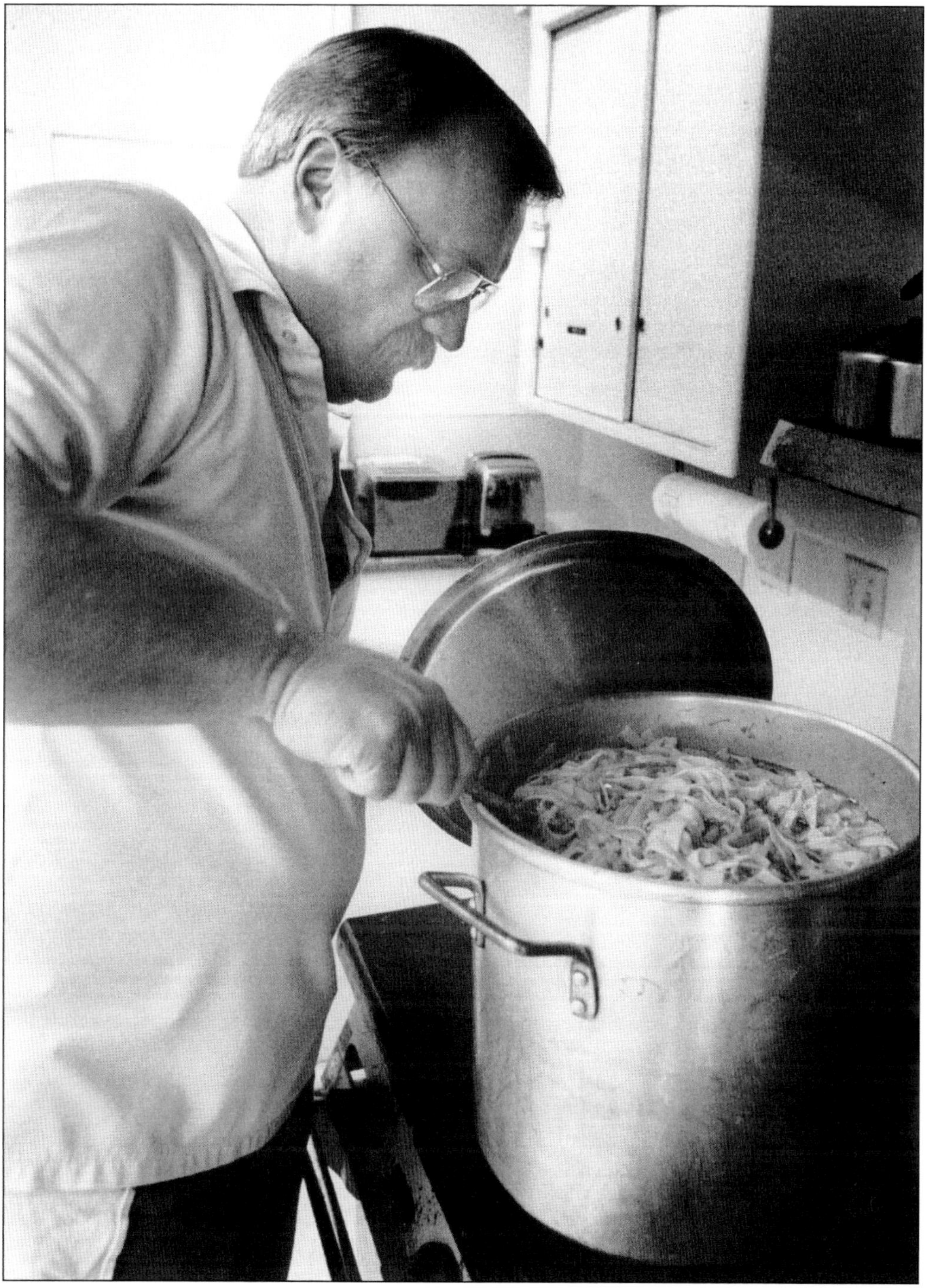

Vista churches have taken turns serving free hot evening meals to the poor and homeless for many years. In this June 1988 photograph, Mike Lourey, pastor of Faith Chapel, prepares a big pot of chicken and noodles that will be transported and served at the soup kitchen at Community Church of Vista. (Courtesy of *Escondido Times-Advocate*.)

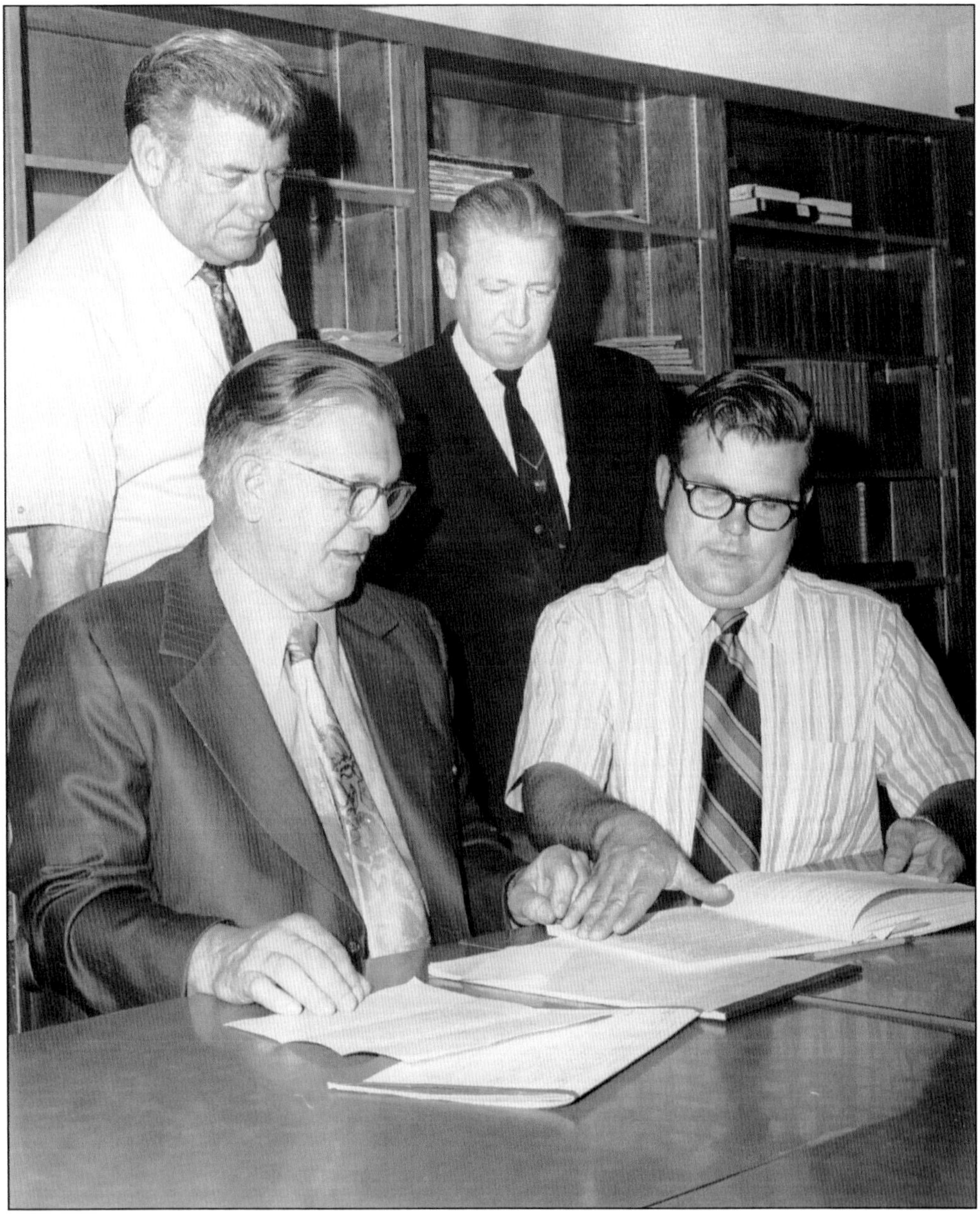

The Vista Drug Coalition was formed in the early 1970s as a joint effort to promote drug use education and prevention measures for the city's youth. From left to right are (seated) Mayor Frank Meyer, representing the City of Vista, and Howard Amend, Vista Boys' Club director; (standing) Tom Banning of the sheriff's department and John Downey, representing the Vista Unified School District.

Regular visitors to the *Vista Press* newsroom for many years were the Fairest of the Fair (name unknown) and Don Diego, goodwill ambassadors for the Del Mar Fair. Also known as the Southern California Exposition at Del Mar, the fair is held annually from mid-June to early July. Joining the pair in this 1966 photograph, taken in front of the newspaper's awards wall, was newly elected Mayor Harrison Doyle (center).

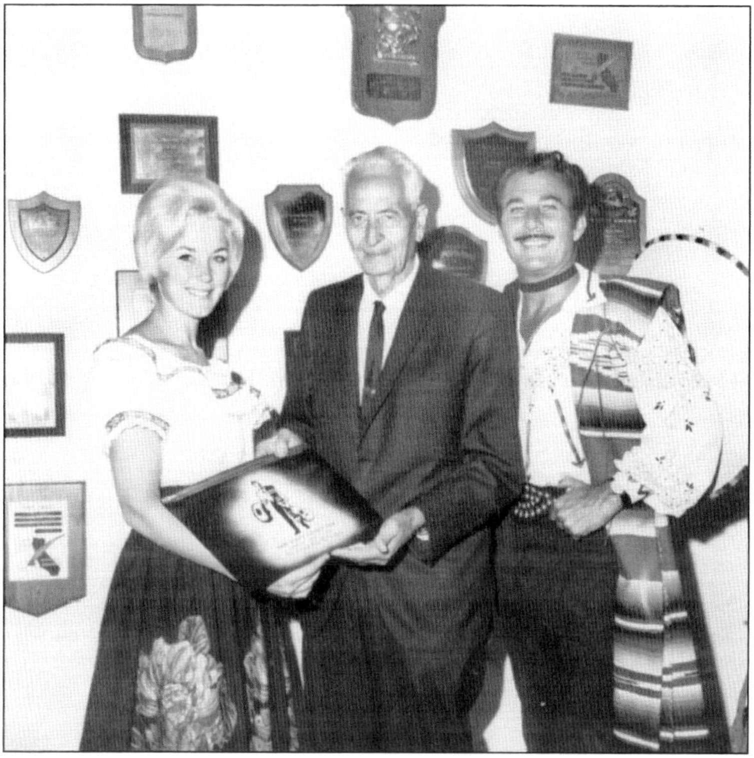

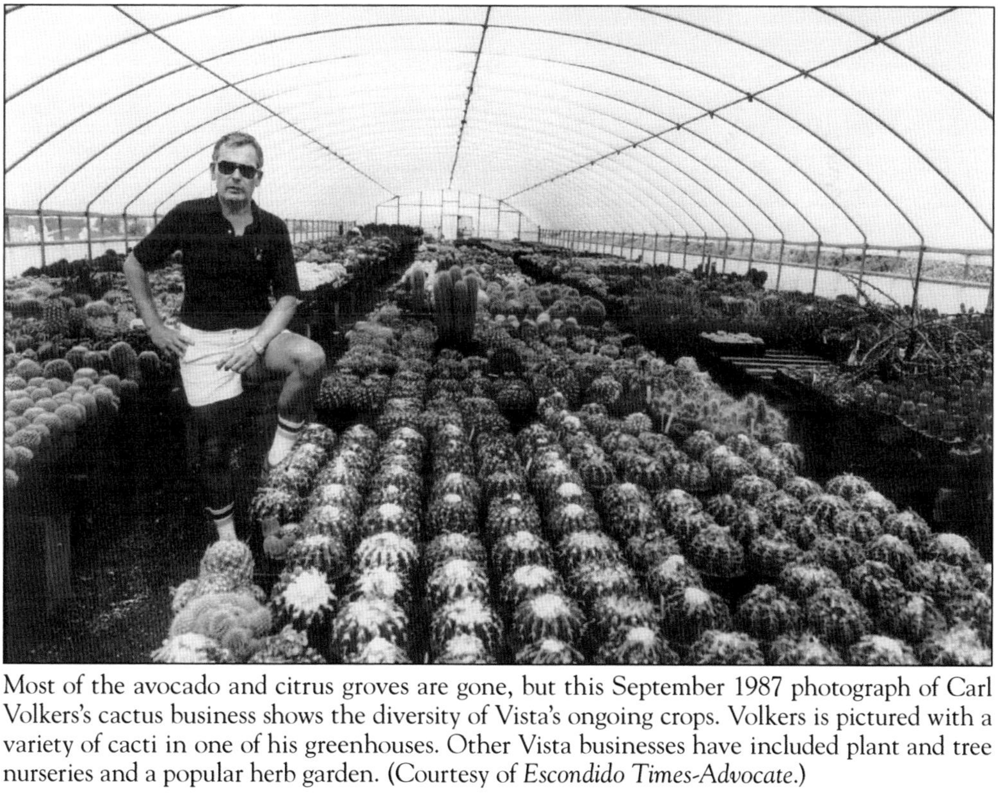

Most of the avocado and citrus groves are gone, but this September 1987 photograph of Carl Volkers's cactus business shows the diversity of Vista's ongoing crops. Volkers is pictured with a variety of cacti in one of his greenhouses. Other Vista businesses have included plant and tree nurseries and a popular herb garden. (Courtesy of *Escondido Times-Advocate*.)

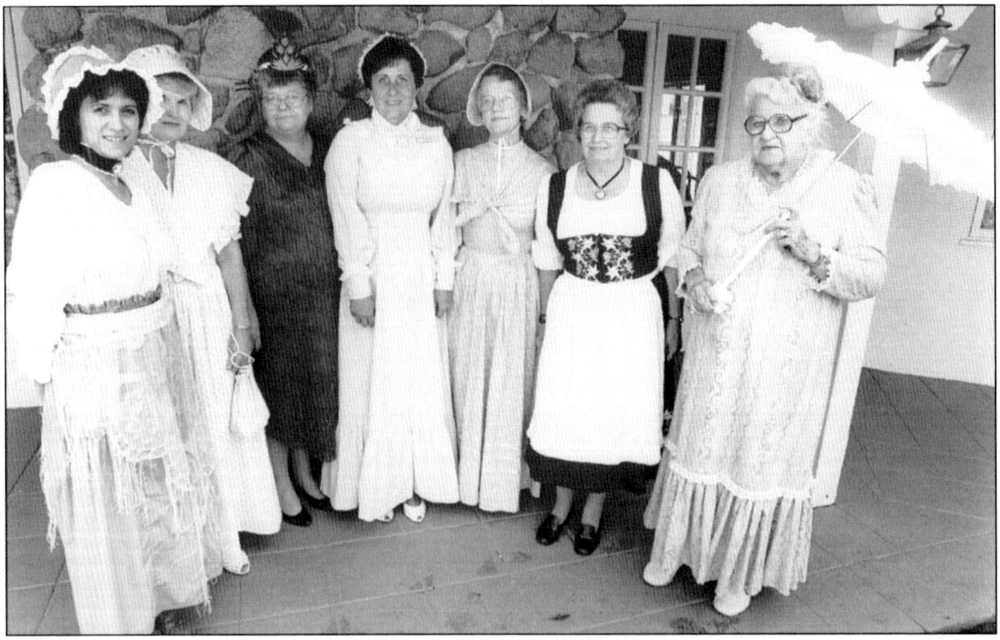

Vista celebrated Heritage Week in the 1980s, with organizations and schools taking part in weeklong activities and a downtown festival featuring folk dancing, food, and information booths. Dressed in costumes celebrating their heritage are, from left to right, Rosemarie Fournier, LaVonne Hurley, Ginny Sharpell, Wanda Cramer, Wyvetta Wilson, Rena Fecho, and Meta Royer.

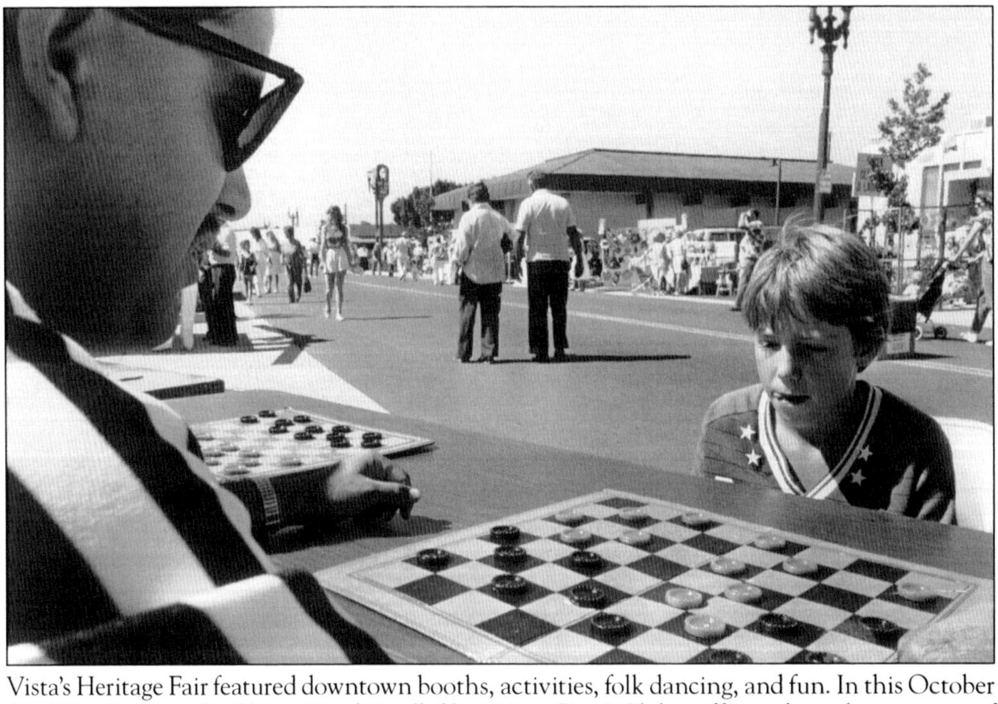

Vista's Heritage Fair featured downtown booths, activities, folk dancing, and fun. In this October 8, 1988, photograph, Chico Cendejas (left), a Vista Boys' Club staff member, plays a game of checkers with David Mitchell, 10, a Boys' Club member. (David won.) The popular Vista facility on California Avenue later became the Boys' and Girls' Club.

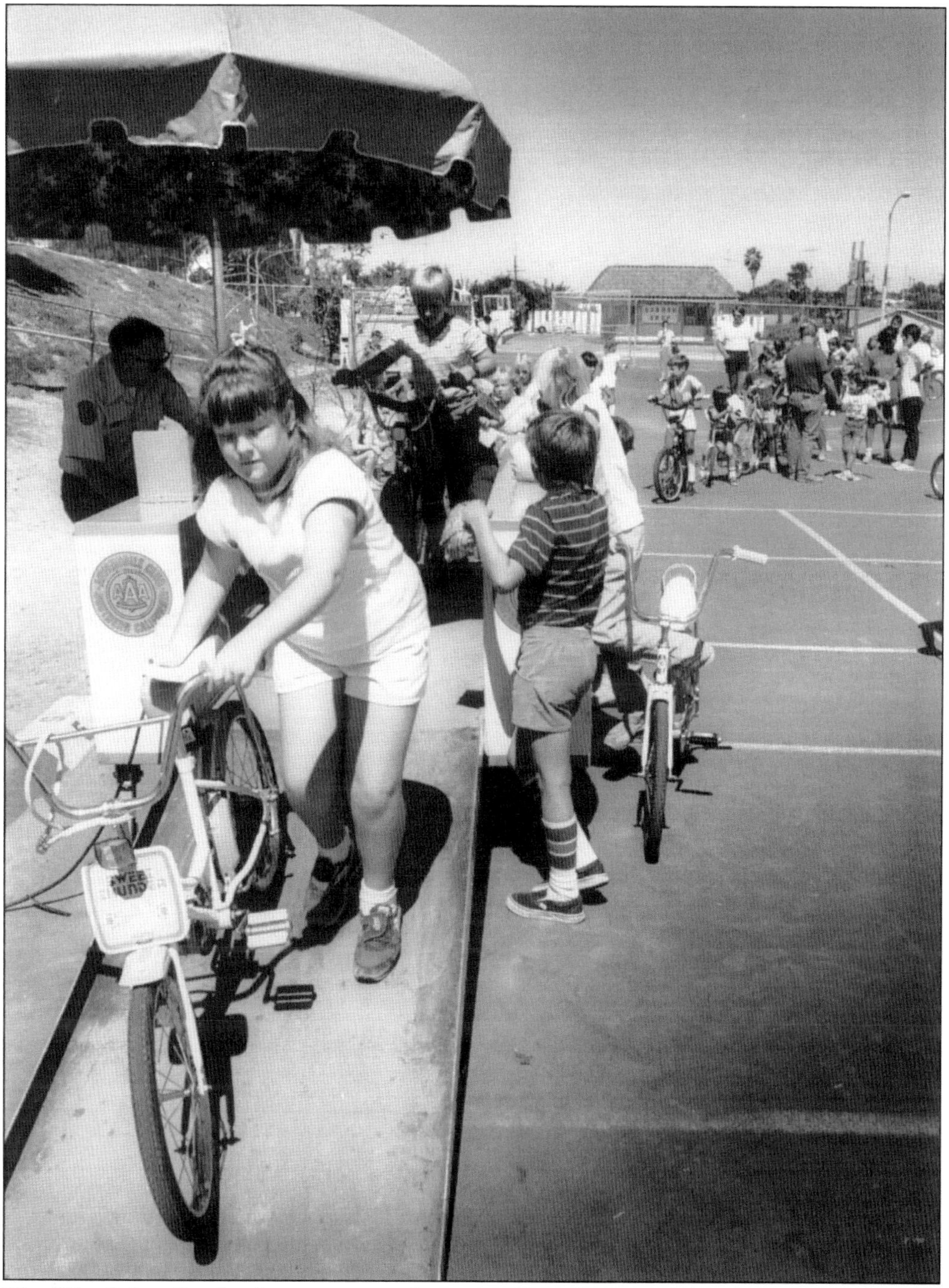

The Bike Safety Fair has been an annual event in Vista for several decades, with educational activities and each child's bicycle carefully inspected for possibly dangerous equipment flaws. After inspection, the owner received a bicycle license. The event was sponsored over the years by the Vista substation of the sheriff's department and the Automobile Club of Southern California. Pictured here on September 25, 1985, children move through the line at AAA's Bicycle Safety Rodeo at Bobier Elementary School.

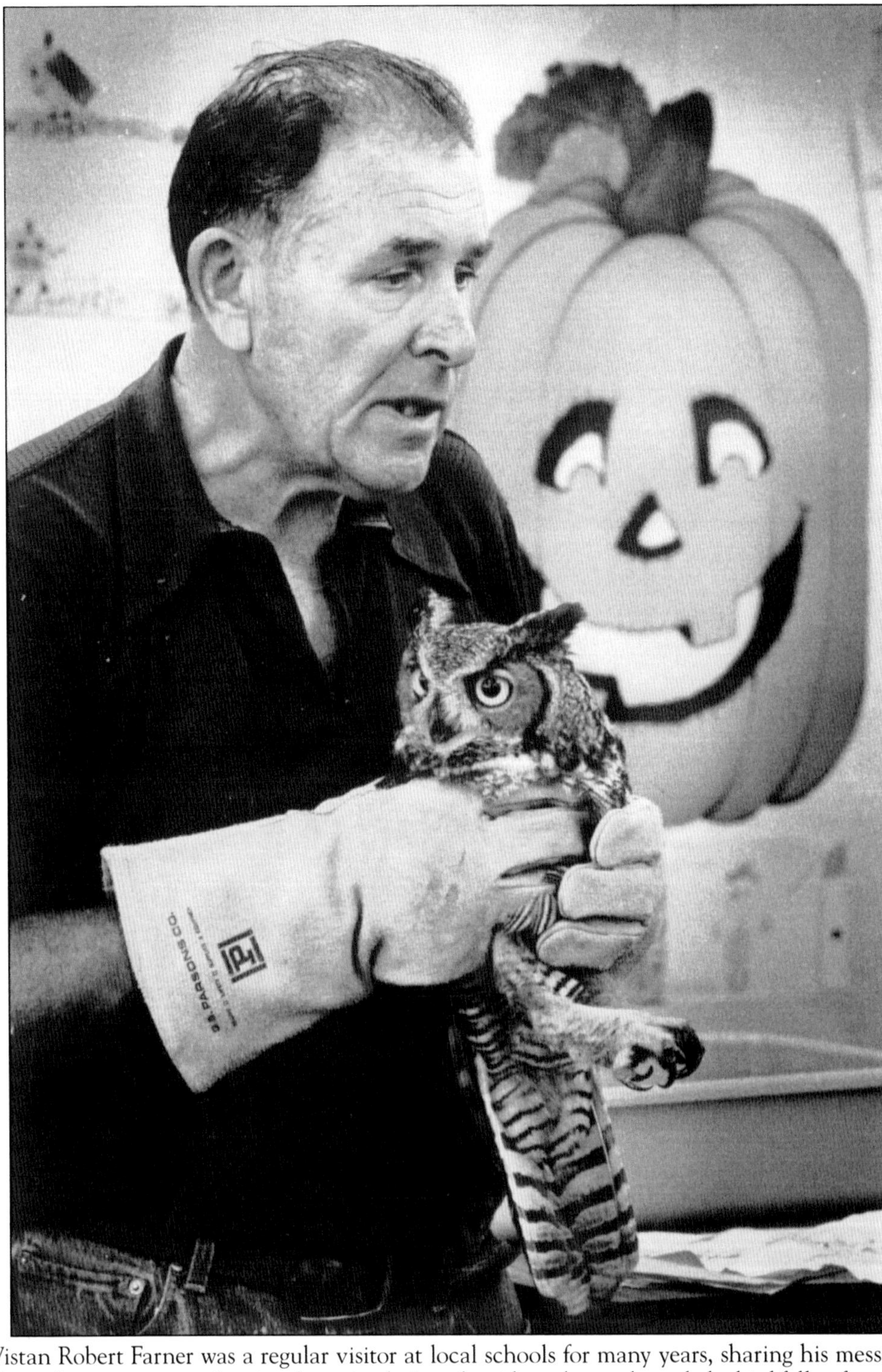

Vistan Robert Farner was a regular visitor at local schools for many years, sharing his message about the importance of caring for animals. Local residents knew that a baby bird fallen from its nest or a homeless bunny could be taken to Farner, day or night, for care and advice. He is pictured in a classroom showing children his pet horned owl in this October 1985 photograph.

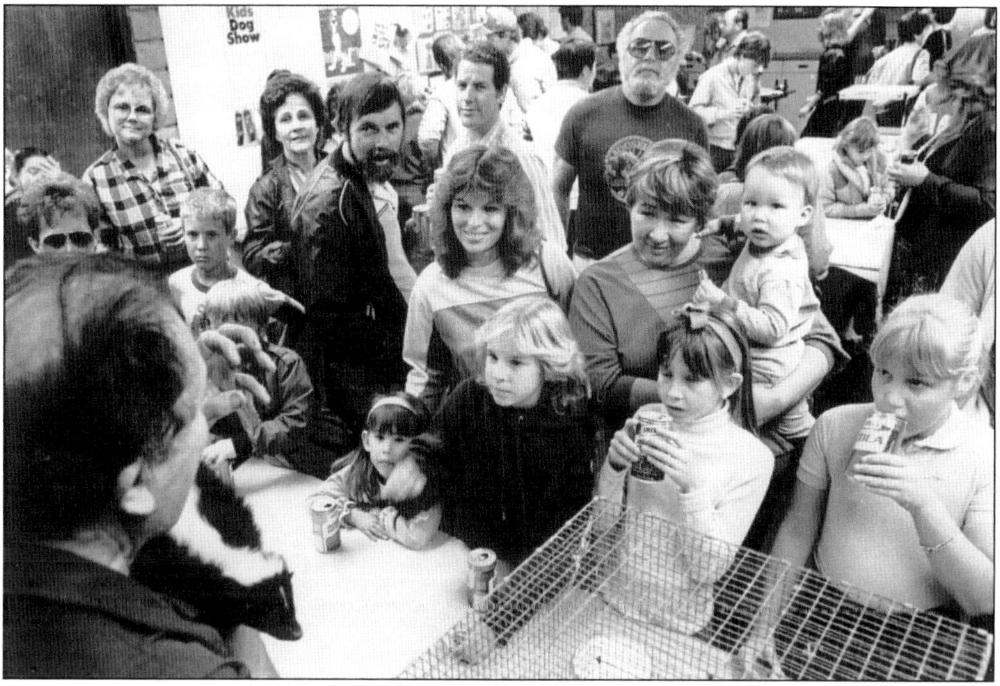

No one seems to mind that the animal Robert Farner is holding is a skunk. Parents and children gather round at the Escondido Humane Society on May 11, 1985, as Farner shares his message of loving and caring for pets of every ilk.

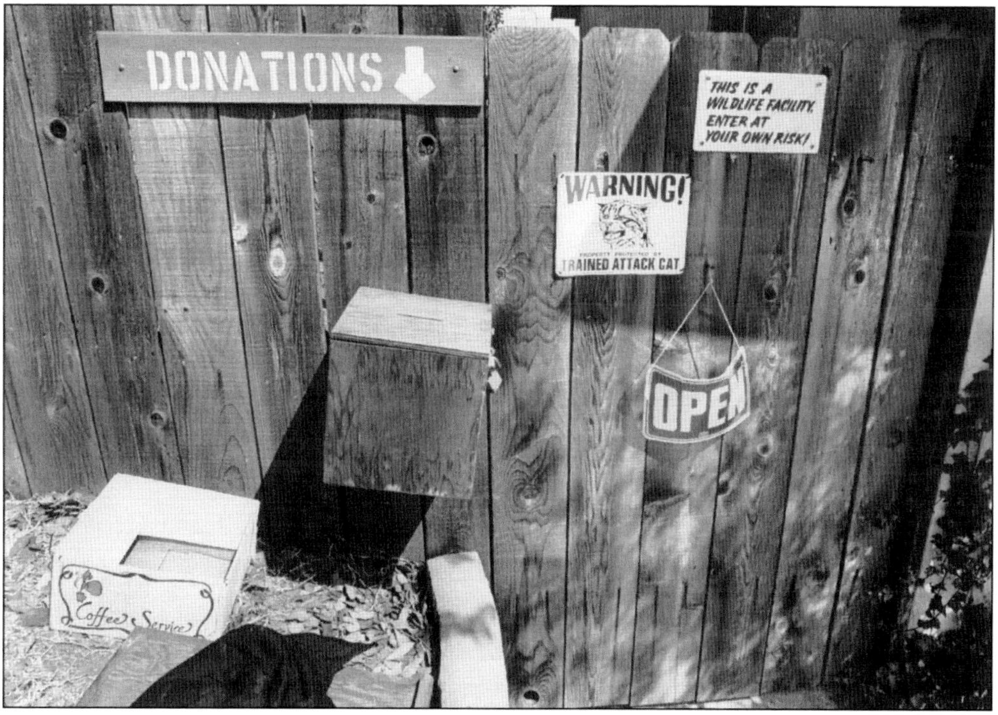

The door was always open at Robert Farner's Wildlife Rescue Education Center in Vista. Farner relied on donations to help feed the many creatures who ended up on his doorstep.

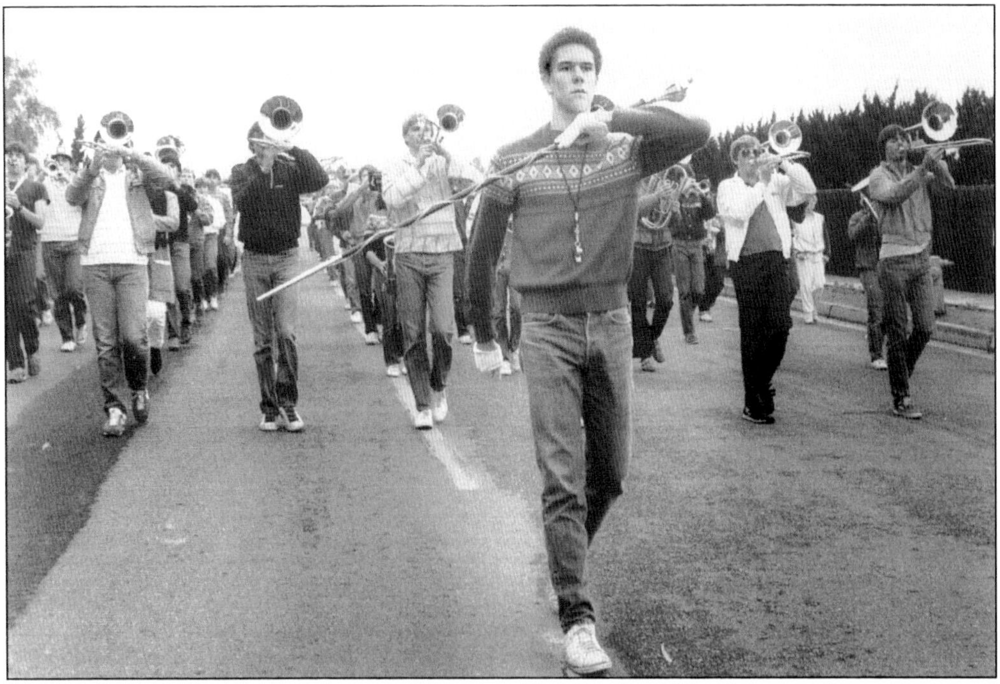

Steve Green, drum major for the Vista High School Panthers band, leads his band down the street as members practice for their appearance in the January 1, 1985, Tournament of Roses Parade in Pasadena. (Courtesy of *Escondido Times-Advocate.*)

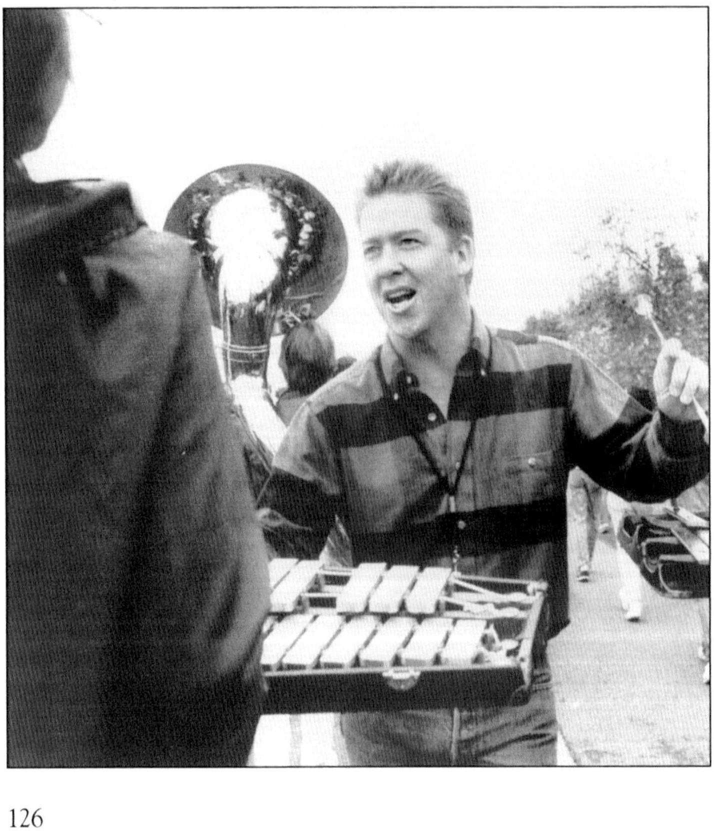

Kenneth Gammie, the Vista High School band director who also has served as conductor for the Moonlight Amphitheatre summer musicals orchestra, directs band members as they prepare for the 1985 Tournament of Roses Parade. (Courtesy of *Escondido Times-Advocate.*)

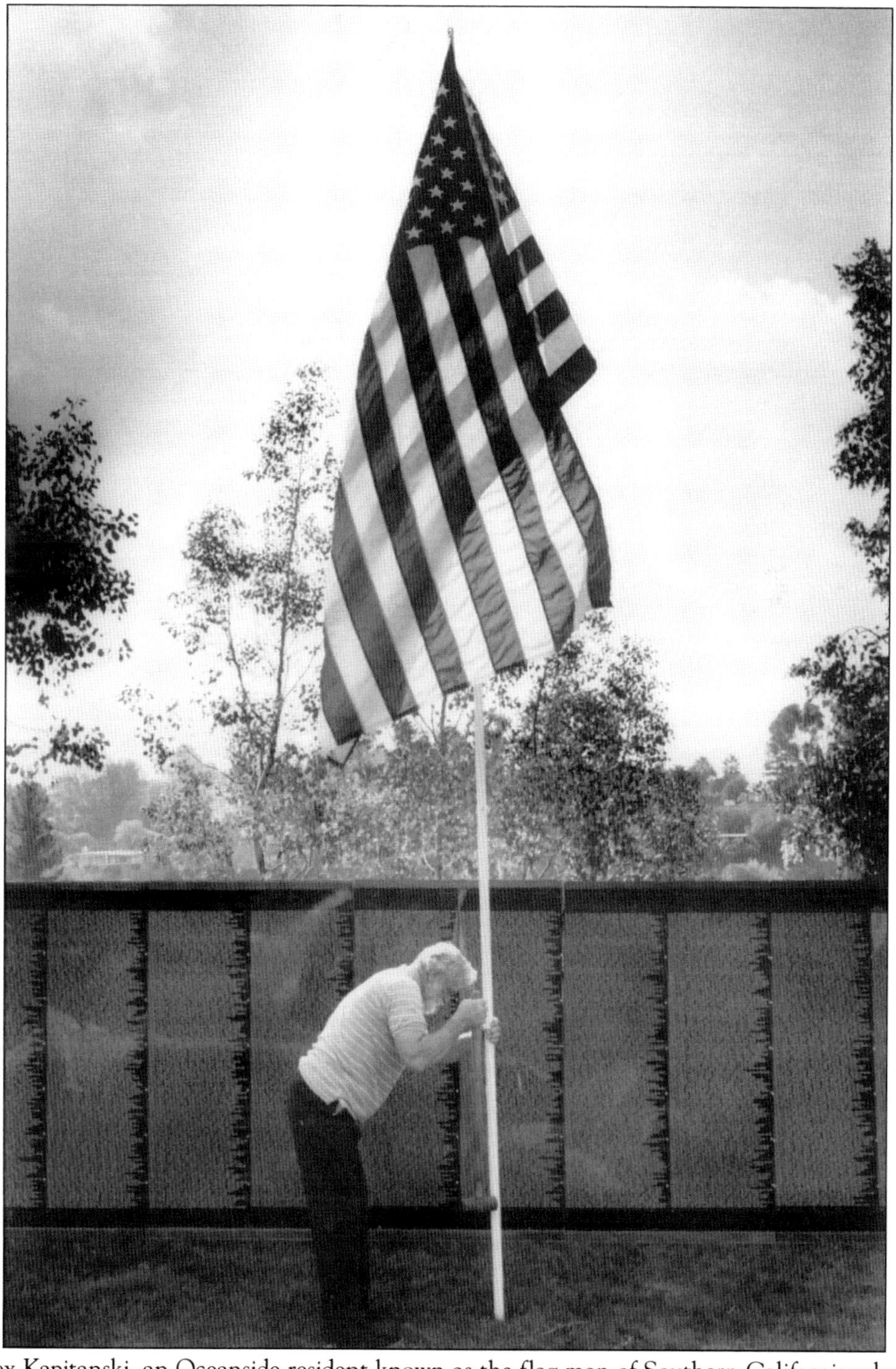

Alex Kapitanski, an Oceanside resident known as the flag man of Southern California, places an American flag at the center of the traveling Vietnam War Memorial on December 8, 1985, when the memorial was on display in Vista. In a city comprised of many servicemen and veterans, and of residents who are active in civic and philanthropic activities, Vistans are known for their patriotism and their pride in their city and their country.